Sight and Insight

SIGHT
AND
INSIGHT

A Prediction of
New Perceptions in Art

RICHARD GUGGENHEIMER

KENNIKAT PRESS, INC./PORT WASHINGTON, N. Y.

Contents

Preface

Great truths and the beauty of great truths must be brought within
e horizons and the reach of multitudes. It must be done without
uting and filtering of spiritual nourishment to suit the frailest diges-
n. This work seeks to propagate a dynamic conviction that art and
an can and must ascend toward the maturity of total communion.
til this occurs, both are constrained to relative frustration. Every
ortal has his role to play in this ascension. The awkwardness of a single
ul tends to break the continuity of process. With the miracle of life for
bject matter and the miracle of the human mind for activating agent,
ery human being is potentially a poet.

The mysteries of aesthetics have challenged sensitive minds for sev-
al thousands of years. But because the finest art of man is subtle,
cause beauty is generally an affair of nuance, an atmosphere of special
eparation and erudition has enveloped the world of art. Furthermore,
has become an increasingly troublesome fact that as modern life has
en compartmentalized into ever-multiplying categories of specializa-
n, there are more and more circumscribed groups of people who un-
ittingly trade much of their potentially wide sensibility for the narrow
plication of their energies to practical purposes. In other words, to
great number of persons, beauty seems to be a pleasant ornamental
xury that graces life from time to time, but which bears no integrated
lationship to daily living.

In his vast preoccupation with the practical, and with all the mounting
ewilderment and spiritual chaos that has resulted from this preoccupa-
on, man has lost sight of the miracle that is inherent in every instant
being. He has grown so familiar with the materials of his little island
life, to which he drifted but a few wispy years ago out of eternity
d infinity, that he is blind to the incessant wonder of it. Every now

and then he is startled out of his blindness by the inspiring gesture of
artist who gets excited about what may seem to be the merest shad
of a trifle and discloses its identity as part of the universal mystery,
adding his own insight to the jaded sight of his fellow man. The gen
invents nothing; he reveals. But his revelation cries out for recept
understanding.

We seek a solution to the problem of how to get man's highest in
itions successfully communicated to the general public without dim
ishing the quality of the thing communicated. Obviously the first nec
sity is to raise the level of the community's capacity for understandi
its sensitivity. Before this process can be greatly speeded up, the pul
must be made further aware of its shortcomings, and, above all, of
important fact that these shortcomings are not inherent infirmities l
surmountable impediments. The better self to which man's inner c
science so healthily aspires depends upon the resolute development
his most neglected faculty, aesthetic literacy. That this is becoming e
more evident to contemporary thinkers is well-illustrated by the br
statement of one who says, "To provide aesthetic experience abundan
is the first and last task of civilization" (*Art and Freedom*, by Hor
Kallen).

The main thesis of this work is that, since our major sentiency
ocular, we should bestir ourselves to a livelier, fuller, more mat
capacity for the visual arts. There are many ways of seeing, as there
many ways of being. There are ways of learning to see more and to
better as there are ways of learning to be more and be better. It i
shame that so many of us see much less than is visible. If a man co
buy a pair of spectacles guaranteed to reveal everything to him in a
more wonderful light than he had known before, he would rush to p
chase them. If a man can learn to see more than he now sees, and
further, and see more beauty, and see more clearly the shape of his o
nature and destiny, then he should not hesitate to start learning.

Since this is exactly the case, since there are certain people who
wonderfully well and who are great teachers by the grace of their go
vision, there is the possibility of learning from them. And there is t
obligation. The advantage of their special talent is not to add a lit

:ury to life but to reveal the supernal truth that beauty is not an occa-
ɪnal invention of man or condition in nature, but is the natural and
ɪiversal attribute of every instant of being when viewed by the virtue
 insight. It is not rarified and remote. It is Here and Now.

It is expected of most works on aesthetics that they will seek to define
e beautiful. This work prefers the approach of reverence, which is not
thout possibilities of revealment. What it does seek to define are the
ɪman virtues which it considers essential to the creation and apprecia-
ɪn of fine art. It concludes that art will play a mighty and prophetic
le in the coming restoration of man's faith in himself and thus in the
.otherhood of man, and in the intrinsic virtue of the human soul.

ɪarcliff Manor   R. G.
 ew York, September 23, 1944.

Chapter I

COMMUNICATIVE FUNCTIONS OF ART

B Y THE exercise of every art within his ingenuity, man seeks to extend the scope of his vision and to communicate his findings. A most exalted expression of this effort and achievement is found in is fine arts. It is regrettable that these, representing so important an ement of man's high attainment, should remain relatively obscure to 1e majority of human beings. For, if we are honest about the matter, nly a pitifully small audience enjoys their full benefit. We have fallen 1to the depressive habit of accepting this state of affairs as more or less nalterable. Yet clearly it becomes more urgent every day that we dis- ɔuse ourselves of this fallacy. Our growing understanding of the human ɔsyche reveals convincingly that human sensibilities are not so constitu- onally limited, either quantitatively or qualitatively, as they have often :emed to be. They are retarded; they are obstructed; but they have an calculable potential when liberated, exercised and developed. The de- :ee of their refinement measures the extent of our culture. It determines 1e dimension of our mental stature and our spiritual grace.

The sensibilities of most of us are cultivated to only a fraction of eir capacity, so that we live the greater part of our lives under the 1yopic delusion that our experience ranges around the usual levels of hat we call the commonplace, only occasionally rising to the rare alti- des of the extraordinary, the wonderful, the beautiful. Whereas the etter cultivated individual, sensitized to the dynamics of nuance, finds very instant of existence to be unique and revelatory. For him the com- 1onplace is nonexistent; everything under the sun is new. The freshness f his vision fills him with an incessant delight, and he becomes obsessed ith the necessity of communicating his emotion. His eyes have been ɔened to the perpetual miracle of being. As long as they are thus

1

opened, he never sees less than beautifully. He dwells in the felicity his own and of nature's spontaneity.

Never has there been a more desperate need for man to rise to t higher levels of his capacity than now. Reduced once again to the mc strous turmoil and frustration of being at war with himself, his bett nature is resolved to seek the spiritual maturity toward which he h always dedicated his underlying purpose. He understands the interm tent tragedies to which his divided nature subjects him. As long as the is to be an insensitive side powerful enough to take the ascendancy, knows that he must be torn between his destructive and his creati powers. The violence of the contemporary conflict warns him m poignantly than ever that only the cultivation of his highest capacit and integrity can propel him toward the brighter destiny that his int tion surmises as a possibility.

The gravity of the situation is apparent, and it serves to intensify t process of self-criticism which had been gaining headway even bef we emerged into open strife. This critical sense had been asserting its in all phases of the arts and sciences, and most exuberantly in the fi of aesthetics, where it assumed many serious and many quaint forr Probably at no other period in the history of artistic endeavor had m been as analytical about his own processes and the logic surroundi the entire realm of human expression as in the past half century. Psyc logical research has added its impetus. Self-awareness and a vigorc probing into new-found depths of the human personality give promise a renewed intellectual integrity. We are reaching a stage of self-scruti that will not tolerate deviation from veracity. We seek to re-evalu ourselves, our potentialities, our purport, in terms of contemporary c cernment.

Our intuition tells us that the truths of our deepest searching me into a mystical sort of identity with that which we call the beautif In fact, this intuition has been materially reinforced by a mounting ac mulation of persuasive evidence. It is a poor philosophy nowadays t does not take account of the mystery of aesthetics, and it is poor that does not culminate in forms of transcendent disclosure. "The pl: to seek for reality," writes Irwin Edman, "is not in some metaphys

mula, but in the unimpeachable realities in works of art. It was some-
ng of this nature that Bergson realized when he told us that the
uition of the poet is a surer revelation of reality than the analysis of
: metaphysician. It is this that Croce means by insisting that the whole
iction of the artist is subsumed under the word 'intuition.' " Perhaps
s partially because at this time we are so acutely conscious of our moral
erioration in a setting of keen intellectuality and scientific acumen,
it we turn our hopes toward the final virtue of the arts. Upon the
namics of good art and good religion much will depend. In their high-
functions they are similar forces.

Intelligence and its end product, wisdom, are essentially a collabo-
ive achievement of human beings, based upon successful communica-
n of impressions and ideas. To impede communion is to limit intel-
ence, and it is wishful thinking to suppose that our ultimate spiritu-
ty is independent of it. The evolutionary process of the human soul
ims to be founded upon a principle of shared experience. If the vision
the clearest and the farthest-seeing can be conveyed to the multitudes
10 see less well, the standard of human vision rises, and with it the
vel of mutual participation. We have a shared responsibility to enter
to this process of shared experience at the highest capacity to which
: can elevate our sensibilities.

Practically no human beings are equally sensitive, either creatively
receptively, to all the art mediums. In fact, the ability to practice many
verse arts is considered to be so dubious that the term "dilettante" is
iplied to those who attempt it. As Alexander Pope's couplet has it:
One science only will one genius fit; so vast is art, so narrow human
it." We also know, in our most honest and intelligent moments, that
ost of us delude ourselves as to the degree of comprehension we enjoy
. the role of audience to the arts. There is a vast amount of quibbling
. this matter, issuing from reluctance to acknowledge our deficiencies
id from degrees of inability or unwillingness to imagine states of en-
ghtenment beyond our own. Our vanity imposes more deceptions
pon us than our incompetence. "A genuine inability to believe the
iings that one knows are not true, would bring about the greatest
volution that society has ever known," writes Leo Stein, in his

A. B. C. of Aesthetics. When we listen to a Mozart sonata, our equi
ment for being in communion with the universe of Mozart varies
infinitesimal shadings all the way from that of the most obtuse to t
most perceptive, depending upon our capacities and how they ha
been developed. And Mozart himself may have been relatively bli
to Chardin. However, the likelihood is that he would have been awa
of that blindness, because he could have measured the intensity of
experience with painting against that of his experience with music.

Probably the majority of us measure our reaction to most things
ultimate terms of verbalized thought. We reduce our sentiment to t
common denominator of the spoken word. It is this mechanism whi
prompts us to talk about nonverbal works of art and to make ourselv
as articulate as possible in the process of "speaking our profounde
thoughts." Despite the fact that the nonliterary arts are untranslatab
into words, as untranslatable as Shakespeare is into sculpture, still v
find it profitable to talk about them in our effort to assay the substan
and the spirit of their grace. This is so because in our infancy we a
all conditioned to speech as the primary implement of expression,
the most reliable instrument of our groping intelligence. Many perso
never outgrow this assumption of the verbal medium as the prima
and basic mode of thought and of expression. Sometimes they do n
even discover for themselves that in actuality they happen to be po
sessed of a far higher potential in other terms of apprehension, visua
plastic, auditory. Hence many people struggle all their lives to tran
mute their pure intuitions of a nonverbal category into the idiom
words. They are victims of a compulsive verbal habituation, and ma
be compared to aliens perpetually fumbling with language not nativ
to them.

Since the initial and prevailing elements of our life experience ar
largely visual and tactile, it is not surprising that our graphic, plast
arts play a vast role in the spiritual metabolism of those to whom th
way of the word is not the only way. But the rational quality of our ag
leaves these arts rather inaccessible to all except those few who seem
by creative or perceptive temperament, peculiarly receptive to them
That is why, at this time, there is a great need to explain to a predom

antly intellectualized society the urgency of cultivating all the lan-
ages with which God has graced our sentiency; for he speaks to us
 parables of other terms than merely Words! For example, let us
en truly wide our eyes, that we may see something more of the infin-
 within which we have our being, and which is within us.

The art of seeing is still young. Consequently, so is the art of paint-
g. No doubt, such statements seem naïve in the face of the accumu-
tion of master works that we venerate and love. But the probability
mains that the totality of superb craftsmanship and exquisite spiritu-
ity achieved thus far by our beloved artists represents only a startling
timation of what is in the process of becoming. Every minutest reve-
tion of human genius retains the grandeur of its authentic beauty, but
ir prophetic insight tells us that we are growing children, still blind
 all but a fractional glimmering of that ultimate radiance which, like
universal sun, draws and unfolds us along the evolutionary course of
ir awakening. Some of the recent art of painters and some of the
cent thought of scientists, philosophers and metaphysicians confirm
id invigorate the substance and spirit of this assumption.

The advent of Henri Bergson, for instance, brings us a whole new
erspective and equipment for dealing with concepts of time and of
ace, especially in that most puzzling and important problem of
uration and extension in space. It is in this particular phenomenon
f duration and extension that so delicate a phase of contemporary
udy of aesthetics inevitably lies. The spontaneous immateriality to
hich modern science has reduced the illusion of matter has opened our
inds to new motilities and spatialities. Out of this advanced physics
ill unquestionably come new thought. And, however "intellectual" it
ay seem at its points of origin, explorative thinking opens new hori-
ons for the artist's vision. The artist himself may not consciously be a
etaphysician; in fact, he often distrusts the ways of intellectuality.
ut that is because he senses the need for amplifying the powers of
itelligence and surmounting the obstacles of cerebral limitation. For
hat matter, nearly all of us are far more emotionally aroused by the
ncessant miracle of life than we ever succeed in putting into adequate
vords.

In the field of the pictorial arts, the general quality of appreciati
is far behind the quality of creativity. The special function of this gr
art is lost to all but a few highly qualified individuals. There is a co
mon notion in the minds of many intelligent persons that a painti
no matter how superbly executed, stops short at a certain achieveme
of loveliness, and that it cannot possibly signify to a spectator any
those further, subtler conceptions that are so powerfully convey
through the apparently "more intellectual" expressions at our dispos
At the altitudes of its significance, the art of painting remains relativ
esoteric. But this state of affairs shows signs of improving. Modern m
is becoming increasingly aware of how different the visual experience
each individual is, and he is beginning to understand the revelato
value of relating these experiences into as universally shared a partici
tion as possible. He seeks to develop as complete an interchange
impression and sentiment among human beings as all the arts and scienc
will permit. He also understands more profoundly than ever the imp
tant difference between superficial seeing and fundamental seeing. Th
growing perceptiveness is the natural result of an ever more exacti
demand for the purest possible experience of communion.

In the conveying of thought from person to person, a variety of mea
can be employed. Perhaps the most interesting as well as the mo
exact manner of examining this function of thought conveyance is
close observation of children. Even at this early stage, we find ourselv
confronted with behavior that fluctuates between involuntary a
voluntary activity. Facial expression and gesturing are among the earlie
manifestations, and, as the power of speech develops, these becom
accessories serving to qualify verbal statement in a marvelous fashio
In fact, in the later stages of mature expression, the "manner" surroun
ing the delivery of a remark may often convey more special significan
than the literal meaning of the words. Here we have one of the intere
ing motivations behind much of the modern trend toward radic
stylistic experimentation. In the realm of verbal expression a thre
of staleness hangs over our vocabularies, and there are consequent d
satisfactions with language as a medium for the fullest possible co
veyance of the essence of mood, emotion or idea.

Only the most fortunately gifted poet finds words and images to render in their full significance the thoughts that he wishes to share with others; and the less gifted mortal never seems to have at his command words that will describe to his satisfaction the feelings that surge within him. And yet, how deeply we yearn to share these thoughts in all their treasured perfection of being so peculiarly ours—unique in the sense that every mortal differs from every other in the life flow of his experience and is eternally striving to reveal depths that remain lost in tragic and unwilling secrecy. We shall be forever working on these secrets that we cannot tell, for in their revelation lies all the radiant truth of our innermost natures. And what we cannot say in words we sometimes retain in pent-up feeling, constantly struggling to declare itself, staring out from our mysteriously expressive eyes.

The first objective of every contemplative mind in developing its conceptions is to reveal those processes and their resultant conclusions to other minds, and thus to seek a harmony of opinion. This instinct to achieve unanimity of judgment is a basic characteristic of human mentality, as natural as the logic of the syllogism, and even more compelling, because of man's emotional yearning to establish complete accord with his fellow man. Indeed, the most fervent effort in all the category of human endeavor is the fanatical urgency of an ardent believer to exercise every eloquence in his power to overcome resistance in others and to make them see, as though with his own eyes, the "light." Let a man be once convinced that he has found a truth, and it will become his firmest resolution as well as keenest exertion to exact its recognition from all the world.

How great a multitude of hysterical, exalted spirits are forever seeking to impose their feverish visions on their neighbors, the whole drive and fire of their lives devoted to that alone. And then there are the meditative ones, serene in their searchings, serene in their resignations; they too find comfort in the tranquil sympathy of friends who think as they do. We all love the fortifying stimulus of a communal spirit. At bottom we are terrified at the vastness of apparently impenetrable distances that separate us from even our dearest friends. Our inscrutable recesses and our ultimate destinies seem to whirl us into relentless solitudes. And we are eternally reaching out, some of us in hope, some in despair, stretching every fiber of our resourcefulness to make contact with our fellow man, to relate our identities, to tear away the dark wrappings that engulf us. At rare and mighty moments we succeed.

And so, while it has become a simple matter for us to accomplish the indispensable little exchanges of ideas that occur in the performance of ordinary affairs, nevertheless, as soon as any matter rises a shade above routine character we grow wary, like an animal that, sensing a challenge in the offing, stands tense and alert. Our minds actually work harder then, and we exert every effort to meet the situation, to understand its full significance, all its implications, in order to deal with it to the best of our ability. Under difficult circumstances we frequently consult with others and slowly erect as infallible a judgment as can be gathered from a community of opinion. In this way, day after day, all our lives long, we are forming the structures of our own character and influencing others, through this constant process of contact, involving as it does not only mutual crystallization of thought, but great radiation of emotion as well.

This brings us to the vital and unique function of artistic endeavor, which might be described as the effort of man to transmit an idea or an emotion particularly graced by attributes of beauty. Thus it is differentiated from the purely philosophic and metaphysical endeavor, which seeks to inquire into as many of the essential facts and processes of nature as possible, in order to discover whatever there may be of purpose and design and conceivable direction to existence. And thus, too, it is differentiated from the scientific endeavor which examines facts and processes in order to direct and control them, and generally to extend the power of human will over their operation. Our philosophic inquiries are calculated also to provide us with principles of moral and practicable conduct, and our scientific research tends to expand the scope not only of our control over material function, but of our insight into noumenal finalities. Both fields of investigation at their highest point of attainment reward us, if not with absolute revelation, at least with penetrating intimations of the ultimate nature and working of our selves and of our universe. And it is at this exquisite apex of all human endeavor, when the individual and solitary mind strikes a momentary accord with the rhythm of the great unknown, when it has an intuitive flash of vision into the perfection that it has eternally sensed and never seen, and when it feels the inexpressible thrill of even the most ephemeral fusion of identity with the infinite, that man achieves his fullest gratification. This he calls "truth"; and he calls it "beauty" too, in the immortal verdict of Keats who has said "Beauty is truth, truth beauty." And this brings us to the explanation of the dominant motivation behind the creation of works of art.

At these stirring moments of illumination when, through a combination of circumstance and his own efforts, man is privileged to experience the majesty of truth in any smallest phase of its entirety, his first reaction is one of awesome delight. Indeed, in the case of deeply religious spirits, their sense of communion with the infinite Verity and of occasional mystic revelation has been known to deliver them into transports of reverential ecstasy. And invariably this responsive emotion is accompanied by a rapturous sense of the beautiful. Apparently the human spirit derives immense gratification whenever it senses or perceives the measured perfection inherent in any manifestation of the true workings of things, and it has never failed therein to find great beauty. In fact, man's prevailing idea of beauty seems to involve this specific sense of a certain measured or proportioned flow, which perhaps he recognizes as that eternal, omnipresent quality characterizing truth in every aspect to which he has ever been able to penetrate. This special sense of measured flow or rhythm, implying as it does a complete state of smooth, uninterrupted being, may well be man's nearest approach to expressing his intuition of the true universal state of affairs —an utterly timeless process of effortless serenity, a complete resolution of all discord into harmony. We know that the most apparently haphazard and accidental incident becomes resolved into the highly ordered form of universal flow when fully comprehended, that every act and gesture, sight and sound of nature, however seemingly unrelated, fits into the one and only context. To the exposition of this truth, a work of art, with its particular representational properties, is one of the most apposite means, and I shall devote much space to the explanation of how and when this is accomplished.

There is a perplexing gap between the intuition of man and his intelligence. The whole evolution of human knowledge has been a progression from the speculative hypotheses of metaphysicians, down through ages of patiently systematized research, to ultimate scientific confirmation. In other words, we "feel" the truth of many of our ideas long before we are able to corroborate them with intelligent proofs; and many of these feelings, or intuitions, do not even emerge into tangible, expressible concepts until the faculties of intelligence, by the authority of rationalization, have rendered them credible and authentic. Therefore, behind the mounting façade of our slowly accumulated knowledge stands the elusive and sublime structure of our prophetic insight. It is the compulsion of this visionary unfolding that maintains in the human spirit a dauntless will to penetrate and to disclose the entire mystery. It is that dauntless will of the human spirit which is forever combating and overcoming the inertia of the human mentality, so heavily weighed down at times by the burden of its own frailties and imperfections. Thus, it frequently happens that a man is possessed of a far greater urge to communicate than of a capacity for so doing. It is at such times that he will grasp at every straw in his anxiety to articulate that for which he can find no adequate terms, resorting to signs and gestures, to any means by which he may contrive to make known the inexpressible. Sometimes he fails and ends with a ludicrous gesture of resignation, or a heart-rending movement of supplication for further powers. Sometimes he succeeds by resourcefully implying what he cannot directly state. Indeed, the arts in general, and the "plastic art" in particular, have become man's supreme instrument in this struggle to prefigure or ideate his intimations.

An intimation is more of a felt or suspected truth than a completely established fact. Words failing us, we often call it a feeling; and we are as emotionally disposed to credit such feelings as we are intellectually disposed to rely upon facts. After all, the manifest reality of a fact depends upon the evidence of our senses and the logic of our reasoning power. The essential nature of our intelligence does not permit or encourage us readily to accept as factual anything that we have not either literally perceived or rationally confirmed. And yet, instinctively we recognize, both intellectually and emotionally, that many of our ideas cannot be ruled out of all bounds of possibility simply because they have not traversed the narrow fields of our senses. Science has long since enabled us to infer from our small knowledge the existence of myriads of entities, forces and activities far beyond the relatively infinitesimal portion perceptible to vision. And some of the mightiest experience of mankind has arisen out of its firm belief in unsubstantial notions. This elevated category of persuasion is known as faith; it is conviction permeated by feeling, by fervent sentiment. It is not knowledge, and yet it exerts an incalculable influence. For the intellect, while constantly extending its empire over the intelligible matter of life, is powerless to operate in those domains of the imperceptible and imponderable that are beyond its reach. And yet, this intellect is most unwilling to resign itself to these limitations. Nor is it inclined to accept these convictions on faith alone, however alluring they may be. That is why man has turned to the practice of the art of aesthetics as a further attempt to translate his ineffable feelings into perceptible reality. Aspects of the truth to which he cannot penetrate with his reason he may discern by way of his aesthetic sense, which is a mode of perception by feeling. Thus, where he may not unveil the full logic of truth he may reveal the beauty of it. To see its beauty is to disclose the very soul of truth.

Chapter II

FORM, TO THE EYES AND THE FINGER TIPS

〰〰

THE earliest sign of man's will to make contact with his environment and his fellow beings is visible in infancy. Soon after birth, and aside from what may be called his physiochemical instinct toward the mother's radiation of warmth and nourishment, he begins to reach out toward objects within his sight. He wishes to touch them. This infantile urge to touch things is the first clear evidence of human curiosity; it is primitive interrogation, and marks the beginning of lifelong investigation. The pleasurable sense of satisfaction that the infant derives from this tactile inquiry comprises his first intellectual and aesthetic experience. And thus, it is the study of texture and form that is the very inception of the process of human knowledge and understanding.

Furthermore, it is at this same early stage that the infant mentality establishes its contact with fellow beings. Long before he develops the advanced power of speech, the infant looks into our eyes and speaks volumes with a smile. This is incipient language, and the smile is man's first positive display of a social consciousness. By means of facial expression, imitative in origin, he intentionally accomplishes a definite purpose, which is to convey his sense of pleasure and participation to those around him. It is his first exchange of sentiment.

In the fact that our earliest cognition is derived from tactual impression lies the elemental importance of the phenomenon of Form. In its deepest significance this term embraces the entire structural integration of matter and of transcendent idea. By form, in its highest sense, we mean to indicate far more than mere shape or mere configuration. And yet, by the fact that we start out upon our earliest experience observing and conceiving existence in terms of finite shapes and distances we are restricted in our efforts to burst the confinement of this

pallingly limited language of appearances. How far can true under-
nding transcend the processes of thought which are its implements?
: what point does our concrete intelligence of form fall short of our
·stract apprehension of it? How stunted is our capacity for conceiving
e full harmony of what we call the architecture of the universe?

To answer these questions it is necessary, first of all, to observe the
·olution of our experience with form. It is a vast subject. Starting in
·fancy with the haziest impression of the presence of objects, we
·adually develop a discriminating sense of contour, of divisibility of
·asses, of depth, of configuration, until eventually at highest maturity
·e become aware of some abstruse further facts that lift our notion of
·rm altogether out of the realm of finite matter into a continuum of
·divisible, evolutionary movement. This passage from the material to
·ne immaterial, from concrete matter to abstract movement, is the crux
·f the problem which will be clarified in succeeding chapters. The final
·mplicity of this matured concept is as elusive to the understanding
·f man as is the first simplicity of a mere three-dimensional mass to
·nat of an infant. That is why, in our effort to comprehend the intan-
·ible quality of form in its ultimate essence, we seek once again to
·educe it to a palpable representation of itself. As in our infancy we
·ouched the things about us in order to consolidate an idea of them, so
·n our maturity, reverting instinctively to the same logical mode of
·nquiry, we try to "touch" our ultimate ideas in order to "grasp" them.
·he important fact is that, long before we thought about things in
·erms of words, we sensed them in terms of feeling. Long before we
·earned to articulate our notions of objects in verbal terms of soft,
·ard, smooth, rough, large, small, heavy, light, hot, cold, dark, light,
·hick, thin, round, square, near, far, etc., etc., we enjoyed substantial
·ontemplation of them and gradually formed effective judgments with-
·ut employing the spoken word. Our logic was in our finger tips, as
·t were. Before we acquired a verbal language to amplify our thought
·rocess we already had our reason in busy operation; its language was
·a primary one, and its terms were not yet apt symbols but rather
·nherent sense of intrinsic qualities and essential facts. In place of
·words, our earliest reason dealt in sensations of objects and intervals

with all their qualitative properties; and the discernment of these variables was attained primarily by reaching and touching. Thus we formed our first habitual mode of percept and concept almost exclusively through the medium of tactility.

By reaching from the near into the far, from the self to that which lies beyond the self, we discovered extended space, and by contacting the things encountered in that space, we ascertained their ponderable nature. It must have taken a considerable experience of this sort of activity before we even came to the important conclusion that our self and our environment are two different things, two separate categories of being. In the beginning, it is probable that the infant mind identifies itself completely with everything that enters into its experience, so that its world and itself are one. And this too is a sensation that never thoroughly dissolves, but stays with us despite every rational evidence to the contrary. We have a natural tendency to identify ourselves with the time and space surrounding us, and we continue inescapably to attribute dimensions to them, as though their duration and extension must inevitably conform to the same sort of finite divisibility and pattern as seem to characterize the objects and intervals of our primitive experience. Objects and intervals—these are the earliest hints we have of a structural world outside ourselves. "Little children," says Gardner Murphy, "may indeed have some innate capacity for space-perception, but their struggle to get control of the third dimension takes years."[1]

And, strangely enough, the further we carry our subsequent investigation of these phenomena the more we become bewildered. For, although our experience tends more and more to externalize them, separating their existence and function from that of our own identity, and breaking them up into successions of individual entities, still our deepest apprehension leads us back to that first mysterious sense of universal mergence. Intellectual analysis, by the very restrictions of its apparatus, divides and divides into tangible particles the whole macrocosm. But it is aware, nevertheless, of the ultimate fallacy in this partitioning of what it knows to be essentially immeasurable, irreducible. It has come to know, in the words of Bergson, that "the mechanism

[1] *General Psychology*, by Gardner Murphy. Harper & Brothers, 1933.

of our usual comprehension is of a cinematographic nature, and that our ordinary perception of form is no more than an instantaneous view taken of a transitional process. Our faculty of intelligence, so skillful in manipulating the inert, proclaims its awkwardness the moment it touches energetic life-activity. Intelligence is characterized by a natural incomprehension of sustained vitality and movement; it attaches itself always to arrested stages of the vital flux, to the immobile. Our instinct, on the other hand, is molded upon the very essential form of life itself. While intelligence treats all things mechanically, instinct proceeds dynamically, so to speak."[2] We know intuitively that absolutely everything is in the eternal motion of an existential current. This fact of continuity in all things, of ceaseless, evolutionary movement, makes any conception of true form inescapably intuitive.

Thus, to reveal form, to render it actually perceptible, we are confronted with the necessity of transforming an intuition, a verbally inexpressible apprehension, into sensible expression. And we have, by an exercise of our highest ingenuity over long ages of effort, evolved certain arts of doing this. Where they do not achieve completely realized demonstrations, they do at least carry the intimation of true form far further than can be done intellectually.

And so, form, which to the naïve is so dreadfully dwarfed into the abbreviated shadow of its fullest significance, is the very word, the absolute terminology of Being. It is our language from the beginning of our sense of being. And in its widest scope of applicability, it embraces the whole mystery of eternal flux. Therefore, when small minds dispatch it as evidence merely of felicitously balanced structure, of good taste in organization of shapely masses, of harmonious orientation of objects in space, we must attribute such myopic vision more to intellectual infirmity than to spiritual blindness.

Intuition and intelligence, according to Henri Bergson, represent two opposite directions in the labor of understanding; intuition travels the way of life itself, along the self-evolving, uninterruptible mobility of being; intelligence goes inversely toward a process of analyzing that elusive mobility, by breaking it up into a hypothetical succession of

[2] *Durée et Simultanéité*, by Henri Bergson. Librairie Félix Alcan, 1934.

static stages in material juxtaposition. A complete and perfect humanity would be one wherein these two forms of conscious activity should attain their full development.

I have sought merely to indicate the significance of form in the abstract, and yet how it has its roots in our primitive sense of touch. The language of our earliest thoughts lay in our finger tips, and even our sense of sight was secondary to the corroboration of the sense of touch. We literally felt our way toward the truth, and our nearest approach to it then was to touch it. How intimate a connection there is between this fact and Bernard Berenson's statement of the purpose and procedure of art! In his study of *Italian Painters of the Renaissance*, he writes that "the purpose of art is to produce a direct effect of life enhancement," and that "the principal if not sole sources of life enhancement are Tactile Values, Movement, Space-Composition, . . by which I mean ideated sensations of contact, of texture, of weight, of support, of energy, and of union with one's surroundings. Let any of these sources fail, and by that much the art is diminished. Let several fail and the art may at best survive as an arabesque. If all be dried up, art will perish."

He says furthermore that this space composition "woos us away from our tight, painfully limited selves, dissolves us into the space presented, until at last we seem to become its permeating, indwelling spirit. In other words, this wonderful art can take us away from ourselves and give us, while we are under its spell, the feeling of being identified with the universe, perhaps even of being the soul of the universe. This sense of identification with the universe is of the very essence of the religious emotion—an emotion, by the way, as independent of belief and conduct as love itself."

Now the movement implicit in form, the "plasticity" of which artists and scholars and laymen so frequently and so unsatisfactorily speak, is as irrefragable an aesthetic inference as atomic motion is a scientific inference. And it is, physically, just as unapparent. I purpose, later in this work, to explain how the artist breathlessly seizes with his intuition the stirring truth of this motion, and how he conveys his feeling of it to others. He is perpetually actuated by his yearning to spread the

th about him, according to Bergson, and for him eternity no longer
ats transcendent above time, like an abstraction; it becomes the
tual substance and reality of it.

Ordinarily we feel like helpless, accidental creatures, fated to live a
oment on the isolated island of our mortality, surrounded on all
ores by the heedless surf of eternity's oceans, and destined at the
xt instant to sink into the same indifferent deeps from which
ysteriously we rose. But at times, with the very tidal flux and rhythm
at environs us, we feel a consonance of being. The ebb and flow of
iiversal process, as seen in the endless equilibrium between weight
id support, burden and sustaining power, inertia and energy, is so
ofoundly parallel to our own breathing existence of expiration and
spiration, negation and affirmation, apathy and volition, despair and
ope, that we sense a unison in these dualistic balancings of universal
iotions and human emotions.

The Greek civilization reached exalted understanding of this implied
nison. The serene perfection of Greek form still stirs us with a sense
f calm and of elevated wisdom. To many of us it marks an apogee
f architectural expression. It communicates to us, quietly and com-
ellingly, the magnitude of the intellectual penetration and spiritual
isight that grace human mentality at its heights. And all this is
chieved with the most astonishing economy of means. The inscrutable
iajesty of idea that the Greek surmised as transcendent to reality, he
iterpreted in terms of that reality itself. He recognized the natural
quilibrium in the ebb and flow of universal process; and he detected
ts counterpart everywhere in his environment. Whatever he sensed
f the sublime, he suggested through the simple manipulation of
rdinary materials. He possessed a deep intuitional understanding of the
hysical laws governing those materials. And he was particularly sensitive
o the law of adjustment between weight and energy. The temples he
rected achieved an impeccable balance between burden and power
n stone. Thus he drew an analogy between the strangely satisfying
pectacle of material laws at work and his mystifying inner vision of
iniversal process. He erected phases of truth embodied in stone.
Through the beauty of the finite he approached the truth of the infinite.

It is important to understand the psychology of this pleasurable sen sation derived from a sense of balance between burdensome weight and sustaining force. It involves a concomitant sense of symmetry, and also a feeling of resolution of discord. How does this happen? Why does the Greek temple seem so flawless and move us toward a state of rapture? Why does it seem enveloped by a silence and imbued with a serenity, and why do these tranquil qualities delight us so? Once again the explanation starts with close observation of children in their early infancy.

One of the elemental and most terrifying fears of infancy is that of falling. Owing to the lack of muscular development and nervous organization, an infant is helpless in the matter of preserving bodily poise or security. He is dependent upon outside forces for the support of his own weight, for his posture, and for any required change of position. Consequently, a withdrawal of support, or the merest suggestion of disturbed equilibrium, is enough to provoke sudden and intense fright. The infant's sense of maladjustment between his own weight and whatever support should be sustaining him produces his earliest manifestation of fear. Despite absence of any knowledge of space or the logical hazard involved in dropping from a height, he experiences sensations of discomfort whenever his equilibrium is disrupted. During sleep, it has frequently been shown in experiment, even a slight tugging at the blanket under him will arouse every sign of terror equivalent to that displayed while awake and allowed to fall a short space between two pairs of arms. Loss of proper poise is a loss of well-being.

As the infant's musculature develops through nourishment and usage, he learns how to maneuver his own weight by his own efforts, and he begins slowly to see similarity in the behavior of the things around him, which also seem to have weight and tend to fall whenever support is withdrawn. This behavior of objects according to natural laws stimulates his curiosity enormously and, through constant handling and observing, he becomes familiar with it. Subject as these things are to the same laws of gravity and energy as he himself is, he grows aware of the analogy, and this is one of the reasons why, in early childhood, he projects himself into the inanimate objects surrounding him, attributing animate characteristics to them and endowing them with human behavior. He is fascinated with his ability to make a doll sit up or fall down. After the ability to raise and lower himself, and generally to adjust his own posture, this experience of manipulating something outside himself affords him his first sense of power over matter and the behavior of matter.

Then comes a long process of extending this control both over himself and over things. At the stage where he begins to stand erect and to walk, he grows further alive, as it were, to the great difficulty of achieving balance. This is an impressive lesson, and it takes him a number of years to adjust his strength and nervous co-ordination to such a point as will enable him to move with the full poise of easy, graceful equilibrium. And during this procedure of learning he inevitably conceives a real respect for the entire phenomenon of equilibrium. As his capacity for standing and walking grows, he watches growing with it his whole empire over the things around him. At last he begins to measure his ability by his adroitness in applying a minimum of strength to a maximum of exigency. He sees that a little skill often surmounts obstacles that great effort cannot overcome. He understands finally the vital function of this skill in the performance of any act.

And so the whole tremendous idea of effort, that quality so essential to man's activity, is seen to be an endless process of adjustment between strength and weight, energy and inertia. The more perfect the adjustment, the less exertion is required. The more exquisitely man adapts his strength to that which resists it, the easier the consummation of his effort. And this brings us to our first perception of the quality of grace.

The physical attribute or gift of grace in a man is that easy elegance of movement and bearing produced by a well-proportioned body whose strength is finely adapted to its weight. When the child shall have established a complete development and co-ordination of the nerves and muscles that are the implements of balanced movement, then all clumsiness of carriage, gait and gesture disappears; the body bears itself well. It moves easily, with a minimum of effort. It has achieved grace!

Now, the spectacle of graceful bearing and movement fills us with sensations of immense satisfaction and pleasure. Spencer maintained that

the reason lies in nothing but our enjoyment of the saving of effort. B
Henri Bergson, in his work on *Time and Free Will*, makes some coge
contributions to this subject. Comparing grace to the quality of a fin
curved line, and awkwardness to that of a broken, irregular zigzag,
asserts that "if curves are more 'graceful' than broken lines, the reas
is that, while a curved line changes its direction at every moment, ev
new direction is indicated in the preceding one. Thus the perception
ease in motion passes over into the pleasure of mastering the flow of ti
and of holding intimations of the future in the present. If jerky mov
ments are wanting in grace, the reason is that each of them is self-su
cient and does not announce those which are to follow. There is
naturally superior ease in movements which can be foreseen . . .
present attitudes in which future attitudes are, as it were, prefigured. W
could hardly make out why grace affords us such pleasure if it we
nothing but a saving of effort as Spencer maintains. But the truth is th
in everything which we call very graceful we imagine ourselves able
detect, besides the lightness which is a sign of mobility, some suggestic
of a possible movement toward ourselves, of a virtual and even nasce
sympathy. It is this mobile sympathy, always ready to offer itself, whic
is just the essence of higher grace."

Here Bergson has covered vast ground in a few words, because th
represent a summing up of ideas developed earlier in his work. For o
own purposes, we shall have to penetrate slowly into this concept
higher grace, which will carry us eventually to exalted regions of th
human spirit. For the moment, it suffices to understand the fact th
in a graceful form or movement each part is essentially related to i
neighboring parts within a definite context, so that any one of thes
parts will suggest to us what preceded and what follows. A small, isc
lated portion of a curved line is enough to indicate the larger span. An
moment in the stride of a fine runner discloses the measured flow of h
gait. We are lifted up and carried along in the swing and empathic com
pulsion of his grace.

More impressive continuities are to be found in the vital and obscu
realms of atomic motion and in the behavior of all the elemental force
which, once again, are rather apprehended than actually seen. Th

iversal process, the ebb and flow of which we have spoken, seems to
characterized by this same integrity of operation. Leonardo da Vinci
led it "the serpentine line" of existence; he felt it in all things and
all individualities. The faithful observation, the successful rendition
any phase of this line of grace reveals to us further reaches of its
xpressible entirety. The furthest expression of this equilibrated con-
uity, in its subtlest and most revelatory compulsion, lies in the rhyth-
c forms of high art. The whole architecture of music consists of a
ythmic passage of sounds and silences through a duration of time; the
ole structure of painting is composed of a rhythmic movement of
jects and intervals through extended space. The art of drama in its
ghest form, as best exemplified by the Greek tragedy, and the Shake-
earean, is erected upon the same relentless, rhythmic evolution of
aracters and events moving inevitably through time along the course
their unalterable destinies. The dance distributes the symmetry of its
ovement through time and space. That is why the merest fragment,
instance, a hand, or foot, or torso from some superb Greek statuary,
s us with a thrilling intimation of the rest of the form. It is why a few
rases extracted from the context of great music are enough to indicate
e lofty proportions, momentum, and harmony of the composition.
d from a view of the rhythmic operation of forces and events in the
rly periods of such careers as those of Oedipus, Hamlet, Macbeth we
e able to foreshadow by presentiment the whole relentless succession
graduated incidents leading to tragic denouement. The power of
agedy does not reside in emotions of grief and pity aroused by the
ectacle of catastrophe; we are confronted with these, to a milder degree,
roughout our lives. The real wave and impact that surges out upon
, sweeping us along in the current of fatality, is our recognition to a
ightened degree, due to the dramatic contrivance of quickened crys-
llization, of irresistible powers at work. We see persons rushed along
the inexorable flow of cause and effect, contributing personally to an
apersonal process by which they are borne at last to the resolution of
these opposing forces. Over the struggle of human motivations in
in conflict, the higher grace superimposes a final calm of equilibrium.
his may seem calamitous to the frustrated individuals whose discord-

ancies are thus resolved, but it is a breath-taking revelation of t
futility of human effort exerted without the rectitude, the integrity
grace. These uneasy spirits, unbalanced by the burden of their inordin:
desires, overreach themselves by the very excess of their striving; we :
them drawn to their catastrophe by the implacable weight of their o
maladjustment. The life force, the élan vital, disposes of them as thou
by the jujutsu tactics of a wrestler; they are thrown, mainly by the c
proportion of their own effort.

The wise man is one who erects the structure of his behavior upoı
fine equilibrium between the widest knowledge of facts that he c
acquire and the highest skill he can develop in its useful applicatiı
Judgment is the fulcrum by which he manipulates the load of his oı
limitations. Wisdom is one of the culminations of human grace. Oı
again, at these heights, we are confronted with the process of exquis
adjustment between weight and effort. Man's wisdom is his balar
between the opposing forces of his infirmities and his aspirations. By]
wisdom he maintains his poise. By his poise he maintains his natuı
affinity for the absolute. It is his nearest intelligent approach to tł
ultimate resolution of all temporal discord into timeless serenity. We :
back again to his concept of the true and the beautiful, and we :
back again to the Greek temple.

So vast is man's respect for the quality and power of grace that
has gradually exalted its meaning until it has come to signify in its loftiı
sense the divine favor of God. The sublime grace of the temple aspiı
to this same significance of divinity. Through the achievement of
perfect accord between its heavy horizontal burdens and its efficiе
vertical supports, it seeks to suggest by its appearance of consummɛ
harmony a resemblance to the absolute. By virtue of an impeccaɫ
mathematics applied to structure, the Greek created a substantial sı
gestion of truth. The application of mathematics to building was equiı
lent to that of logic to argument. There is an impact of finality to t
result. By erecting a material structure upon the logic of flawless equil
rium, the Greek sought to display in the finished form his sense of t
ultimate. Through the genius of his material touch, he approached

sp of the abstract idea! This is what inspired Edna St. Vincent Millay
exclaim: "Euclid alone has looked on Beauty bare."[3] Thus Greek form
came one of the mightiest metaphorical triumphs of human history;
drew a most persuasive analogy between superb poise of finite matter
d supernal grace of the infinite.

f in our infancy we find pleasure in piling up building blocks, bal-
cing them as best we can, it is not difficult to understand, in maturity,
r admiration for the same performance carried to altitudes of perfec-
n. When, as in a Greek form, we find every separate part contributing
ectually to the one purpose, every minor embellishment interwoven
th the essential design, unimpeded by ornamental distractions or any
umsiness of construction, we thrill to the majesty of it. It is an accom-
shment performed with the highest conceivable effectiveness, and it
permeated with a feeling of easy tranquillity. It has the appearance
effortless and unending felicity. The integrity of evolutionary process
ems here to be realized. We are happy to behold it; we love the
rsuasion of its composure; we eagerly identify ourselves with its per-
ction. In its presence we forget the agitation of our struggles and
aladjustments; we are uplifted and absorbed into a state of peace.
The infant's first real communication with his fellow beings is through
smile. Is not the artist's creation his mature smile to his matured
llows?

[3]
                        Euclid alone
        Has looked on Beauty bare. Fortunate they
        Who, though once only and then but far away,
        Have heard her massive sandal set on stone.

Chapter III

INTERFUSION OF SUBSTANCE AND SPACE

GREEK form is a metaphorical triumph. In the contrivance language, which displays progressively from its origins the m marvelous resourcefulness, we find at the summit of its expr sive power the figure of speech known as metaphor. It is easy to tra the development of this linguistic invention. The earliest function words was limited to identifying simple objects and acts in the ex rience of living. This in itself was a stupendous advance in man's eff to communicate with his fellows. By the utterance of certain spec vocal sounds, gradually fixed by habits of mutual usage, he became a to convey images and ideas. Such expression was, of course, restricted elementary symbols, until man's growing need for richer and more curate statement led him to devise further implements of speech. Af he had extended his range of expression by "naming" as many things a "designating" as many acts as possible, he began to qualify his nou and verbs with adjectives and adverbs. He felt an urge to describe exactly as possible the distinctive qualities of things and their man of being.

This increase of rhetorical skill lifted language toward the altitudes higher art; and, since words are the very stone and mortar of the int lectual edifice, the growth of language was the growth of thought. Fina as even the richest diversity of descriptive wording fell short of wha man needed to illuminate his profoundest sentiments, he began approach their finer shadings by apt comparison and simile. Literatu burst forth then into poetic flashes of further revelation. One can f exultancy in the release toward new horizons of truth; it throbs passi ately in the Biblical prayers and preachings of the devout; it electri and stirs with detonations of Homeric lightning and thunder. Migl images rise like apparitions of the imperceptible. These poets, th

ers of the metaphor, seem to have discovered some of the idiom
ternity.

akespearean words, like musical notes, combine into chords of con-
nce and meaning; their phrases assemble into a vast and revelatory
ic. What is the rapturous compulsion of these metaphors and
les? The Song of Solomon, mounting from an image of sensuality to
tual realms of annunciation, is interpreted to depict the church as
rdent and repentant maiden seeking everywhere a ravishing union
her beloved Saviour. The imperative nobility of Christ's own teach-
spreads its influence over a refractory world mainly through the
uasion of his stirring parables. The astounding impact of a Sappho,
ing only from the mutilated fragments of her lyrical genius, fills us
a breathless recognition of higher cadencies and import. Even her
essions of earthly passion in its more robust aspects break upon us
waves of impulsion. "Love, like a mountain wind upon an oak,
ng upon me, shakes me leaf and bough." These are the vivid means
eaching to us over a space of centuries, setting us into the empathic
ult of this formidable emotion.

he staggering magnitude of Shakespearean genius in this respect elec-
es us constantly throughout his works. His very name evokes a sense
igher language, and when we have heard his transmutation of our
plest words into miracles of meaning, our verbiage sounds trivial.
alchemy of his rhetoric dazzles us. And, marvelous above all else,
find ourselves lifted into the heights of his own vision. We cast aside
paltry talents with which ordinarily we struggle; we become endowed
h more penetrating sight, loftier perceptions, nobler heart. We rise,
it were, from the impediments of our stunted faculties into the
berance of man in full stature. Through Shakespeare's eyes we see
ole worlds illumined to which our own were blind. We feel with his
ater feeling and think his greater thoughts. We dissolve our lowly
kwardness in his higher grace. And as we mount along the way of
se sequential splendors, some of them substantiate for us our own
te intuitions, while others, beyond the horizon of our intimations,
sh upon us their lightning revealment. These poets explain to us with

their metaphors the very smile of the inscrutable. Listen to John K
ponder over the mysterious beauty of a Grecian urn:

> Thou still unravish'd bride of quietness,
> 　Thou foster-child of silence and slow time,
> Sylvan historian, who canst thus express
> 　A flowery tale more sweetly than our rhyme;
> . . . .
> Thou, silent form, dost tease us out of thought
> 　As doth eternity. . . .

How like the simple notes of a pianistic scale is our brief alphabet, f
which can be drawn by a great musician rhapsodies of immeasur
scope. Small wonder that these achievements are surrounded by a
ness; the pure form bounded but by space. We sing our greatest pa
listening to the choir.

And so, the vision of humanity reaches to the distance of its furth
seeing eyes. The poet leads us through nebulous regions of limited
ception, to the unclouded spaces of his sagacity. He intensifies our s
ment and understanding of a thing by showing us one or a host of
tinent images, momentous in their power of enhancement. He is
supreme relativist, disclosing life's superlatives by the evidence o
comparatives, and discovering the invisible by the wake and shado
its passage. His worded thoughts are evocations of supernal grace.
have said the same of perfected equilibrium in Greek form. By t
expressive resemblance to the ineffable, these artistic creations aspir
represent finite aspects of infinity.

The compulsion, then, of such metaphorical achievements lies in t
vivid, descriptive power. They enable us to ascribe appearances to
invisible, tangibility to the impalpable, form to the infinite, and mea
to the eternal. Once again, by the exercise of our art, we reach ou
touch the unknown, to grasp its nature and its implications. Wave
sound beyond the sensitivity of our ears are silence to us. "Heard m
dies are sweet, but those unheard are sweeter . . ." Our spirits, by t
works, become attuned to a music unattended by our mortal ears.
everlasting, measured flow that we sense as the truth of all bein
rendered perceptible by human imitation. The man with the furth

ing vision yearns to spread the view of his horizons everywhere, to
the beauty with his blinder fellows, to make them see as he does.
is the revelation of high art, the mightiest effort within the capacity
an. It is a revelation that mankind is unceasingly demanding as
incing proof of its most treasured intuitions. Hopefully it scans the
of art, and rapturously it acquiesces. Man's instinctive challenge
confronted with any idea incredible to him is immediately a plea
roof. "Show me; prove it to me; let me see it." And so, this intan-
, inspired sense of "something beyond" is "shown" by the poet-
as his answer. He expresses his own vision of it with an integrity
permits his fellow men to see as he sees. This act of higher grace can
an apotheosis of man. There are few higher functions in the cate-
of human endeavor than this inquiry for truth, and the manifesta-
of its beauty. If there is a logical path to the sanctification of the
an will, should it not be along the unfolding of these values?

his brings us at last to the special province of the picture, literally the
t vivid metaphor of all. Here we have not a verbal, but an actual
e. In its beginnings, the picture served merely to identify objects,
he noun does in language. It conveyed no more than might any
le word when extracted from a context. It was merely a crude visual
esentation of superficial shapes, achieved by the interrelation of a
imitative lines. In this rudimentary function it was simply a linear
bol instead of a linguistic one. Long before the art of speech de-
ped an eloquence of its own, such linear improvisations were an early
s for human discourse. To primitive mentality, the device of drawn
s was sufficient for delineating the apparent shapes of things; and
this resourcefulness men were able to communicate and to record
s without the medium of words. The picture served to identify and,
limited way, to describe things. Indeed, one wonders whether the
man could have conveyed nearly so much verbally as he expressed
his artful drawings. Those pictures, however, are already advanced
ond that simplest function which marks the origin of pictorial ex-
ssion. They are no longer merely linear symbols; they are infused with
eeper intention. They display an awakened feeling for certain quali-
in the shapes of things, and a developed capacity for rendering them.

The art of pictorial expression has thus had an evolution simila
that of language. Starting with the barest, awkward delineations, its
advance probably lay along the path of increasing skill which permi
truer, and consequently more satisfactory, portrayal of shapes. N
came the depiction of activity, the liberation from static confinem
This parallels the function of the verb. By observing and faithf
imitating the appearance of objects in their various stages of transit
their outlines came to be drawn in such fashion as to give a semblanc
action. By drawing the accurate outline of a man or an animal,
instance, at any one instant during a sustained movement, an impres
of that activity was created. Once these two functions combined,
art of depiction was greatly enriched, both practically and aesthetic
Practically, it became possible to convey ideas not only of things, bu
life manifestations as revealed by things in action. Aesthetically, it
vided a truer representation of appearances in the grace of their inhe
movement. From the infantile symbolism of a man represented b
few suggestive lines to an outlined effigy portrayed in an instantane
phase of some activity is a considerable progress. And still the effig
but the outer semblance of a man. Its highest quality remains limi
to an elegance of shape, an ostensible symmetry, a specious rhythm.
truth and higher grace of *form* in all the effulgent supremacy of its
is to be found in none of these, however scrupulous, delineations.
long as the depiction is confined to the portrayal of objects, no ma
what magnitudes of skill and passionate zeal may be lavished on
accomplishment, still there is no grace of *form*. However fair the fig
in shapeliness, gracious coloring, felicity of expression, the grace of fc
is not present. Such pictures have no beauty, though they glow w
loveliness; they are animate with all the galaxy of charm. We love tl
pleasing features; hence, their "loveliness." But they are still o
aspects, however exquisite, of *things*. They are not yet aspects of tru
not yet finite versions of the infinite. At best they are moving images
ourselves, but never a conception of ourselves related to context
eternity, the very soul of self. What is this elusive phase of appearan
so indispensable to the grace of true vision, and without which no
ture surmounts the level of a semblance? What further properties

gs must be discovered and displayed before the picture rises from
blance to revelation, from the intelligible to the intuitive? When
; a picture abandon illusory appearances for the real consonance of
ties? The answer is impressive and crystal-clear.

he picture becomes vast and revelatory experience at that momentous
e when it discovers the mutual pervasiveness of substance and space.
:h this discovery comes a flood of revolutionary development. Objects
no longer isolated islands of substance bounded haphazardly by other
cts and by space. Things are no longer related to each other merely
the chance disposal of how they happen to appear in juxtaposition.
denly a new element appears in the visual experience of man, some-
ng that had always been visible but never before observed in its full
ificance. Hitherto preoccupied with the manifold aspects of objects,
now becomes aware of intervals, aspects of space. He awakens to
tremendous consequences of this further insight. The pleasing sym-
ry of shapes that once delighted him shrinks now into disregard.
 symmetry of shape seems but a vulgar and tawdry pleasure com-
d to the new-found grace of form. For here, at long last, is the pic-
 of man's further feeling for the true shape, not of matter but of
ng. This new image does not delineate the shape and structure of
gs, but of things in their spacious context of infinity. The ultimate
ilibrium is unveiled in all the vibrant thrill of its perfection, the
ilibrium between these objects and intervals which are the two
nents of form. And it is the interpenetrating flow of these two ele-
nts in their endless interweavings that we call the plasticity of form.
esembles what our intuition has described as the eternal, effortless
 of the ultimate. And that is why a picture possessed of this specific
sticity of form fills us with a sense of metaphoric revealment. It
kes visions of the imperceptible.

'o speak of the mutual pervasiveness of substance and space, to call
cts and intervals the two elements of form, is perhaps to say over-
ch too briefly. I shall devote considerable space to an explanation of
 how the human mentality became aware of these aesthetic truths,
 how it gradually acquired a skill for displaying them pictorially. And
hall endeavor, in the process of this explanation, to show the most

important fact of all, which is that every time one is privileged to s◄ successfully rendered picture of this ultimate nature one becomes ı teriously involved in the integrity of its consummation. To a suscept person this is quite as lofty a spiritual experience as any of the varic of religious experience. For the present, it is essential to retain the ı of form as consisting of endlessly interweaving substance and space, arrested by contour, which merely serves to punctuate, as it were, successive shapes and intervals composing the plastic movement. other words, the soundest conception of form is that of the evolutioı process itself . . . an unfolding through space and time, seeming proceed out of a mystical adjustment between energies and inertias, ᵥ the energies ever prevailing. For it is never static, always dynamic.

This explains what was intended when I spoke of the special provi of the picture, calling it literally the most vivid metaphor of all. ˈ painted picture has a special and unique mission, distinguished fronɪ the other arts in one impressive respect. This is its quality of immedi It is the only instantaneous expression of duration, of movement thro◄ extended space. Here is a resemblance to lightning revelation. The wⁱ illusion of duration in time and extension in space is revealed in a ſ of simultaneity. In a single instant of beholding, one perceives the wⁱ form in pictures; whereas such form may be disclosed by all the oᵗ arts only through the lengths of time that it takes for them to be ı or heard or seen. The picture happens all at once, so to speak. ˈ plastic arts of sculpture and architecture must be considered as phase this same sort of experience, though impeded by certain disadvantᵢ later to be examined.

The procedure of music, of poetry, prose, drama, and of the da involves, in each case, a passage of time. It is for this reason that exp sion in literature and music seems to some to be a more intellec process than that of the plastic arts. The procedure of these expressⁱ resembles the procedure of thinking itself, which is always breaking the flow of experience into a sequence of component parts. In tⁱ forms there is a progression from a beginning to an end, requiring tained attention through stages of development. Only at the conclus can the mind grasp the full significance, the full form, that has haᵈ

ne to it gradually, extended over a "space of time." None of them
opens instantaneously; they all reveal themselves progressively, so
t at any given moment only a fraction of the form is perceptible, and
faculty of memory plays an indispensable role in the integration of
whole form. Hence the startling impact of a great picture that dis-
ses in an instant of looking as much as may be found in other forms
art only after protracted assimilation.

Chapter IV

THE GRACE OF CONTINUITY

O NE may well be reproached for introducing metaphysics i
the study or the appreciation of works of art. Resentment
quently and understandably arises when a "pure emotic
expressed by some "intuitive" artist is subjected to tampering analysis
the hands of inquiring "intellectuals." This revulsion against dissect
of the mysterious flower is similar to the pain one might feel if an
quisitive anatomist were to halt the expressive miracle of an Isad
Duncan in the act of dancing in order to investigate the skeletal pi
esses of her motions. Such investigation would surely yield no expla
tion of her peculiarly exalted grace. Yet an understanding of I
mentality might reveal at least some attributes of the spirit animati
her gestures. For the compulsion, the power to move us, possessed
a great dancer does not lie in the nature of her beautiful body or in t
mere grace of its movement. These qualities may constitute a welco
part of the equipment and functioning of a Duncan but, without t
animating genius behind these gracious accessories, they are capable
producing only the mediocre achievement of a pleasing but uninspir
spectacle.

In this connection, it is interesting to recall from both the Platon
and the Xenophonic dialogues the fact that Socrates himself, despite t
handicap of what seems to have been by his own admission an almc
revoltingly ugly body, endeavored to express himself occasionally throug
the medium of the dance. He insisted that he need feel in no wa
hampered by the apparent disadvantages of an ill-formed body. He w
persuaded that any body, motivated by lofty sentiment, could be t
medium for beautiful expression. Indeed, is it not an obvious fact th
out of the plainest, most ill-favored visage may shine a heavenly ligl
when, from the inner spirit, comes an inspiring and benevolent message

pid and inconsequential remains the prettiness of a merely pretty face;
ring to the depths of the soul will be the countenance animated by
virtues of gentle understanding and illimitable love. Thus, with
rates, it was his logical conviction that if he ardently yearned to
vey a noble sentiment by grace of an "ungraceful" body, the intensity
his will so to do would surmount the handicap of his bodily awkward-
s and achieve a spiritual grace.

This was at the heart of Isadora Duncan's so-called genius, a variety
saintliness that lies at the bottom of so much of humanity's highest
deavor. As mysticism falls away from religion in these modern eras
science and skepticism, the saint of other ages will be found in some
the artists of today. Here is the field of renunciation of worldly
ities, the embracing of the three interchangeable virtues. For, where
e unregenerate worldlings will have, time and again, rejected goodness
t of vanity, and ignored truth out of willfulness, they are still touched
beauty and inspired, if only ephemerally, to a renewed love of virtue.
pointed illustration of the intimate connection between the concepts
beauty and virtue is contained in the *Causeries Florentins* of Klaczko:
The short epoch which traverses the times of Leonardo to the death of
phael was one of the most radiant of human history. The matter of
auty preoccupied almost exclusively, animated and bore along the
eatest and most elevated spirits; it had become the unique end, the
st business and ultimate reason in all things. And it is from this period,
I am not mistaken, that art, ingenuity, skill acquired amongst us so
nerally the name of Virtue." Once again we see that beauty may
anifestly be a visible radiation of the form of Truth, of God, of what-
er humanity may choose to call the ineffable Virtue.

Isadora liked to consider the human soul in the vernacular of her own
me, as a radio receiver and transmitter. Her message of universal love,
e believed, was best conveyed far and wide by her "tuning in" on the
hereal omniscience, and radiating out of herself to her fellow beings
e love impulse that she sensed to be the humanized version of this
dly vibration. She felt this comprehension to be unutterable in words,
ut believed that it could be shown, or at least implied, by gestures of
human body receptive to the impulse of this ineffable power and

capable of becoming a medium for its transmission. Nor did she f
this capability to be anything more special than a consecration of
human will. As with so many saintly characters, her fanatical devotion
this specific concept endowed her with ever-growing persuasiveness,
that gradually her vision gained vast empire over herself and over th
who were privileged to receive her communication. The result was t
finally she had but to make a simple gesture, without even the necess
to move her feet, and there came forth from her almost station
dancing a hypnotic force laden with gifts of purifying magic. This wa
religious experience of the most elevated nature; to behold this type
transport is to be lifted out of all the selfish encumbrances of wo
preoccupation, of inertia, of fear, of all the manifold obstructions
which the spirit ordinarily is subjected by the substance; and, transcen
ing these, to answer love with love, bereft of any other passion, render
too pure in essence to give or to receive any radiation other than t
most ultimate grace.

It will not be digressive to study for a moment the mental proces
which nurtured the talent and fructified the genius of such an artist
Isadora Duncan. According to her own description, she was animat
by the dominant conviction that love is the essential force by whi
human nature can and must fulfill its highest destiny. She regarded
obstacles to the sustained possession of this dynamic sentiment as sym
tomatic of the world neurosis from which we all suffer to greater a
lesser degree. She wished, above all else, to purge her fellow beings a
to purge herself of the multitudes of obstructive vanities and fears whi
so encumber and so vitiate the conduct of worthy lives. She understo
intuitively as a psychiatrist understands analytically the obsessive fea
and lusts which envelop us in such unhappy, dark confusion. She fe
that, in succumbing to these incapacitating degenerations of our spiritu
stamina, we bind ourselves hopelessly in the fetters of our own maligna
folly. And so it was clear to her that if she could demonstrate t
futility of selfishness she would deliver humanity from frustration in
a regenerative flowering. It is neither necessary nor fitting to investiga
here the logic by which Isadora persuaded herself and her communican
of the divine indispensability of this truth, since it is an ethic that h

n beatifically revealed and expounded to the world of lethargic
rtals time and again by its loftiest and most inspired thinkers. This
; the vast blessing that Jesus strove with all his anguished heart to
e to us.

sadora was sensitive to the analogy between the morally and the
thetically noxious. The offensive behavior of the impure human being
istitutes a blemish on the pattern of what is good, and the corruption
the pattern of goodness is as ugly a catastrophe as can befall a God-
iring world. In other words, an unloving spirit is an unlovely spirit,
d the world of unlovely spirits is an ugly thing. It is probable that
en Isadora was a young girl starting upon her difficult career as a
ncer, few if any of these thoughts were in her mind. At that time she
s more virginally unaware of her deep intuitions and not analytical of
em. She loved the idea of the dance and she wanted to dance as
autifully as she could. She studied the figures on ancient Grecian
ses, feeling that she derived much inspiration from the elevated
hievement of the classical age. The dynamic quality of her tempera-
ent ensured her against any tendency to mere imitations or sterile
surrections of past splendors. She was simply beginning her own young
e with a healthy susceptibility to the almost hypnotic communication
at comes to all sensitive earthlings from the creativity of their fore-
ars. This, contrary to much illusory cavil on the part of individuals
ho dread an empire of the past over the present, has always been the
ay of growth in the evolution of human genius. Our Cézanne and our
an Gogh were as mightily enamored of what they sought and found in
e Musée du Louvre as many an uncreative amateur, and the structure
f their own original works was only enhanced by these stirring messages
om their fathers and their brothers. As the infant matures by the ac-
mulation of its own experience, so does the human race; and every one
f its creative members emerges in the advancing flow, by the cumulative
rce of the historic current plus his own striving. So it was with Isadora.
y every means available to her, out of the past and from her contem-
oraries, she sought to make of herself as good a dancer as by the grace
f God, of man, and of her own efforts she possibly could. She knew that

she yearned to dance beautifully and she did not at that time grea question why.

And she did dance beautifully, to such an extent that her name v celebrated and loved. The art of the dance was revived by her into experience that stirred great numbers to a quickened enthusiasm. T current of her artistry charged her audiences with responsive emoti as though electrified, and the whole metabolism of their souls arose a new vigor. And as she went on accomplishing this fine performing the early flower of her youth, she did little philosophizing about her and little proselytizing. Her message at this time was in the form o great, spontaneous outpouring of pure movement. In her hour on t stage she sought, by the exquisitely responsive medium of her body, execute a noble architecture in time and space. The unimpeded gra with which her motion suggested a transcendent rhythm released l audiences from their self-imposed bondage of egoistic restraints a anxieties. By an empathic surge they felt themselves drawn and lift into an effortless communion and identification with the dancer.

We are all more or less acquainted with the illusion of ease that great artist produces by the perfection of his own performance. A bea tiful singer makes us feel that we ourselves have but to open wide o eager mouths to sing as well. In the hearing of operatic cadences o sometimes has to exert a self-restraint, so great is the impulsion to fli oneself into the gloriously fluent stream of sound. One reads a sonnet Dante, of Milton, of Shakespeare, and one feels ready to add a sonnet one's own. In a less restricted field, what mediocre amateur of tenr has not felt, when watching a Tilden in the easy stride and swing his masterly performing, that he might readily step upon the cou and enter into an exalted version of his usual game? The compelli grace of the master tends to lift us out of our frustrating sense of medic rity. Nor is this merely tempting us into a momentarily happy illusic from which we are to be rudely awakened each time into the sord reality of our little selves again. If this is all the artist could do for us raise us up a moment to the airy altitudes of his attainment and drc us down again to the depressive level of our everyday torpidity—v could not profit greatly. Fortunately, the contrary is the case. Eve

ne an average mortal is privileged to come within the aura or direct
fluence of a more articulate, superior mortal he is affected by the
perience. We are all to a great extent the products of our environ-
ent. If we wish to be connoisseurs of good wine we have to do much
ne tasting in order to emerge from complete ignorance of wines to
tensive familiarity with them. If we wish to know enough about the
: of music or of painting or of any human expression to be enabled to
ceive from music, paintings or other communications what they have to
ve to us, we must hear much music, see many pictures, make many
orts to increase our capacity of comprehension. And similarly, the more
ten and the more intensively we are exposed to the influential grace of
ine artist the more apt we become to assimilate and to reincarnate much
that grace. Hence those who saw Isadora dance only once had already
inkling of some further dimension to the human soul, and those who
w her many times expanded that much further into the wider spaces
' her reaching.

It is not surprising that Isadora found in Walt Whitman a kindred
irit. Here was a pioneer American poet who sang at the top of his lusty
ice about his beloved America dancing with all the fervor of its
outhful strength. He too felt that the young and pure of heart must
ance their dreams, in the full joy of universal love. All men were his
rothers, children under the same sky and out of the same mother earth;
nd if he could fling aside the encumbering robes of selfishness in which
e all-too-often wrap ourselves, freeing himself for the exuberant way of
fe, why not all his brothers and his sisters? He identified himself with
ll of them, he loved them all, and wanted all of them to love as he
oved. To move with love is to dance, is to sing, is to be gay. And so
Walt Whitman called out to all America and to all the world to join the
ance of the good life. He lifted up the lame and the halt by the strength
f his fellowship and by the force of his will. There was an exhilarating
nd a healing energy in his joyful wisdom that swept through the stiff
oints and interstices of many a diseased spirit, restoring it to health and
appiness. This was the "gai savoir" of which Nietzsche at times so wist-
ully and at times so feverishly sang.

One of the earliest as well as most enduring impulses of man seems

to be this gesturing with his body as a means of expressing emotio
exorcising demons, supplicating gods. It is one of our earliest and mo
elemental languages. And at the summit of its perfection it affords
tangible display of human grace in fullest actuality. It is so potent a
instinct that its semblance often appears in other forms of art. F
instance, this same majestic dance rhythm so literally rendered by a
Isadora is to be found almost ecstatically revealed in the marvels of I
Greco. In his paintings, Christ and his apostles are in an endless swirl
what, in the behavior of ordinary people, would seem to be an excessi
movement. It is true that "ordinary people" do not move like tha
When they walk they do not seem to dance, nor when they are eag
do they soar like flames. But El Greco's Christians dance and soar b
cause they and El Greco are not "ordinary people." They are imbuc
with that vehemence of character which, in men of lesser wisdom ar
integrity, is called fanaticism. The ardor with which they seek to puri
themselves and their fellow beings, to transcend the paralyzing effec
of mortal iniquity, causes them to think and to act in a mood of urgenc
They live in the conviction that every transgression is a morbid profani
of the life that is given man to live, and their own accelerated activi
is the result of their striving to purge humanity of its inherent poison
The tremendous exercise of will required by a sound mind to guide a
impaired mind toward health, the torment that so inevitably accon
panies this herculean task of overcoming resistance and inertia, rous
the stronger will to a higher and higher pitch of endeavor.

This, at bottom, is the motivating power of the saint, dominated b
the unique resolve to free himself and his brothers of every impedimer
which from the impure flesh confounds the spirit. And in the ultima
sense of the words, it is the ascension from death to life. Is there muc
wonder, then, that men like these, bent upon celestial business a
their lives, should acquire some of the heavenly idiom? Is it not to b
expected that these men who come to understand the grace of humb
love and wisdom will move with grace along the ways of their benev
lence? Thus, in the human idiom, to move with grace is to danc
particularly when it is a movement of aspirational intensity and joyf
reward. A child will leap and dance for joy, and so, by his own test

ony, did Socrates. Why, then, will he not dance in the fervid exertion
his spiritual flight? El Greco says he will, and he shows us Jesus in
passion against the sinners who violate the temple. In a transport of
ghteous indignation Christ lashes out at the impurity of mankind,
ourging and purging himself as well as his brother men of the cor-
ptions that impede a better human destiny. For he loves them as he
ves his Father, and the greater his love the more violent the ecstasy
his castigation. His exalted emotion is pictured by El Greco in a
multuous creativity of ethereal motion, essentially a dance of good
rmounting evil, of life casting out death. Here is form beyond
sthetic, Nature in her divinely plastic mood!

As the spirit and mentality of Isadora emerged from the chaste
rtues of adolescence into the more matured experience of adult years,
er art expanded. Virtuosity became less and less sufficient to the
onscience of the artist. As she encountered the passions and prejudices
f a troubled world, she was no longer content with the enthusiastic
ut rather sterile reactions of her audiences. She wanted her dancing
o produce more than acclamation. She was ashamed of the vanity in
er that caused her to enjoy the triumph of wild applause. Her con-
cience did not want applause. The doctor does not seek applause from
is patient, nor the teacher from his pupil, nor God from his children.
Iumble silence were a better sign. Beauty and truth prosper best in
he tranquillity of listening spirits. She became distrustful of the prima
onna role that life was forcing upon her. And it was by the combina-
ion of this pure intuition and the sorrowful tribulations to which her
ensitive spirit was subjected by the accidents and incidents of her life
hat Isadora at last mounted to the apogee of her genius. With a brief
lescription of this final phase of her being I shall be describing at the
ame time the process by which so much of the world's best genius
as flowered.

Isadora's final hope was to induce all humanity to dance as she
lanced, and so to be in a universal communion of feeling and gesture.
She believed that it was most practical to start with little children, and
he envisaged a dance of mutual love spreading over the world, bearing
vith it the blessings of serenity and self-evolving felicity. When asked

how she hoped to be able to teach any ordinary child to dance beautifully as she danced, and by just what process this might be done her explanation was simpler than the achievement. Because she d not always see how little of her own integrity and generosity could permanently inculcated into the frail vessels that were her brother an sister children. However, though we cannot all be Isadoras, we can receive and give forth in the measure of our individual capacities t grace of her ampler benevolence. Her explanation of how to dan involved no systematic physical training, no program of laborio technique. This she felt would develop of itself by the constant exerci of the body in pursuit of and in response to its motivating idea. Th first thing she taught each child was to consider that the motivatir force of a human being, the soul, or whatever one might call it, situated at the center of one's breast, and then she had each chi hold her hands one upon the other over this central place. She the explained that there were children all over the world who, though the spoke different languages and lived materially separated lives, neverth less stood in the same way with their hands gently folded over the breasts. These were all brothers and sisters, everywhere and at all time And the first gesture she asked them to make was to reach forth the arms to these brothers and sisters with only one idea in their mind that this stretching forth of arms was a greeting, a silent, far-reachir message of love. Animated by this thought, and this thought alon the gesture was always a beautiful one. It is amazing to see with wha grace the most untutored person will perform such a gesture whe actuated by this impelling mood, automatically released from th awkward restraints of self-consciousness and the other impediments c habitual egoism. Whereas if one were to set about making the sam gracious movement by skill alone, uninspired by the urgency of th communication, the result might be what we call pretty but it woul not be beautiful. It would be only the copy of an original, without an of the sublime emotional impact.

On this alone a volume might be written, and we have but to loo at a Parisian Madeleine or a New York St. Patrick's Cathedral in con trast to a Grecian temple and a cathedral at Chartres to understan

e full implication. Even a certain vulgar mawkishness of a well-
tentioned but shallow Murillo when compared to such spirits as
imabue, Duccio, Giotto, Fra Angelico—to mention only an outstand-
g few of the galaxy of love-inspired ones—illustrates the world of
ifference between talent and genius, skill and spontaneity. The flower
f grace has to be watered with tears of love. And that is why Isadora
eld out her hands to give herself to her children and to receive them
a her arms. This was her mature smile.

Chapter V

POWER OF WILL IN CREATIVITY

~~~~~~

METAPHYSICAL considerations have not yet been introduce because it has not been necessary to do so. However, if had wanted to increase our understanding of the who phenomenon of an Isadora Duncan, if we had desired to pursue t mystery of her power and her beauty to the point of its inscrutabilit we should most certainly have found ourselves traversing the fields metaphysical inquiry. We were already approaching the moment whe we would be tempted to talk about the aesthetic values of Isadora art in terms of form, apart from the psychological and spiritu causation. And this would inevitably have brought us back to a rema about form made in Chapter Three, which seems to apply as well form in the dance as to that in any other medium. If we visualize t movement of Isadora as we reread this remark, it will certainly bear visible resemblance to the abstract process previously describe ". . . the soundest conception of form is that of the evolutiona process itself . . . an unfolding through space and time, seeming proceed out of a mystical adjustment between energies and inertia with the energies ever prevailing. For it is never static, always dynamic

A great part of the preceding chapter was devoted to emphasizing t importance of motivating idea. I was anxious to stress the significance Socrates' and Duncan's insistence upon the relative unimportance one's physical equipment as compared to the creative potentiality a forceful idea. And, after all, it is easy to see that the world is fu of women who happen to be far more strikingly beautiful to look at, the ordinary sense of the word, than Isadora happened to be. The are always countless women who possess more elegantly shaped bodie more radiant complexions, more comely hair, a generally more allurir emanation in many respects, than may have been possessed by a

adora, a Sarah Bernhardt, or an Eleonora Duse. It is doubtful that
any one of these three beautiful persons would have even qualified
. an Atlantic City beauty contest! Yet, when we behold any one of
.em in the majestic atmosphere of her own element, radiating the
.quisite luminosity of her specially endowed nature, the beauty-contest
.nners by contrast only glitter in a vapid, sensual sort of way. No one
: them could ever dance as Isadora danced until, like all of Isadora's
.ildren, she stretched forth her not merely lovely but loving arms to
.r brothers and sisters everywhere. And this truth applies to every
.alm of human effort. He who is possessed of a pleasing voice is not
.erefore a beautiful singer nor even a fine talker, though multitudes
.ay be misled and deceived by the apparent authority of the gift. Nor
. any skill likely to be of far-reaching consequence save in its valuable
.pacity as auxiliary to the higher impulse of an exalted idea. From the
.me of Plato, the function of idea has become increasingly recognized
.nd appreciated.

The next vital ingredient in human creativity, the dynamic element
.f the process, is what we commonly call "force of will." "Idea" might
.e termed the potential and "will" the kinetic energy of spontaneous
.reativity. Schopenhauer sees the whole evolutionary current as a
.Vorld of Will and Idea. Once we have established a clear picture of
.hese two mutually stimulating elements as they operate in constantly
.nterpenetrating agency we shall be better equipped to understand
.hat takes place in the fulminating process of creativity.

The human will is an element so pervasive and so constantly essential
.n the life process that, as in the case of the air we breathe or the
.nvoluntary heart and other vital functions of the body, we tend to
.gnore its indispensable role. This is true of the human will not only
.s an indispensable implement for getting things done, but also as an
.qually necessary element in the mere matter of human existence and
.urvival. Furthermore, I do not mean this only in the Darwinian sense
.f the need for its exertion against the competitive forces that threaten
.s with extinction at every phase and instant of existence; I mean
.terally that the human will must function in each individual who is
.o live in any reasonably healthy state. I mention this in analogy to the

biological operation of breathing because, since we take this habitu
activity of ours for granted, and since it is automatic requiring ı
awareness on our part, we have no occasion to evaluate the act
breathing until scientific curiosity leads us to investigate its vital impo
tance. It then becomes empirically obvious that we live neither co.
fortably nor long if our breathing is inhibited or stopped. However, tl
fact that this is one of the involuntary operations of our being a.
that it and all the other vital physical functions are so organica.
intrinsic to the life process make them easily seen, easily understo
and fully appreciated. Whereas the function of something inorgan
and less tangible, like the human will, is not so easily assessed. Its va
empire and its indispensability are only manifest where it is eith
depressed or exalted beyond normal levels. The result of such deviatic
is destructive or creative in proportion to the degree of fluctuatio
and dependent also, of course, upon the nature of the mentality f.
which the particular will is an instrument.

The clearest examples of this fact are to be found, therefore, in tl
morbid deteriorations or excesses of the will, because in these extrem
of behavior we have an accelerated and magnified view of the co.
dition. In observing, for example, the depressing spectacle of a nervo.
breakdown, we can see a human being sometimes in such a paralyzi
state of apathy that he is apparently bereft of all will to live. Such
person is momentarily incapable of contributing the slightest effort
the normal requirements of survival; only his involuntary functioni.
continues. In extreme cases, it is only with the utmost difficulty th.
such a person can be urged to swallow nourishment. Sometimes it ha
to be forcibly or artificially administered. The net result is that life
being preserved in such an individual not by his own will to live b.
by the will power of auxiliary egos, of benefactors, in the shape
either professional or amateur lifesavers. In other words, by the resolu.
exertions of doctors, nurses, family and friends, the patient may possib.
survive and overcome his self-destructive inanition.

An even more radical phase of this sort of malady consists of
perversion of the will to a destructively negative volition, a conscio.
or subconscious drift toward suicide. This type of morbidity ma

verse a whole series of intensities from mild neurasthenia through
the tragic gradations of disease to the most desperate and fatal
niacal frenzies. In these pathologies we have lamentably cogent
oofs of the negatory potentiality of the human will. And in the cure
these ills we have equally cogent proof of the efficacy of the affirma-
e will, which exercises its ingenuity to heal. This is, indeed, another
tance of that kind of saintliness which seems to arise wherever there
sore need for the strong to uplift the weak. Anyone who has even
ght knowledge of the anguishing continuity of effort, of the self-
rificing nobility of physical and mental labor endlessly expended in
e attempt to impose some restorative spiritual buoyancy upon these
king souls, will understand the heroism involved. And he will under-
nd a little better the mystery of will power and what it can accomplish.
ese immeasurable exertions of the good, the true, the beautiful
irits of the world to regenerate their feebler brothers and sisters are
unending glory and testimony to the dignity of the human race.
d, more to the present point, they constitute a salutary evidence of
e ebb and flow of the spiritual macrocosm under the influence of
s mighty power of will.

From the smallest social units through all the galaxies of minor and
ajor groupings to world-wide dimension there is a constant interplay
individual and group volition producing an endless seething and
urning of human constellations. The palpitating commotions and
e smooth, steady flux of social evolution derive their momentum
om this perpetual interaction of volitional drives. At times, we are
minated by the special force of some unique personality endowed
th a compelling abundance of this drive. At times, the course of our
es is frightfully shaken by the tumult and upheaval resulting from
e inordinate influence of a morbidly disposed willfulness. Con-
mporary students of psychology and psychiatry are ever more aware
the profound implications of this undisciplined and unchanneled
wer. They envisage tremendous ameliorative and creative possibilities
a science that may measure and direct this unruly giant. An enormous
rcentage of this valuable energy is, at our present stage of develop-
ent, wastefully dissipated and mischievously misapplied. Misdirected

purposiveness engenders the most tragic devastations and frustratic of both personal and group existences. We can attribute a sorrow catalogue of world calamities to the ill-motivated exploitation of t formidable weapon. The drastic consequences of its misuse must ı blind us to the miracles of happy achievement that are the issue of t same force when benevolently employed. Our destinies depend up the marriage of good ideas to strong will.

It will be profitable to dwell a little longer on the various manifes tions of human will, because the subject is so intimately related to ı next phenomenon of human behavior which we will encounter in ɛ approach to the very source and matrix of artful creativity. This n phenomenon of which I speak seems to be an almost invariable attribu an inherent characteristic of the so-called genius types. In an interesti study of the Man of Genius by Cesare Lombroso, it is demonstrated the cases of men of every kind of genius, from the scientific to ı political to the fine arts, that this particular characteristic, in one ph or another of its quality, is common to all of them. It is a state of bei know as hyperaesthesia, a state of exalted, or morbidly excessi sensibility. Here, too, we have a delicate proximity of creativity destructibility, of genius to madness. The exalted sensibility is a posit asset in the creative process of communication and assimilation; but its morbid stages it involves a degeneration of the positive faculties a a somber discontinuity with practical reality. It is in connection w this relativity of sensibility that I should like to pursue a little furtl the varying intensities and capacities of will power.

As a dominant element in the operation of human behavior, ı unique role of the will has, of course, long been recognized. Oı recently however, has it come to the forefront in a scientific light tl has illuminated some further recesses and horizons. The classical Grɛ dramatists regarded it intuitively as a prime factor in the patterns destiny. The Greek tragedian constructed examples of human beiı who, through the excessive passions or limitations of their own w hurled themselves unavoidably toward catastrophe—victims of ı relentless forces of their own misguided energies. Frequently, too, ı nature of Greek comedies was based on similar extravagances of voliti except that, in the case of comedy, the outcome turns toward the ludicrous instead of the calamitous. Unfortunately, calamity is by far the more frequent consequence of these inordinate desires, lusts, ambitions, and that is probably why the word "catastrophe" has gradually assumed in our minds a permanently disastrous connotation, whereas its original meaning was simply, following the catastasis, a final event. In comedy or in tragedy, this catastrophe usually involved a subversion of the usual order of things, which might be funny or might be sad depending upon the consequence. Cheerful or grievous, it was always forces of will, will of the gods or will of the human beings, that drove affairs along the path of destiny.

In vast areas of Oriental civilization, it was deemed the better part of wisdom to repress these troublesome human desires, to exercise the faculty of will power upon the unique objective of renouncing all the worldly pleasures that stimulate this same will power to self-destructive excesses. In this philosophy, serenity of spirit represents the highest good, and even though it must be attained through long mental torment and distressful mortifications of the flesh, still, once the soul is emancipated from the afflictions of its material desires, it mounts to a Nirvana of enduring felicity. Here we had the employment of will as a supreme guardian force over the soul's tranquillity against its own turbulent bodily manifestations. In other words, the higher will was on guard against its lower self, which is a very human picture indeed.

Then along came such figures as Friedrich Nietzsche, who saw the will in its most exalted form as the transcendent force which can and must lift mankind out of its apathy and infirmity to the elevated plane of the superman. Nietzsche envisaged mankind as in a depressive state resembling that of the individual hovering about the areas of nervous breakdown, weighted and inhibited by the emotions of self-pity and inanition. That is why he extolled the violent qualities of ruthlessness; sympathy and compassion of the strong for the weak tend to drag the strong down to the levels of the weak. Pity of one individual for another, when seen as a quality in the characteristic behavior of humanity as a whole, becomes self-pity, a negation of man's "yea-saying" role in nature. For Nietzsche, the only way by which man can raise himself

to the stature of superman is by pitiless self-purification and self-imp
sion. All weakness must be extirpated, all strength glorified. This m
be a good program for self-infliction, but it can be sadly misconstru
and misapplied by presumptuous individuals who extend their pitil
empire over their fellow men with more fervor than discriminatio
and too frequently with more individual sadism than sanctified se
castigation or even sublimated masochism! Unfortunately, the Nietzsc
ean principle, applicable though it be to the world neurosis,
applied by the right psychiatrist, invites the ministrations of too ma
"exaltés," themselves afflicted by phases of the very disease they pr
tend to treat. It is not the manic who will cure the depressive!

In France and in Switzerland toward the end of the nineteen
century, the medical profession revived its interest in suggestibility ar
hypnotism as therapeutic instruments. The results of the experime
tation were interesting from many points of view. As often happen
a great deal was learned about so-called normal behavior by observir
behavior under extreme conditions. Without attempting detailed scr
tiny of the valuable and fascinating researches of Drs. Charcot, Ber
heim, Wundt and their followers, it will be contributive to the preser
theme to note some of their impressive findings. The outstanding fe
tures of these experiments in controlled will were the amazing feats o
physical power and endurance performed by subjects under hypnoti
suggestion. The human body was found to be capable of exertion
and displays of strength surpassing the possibilities of ordinary ci
cumstance. For instance, under hypnotic influence a subject has bee
posed horizontally between two chairs, supported only at the back o
the head and at the heels, with no sustaining prop at any other par
of the body. To maintain oneself in a rigid position under these con
ditions is already far from easy. Yet in this difficult position such
subject has been known to support weights of several hundred pound
on the unsupported abdomen with no apparent signs of strain and n
injurious aftereffects. Thus we find ordinary persons demonstrably able
under certain conditionings of their will, to perform feats of strengt
beyond all normal capacity. Similarly, their nervous organizations may
be so controlled as to permit them to endure all sorts of trials and strain

ich, without hypnotic influence, would provoke reactions of shock
d pain. Long pins have been thrust through the arms of patients,
th no resultant pain, bleeding or infection. After countless experi-
nts it became clear that certain general conclusions could be safely
awn.

It became evident that mankind was still spectacularly far from
ercising the full capacity of its latent powers. Whereas hitherto this
s only an intuitive sort of guess, inspired by the wide spaces observ-
le between the highest and lowest human capabilities as shown by
fferent individuals, now suddenly the fact became known in a new
d startling display of corroborative evidence. Naturally there is tre-
endous impact to this discovery as all the rich implications of it
wn upon us. Here, within the confines and framework of the indi-
dual man, is revealed the immense lapse and hiatus between his cus-
marily casual drive and that maximum power of will which lives sub-
erged, deteriorative, pulsating with a dormant potency, awaiting
e magical moment of release. The pattern of mediocrity is familiar
us and, indeed, respectable in the average community where the
mforts of quiescence are highly prized. But it is a tortured and
usory quiescence, far removed from the true serenity that is the
solution of all discord and is attainable only by the sort of extra
nergy that is the subject of our study.

It also became more clearly perceptible, as a result of these researches,
at a skillfully, energetically and assiduously imposed will power can
stablish great empire over the latent forces of the less aroused indi-
iduals. Hence it became more apparent than ever that the nature of
leas governing the more dominant will powers is profoundly impor-
ant to the well-being of the social community. What better hypnotic
gents for the slumbering world will than the artists and the saints?

The "fine frenzy" of the poet at his peak of creativity is a spiritual
arallel to the physical phenomenon of the berserk rage. The poet
n his "frenzy" finds himself endowed with a prodigious volitional power
vith which he reacts creatively to his heightened sensibilities, a
rodigality of power far exceeding that of the normal man and even of
is own normal self. He warms up to his higher pitch, he climbs to the

summit of his capacities, by surmounting the myriad obstacles of his
lesser self. Each access to the acme of his power is an exalted act
will, a colossal expenditure of spiritual, mental, physical effort, a dee
breathing, exertional process, whence it derives its frequent name
"inspiration."

The phenomenon of the "berserk rage," an Icelandic nomenclatu
recurring in Norse folklore, is simply an access of physical frenzy,
maniacal outburst, during which the "possessed" person is endow
with preternatural force enabling him to perform feats of streng
beyond the capacities of ten or more normal men. It resembles tl
augmented abilities of the hypnotic patient. Since it is clear that the
sudden onsets and evocations of abnormal strength are not due to,
explicable by, any hastily increased muscularity, it is logical to conclu
that they are produced by an intensified concentration of the human wi
Evidently this force is enlarged in direct, or perhaps in acceleratin
proportion to the reduction of its dissipative tendencies. Ordinarily i
energies are scattered over the wide areas of human interest and fru
trated by the multitudes of human conflicts and fearful apprehension
When released from all these inhibitory factors, it leaps to the level
its higher potency as though seeking the exhilarating plane of tra
scendency. This extra invigoration is a result not so much of increa
as of liberation of inherent forces. It is probable that all human bein
are possessed of an inner impulsion capable of an effectiveness that
circumvented by their confounding repressions. And when this inn
impulsion is relieved of its restraints, it bursts forth into the exuberar
surge of spontaneity. Spontaneity is the modus operandi of the unfe
tered spirit. It is probably the originative mode of all being. And whe
one realizes that the apparently intricate period of a million years
scarcely an infinitesimal instant in the awesome concept of eternity,
is easier to apprehend the possibility that even such extended perioc
and involved conformations are essentially spontaneous in origin an
in unfolding. Certainly spontaneity is an absolute requisite to intuitiv
genius. And, consequently, it is one of the most important phases
human development to be cultivated and nurtured.

Out of the eventful process of this cultivation there arises an eminer oneer in the very area of human endeavor where one would most gically expect to find him at this stage of our evolution. A psychiatrist, culiarly endowed with both the analytical clairvoyance of the scientist d the spiritual intuition of the creator, has projected a revelatory agnosis of and therapy for the crucial case of arrested creativity, warted spontaneity. Dr. J. L. Moreno has formulated a radiantly romising design for resurrecting this most vital of all human faculties. ew and hopeful perspectives emerge from his reintegration of the ontaneity factors. "Definitions of creativity," according to Moreno, to date, have been inaccurate because the experience upon which they ere based was incompletely portrayed. But since spontaneity work in a ontrolled environment began [referring to specific psychodramatic erapeutics], our understanding of creativity has broadened. The inuence which cultural patterns have upon specific persons and, vice ersa, the influence which the creativity of specific persons has in the haping of cultural patterns is a problem which occupies the minds of esearch workers in many fields of science. Cultural anthropology, ociology, psychology, and psychiatry are equally concerned. A methodlogy has been worked out [referring to the analysis of a specific artist's roblem] which tries to unfold the process of creativity from its initial pontaneous phases and through the intermediary stages up to the inished product."

"The fate of a culture," he continues, in Creativity and Cultural Conserves, "is finally decided by the creativity of its carriers. If a disease f the creative functions has afflicted the most primary group, the reative men of the human race, then it is of supreme importance that he principle of creativity be redefined and that its perverted forms be ompared with creativity in its original states. This problem has never een properly examined and the solution demonstrated. Creativity as a frame of reference has not been established, and so a basis for a ritique of deviations has been missing. Psychiatry has been limited to he neurosis and psychosis of the average intellect. The patient of reative mentality has been neglected. Analysis of works of genius or f genius in retrospect on the basis of material gained from analysis of patients of average mentality is often misleading and erroneous. The

task of the psychiatrist is therefore to face a person of creative mental
in the midst of his dynamic difficulties."

At this point Moreno proceeds to present the problem of a dist
guished violinist, concert master of a well-known symphony orchest
whose playing before large audiences has become gravely impaired
uncontrollable accesses of trembling, etc. The resolution of this proble
with its consequent restoration of the artist's unimpeded performan
hinges entirely upon the process of discovering and liberating him fro
a whole constellation of inhibitory factors. Once he is released fro
these restraints which are the components of his neurosis he acqui
a spontaneity of expression exceeding even his best efforts prior to l
affliction. The case is a fascinating analogy to the whole, vast structu
of will and idea.

Applied to the idea of religion and of God, this concept of spo
taneity, of maximum will, is in continual operation. I quote again fro
Moreno: "The difference between one thing and another—and th
between God and man—lies in the degree of spontaneity and creativi
which each can summon. The amount of spontaneity and creativi
which God can summon—and which He is required to summon—
so far greater than that of any other that the difference becom
absolute. Indeed, God is the Being who can summon the maximu
of spontaneity and He is the Being whose spontaneity has become
creativity."

One reason why Sigmund Freud and his followers in the psych
analytic school of thought have exercised such a profound influen
lies in this same realm of the recognition and treatment of disorder
volition. The specific advancement to which the analysts have co
tributed a great impetus consists of a new technique for dealing with tl
inhibitory forces of the subconscious. Without yielding to the temp
tation of following the interesting paths of this new science, one must
least pause to appreciate and acknowledge the wonderful further awar
ness it affords us of our innermost depths. Freud has illuminated som
of the darkest recesses of our self-deceptive souls. He has shrewdly an
courageously shown us how our conduct is distorted and profaned by
fear-ridden dishonesty of motive. Furthermore, we shall gradually unde

d that he has resolutely taken away from us the immunity of inno-
ce in which we cloaked ourselves before he came and saw and told!
ce our subconscious is no longer insulated from reality by that
cious sort of inscrutability which it had so cunningly contrived
ough the ages as a protection against the increasing exigencies of
ilization, we are now obliged to "face the facts of life" with a renewed
l healthy integrity. If not at once by our own probing, then by grace
a brother man equipped to do the probing for us, we are now able
root out the deceptions buried below the surface of our consciousness.
e can clearly see the consequences of our past disinclinations to meet
issues uncompromisingly; we find ourselves encumbered with the
alculable burden of our self-abusive frustrations. In many cases we
d the human will to be so morbidly devitalized by these involuntary
tomatic self-wrongs that, like the onanist, it has lost most of its
tural capacity for spirited love and pure initiative. The happy fact
it mankind, in the personalities of these persevering and highly
otivated individuals, continually reintegrates itself along the lacerating
t ever-mounting course of its ascension is a constant assurance of our
ogress toward that sublime spontaneous creativity which was and is
d will be our unalterable essence.

Let us now examine the crucial interdependence of dynamic will
d dynamic art.

Chapter VI

ESSENTIAL SENSITIVITY

wwwwwwwwwwwwwwwwwwwwwwwwwwwwwwwwwwwwwwwwwwwwwwwwwwwwwwwwwwwwwwwwwwwwwwwwwwwwwwww

IN OUR examination of the human will and its effort to retur
ultimately to the pristine powers of its essential spontaneity, ou
thoughts will turn ever and again to the arts, because they are :
closely related to the whole subject. First of all, they resemble in the
own evolution the eventful progress of the will from its infancy throug
all the pangs of its growth. Both the arts and the force of will passe
through their periods of simplicity before they became complicate
by the subtle intricacies of the maturing process. And they both aspi
to regain the direct simplicity from which they were deflected by th
perplexities and trials of adolescence, so to speak. They seem to traver
paths of self-expansion between a sort of first simplicity and last sin
plicity. The will, in its earliest history, functioned only within the na
now orbit of a limited though urgent necessity. That necessity was th
simple one of survival. But since it involved survival in a relative
vegetative existence, the demands upon the will were not exacting. A fe
elementary drives covered the primary needs of nourishment, growt
procreation and whatever self-preservative cunning might be summone
forth to meet a small variety of situations.

It was only with the cultivation of memory that human life bega
to grow more complicated and to require the exercise of much mo
ingenuity in the pursuit of its widening purposes and direction
Similarly, the primitive arts of man consisted of the simplest, mo
spontaneous expressions, brief, unelaborated, rudely direct. This u
adulterated expressiveness is often superficially imitated by individua
and schools in advanced cultures who seek to lift themselves out of th
morass of their confused midway status. They do not realize th
primitive spontaneity was the property of its own age and can be
more successfully reassumed than can the charming style of a child by

own man. Easy, primitive spontaneity has played its role. But every
ge—and, indeed, every instant—may regenerate its own revived and
berated force of creativity; not a moment nor a soul need be deprived
the grace of spontaneity in its own fresh and satisfying version.

F. H. Bradley, in *Appearance and Reality*, gives special point to
is truth in the province of philosophy. "All of us, I presume, more
less, are led beyond the region of ordinary facts," writes Bradley
propos of persons who pursue the study of ultimate truth. "Some in
e way and some in others, we seem to touch and have communion
ith what is beyond the visible world. In various manners we find
mething higher, which both supports and humbles, both chastens
d transports us. And, with certain persons, the intellectual effort to
derstand the universe is a principal way of thus experiencing the
eity." However, Bradley sees the need for the "fresh and satisfying
rsions" of which I spoke above, in an ever-changing world, and that
why he concludes that "Existing philosophies cannot answer the
rpose. For whether there is progress or not, at all events there is
ange; and the changed minds of each generation will require a difrence in what has to satisfy their intellect. Hence there seems as
uch reason for new philosophy as there is for new poetry. In each
se the fresh production is usually much inferior to something already
existence; and yet it answers a purpose if it appeals more personally
the reader. What is really worse may serve better to promote, in
rtain respects and in a certain generation, the exercise of our best
nctions. And that is why, so long as we alter, we shall always want,
d shall always have, new metaphysics."

We shall always have new metaphysics and we shall, for the same
asons, always have new art, since these are all paths toward the same
ith. I quote Bradley once more: "I have been obliged to speak of
ilosophy as a satisfaction of what may be called the mystical side of
r nature—a satisfaction which, by certain persons, cannot be as well
ocured otherwise. And I may have given the impression that I take
e metaphysician to be initiated into something far higher than what
e common herd possesses. Such a doctrine would rest on a most
plorable error, the superstition that the mere intellect is the highest

side of our nature, and the false idea that in the intellectual worl work done on higher subjects is for that reason higher work. Certain the life of one man, in comparison with that of another, may be full of the divine, or, again, may realize it with an intenser consciousnes but there is no calling or pursuit which is a private road to the Deit And assuredly the way through speculation upon ultimate truth though distinct and legitimate, is not superior to others. There is r sin, however prone to it the philosopher may be, which philosop] can justify so little as spiritual pride."[1]

And so, whether we approach the heights by way of intuition or l way of intellect, it is by our ardent wills that we are driven, as by o love inspired. We now arrive at that interesting phenomenon of hype aesthesia mentioned in the preceding chapter as an almost invariab attribute, an inherent characteristic, of the so-called genius types. An since it is these types who are what Moreno has called the "carrier of creativity, it is important to understand the exact nature and exte of their hypersensibility. There has been much frivolous theorizi about this matter, partially due to the fact that the extravagancies behavior so often found in persons of genius are considered to l romantic, whereas a display of similar singularities by ordinary perso would be dismissed as odd, sordid or vexatious. There is a wide gradati of human temperament rising from the dull and phlegmatic toward tl vivacious and creative. At the bottom of the scale the receptive sen will be found to be coarse and unimpressionable to such an exte that it is well-nigh impervious to the influences and stimulations the higher temperament. Toward the summit it becomes exquisit delicate, so that it not only enjoys exalted perception but is also bou to suffer pain from the very acuteness of its susceptibility. As mediu for the transmission of feeling, their qualities are disparate in the sar sense as crude musical tools would be inferior to fine ones, only l more so. The Stradivarius fame is not fortuitous, as any violinist know and if the Lord himself seeks instruments responsive to his immacula touch, he has his Son of man and countless other worthy instrume in every field of art and high endeavor.

[1] *Appearance and Reality*, by F. H. Bradley. George Allen and Unwin, Ltd.

t is worth-while and, as a matter of fact, necessary to scrutinize the
tive abilities and qualities of apprehension among different levels
mentality. Until we do so it is impossible to have any but the
uest notion of just what it is that makes some persons able to
omplish with the greatest ease what others are able to do only badly
h the greatest effort. As soon as we start to investigate this fascinating
stion we learn that no amount of ardently exercised will power on
part of a normal temperament can alone lift that temperament to
effective capacity of a more highly perfected temperament gifted
h pre-eminent aptitude. There are certain inherent gifts, or talents,
specially endowed skills, which enable their possessors to assimilate
re and to give out more, to see more and see better, and to reveal
re. Of course, these talents do not rise to the creativity of genius
less they are driven to those altitudes by the supreme power of will.
t by their very natures these exquisitely attuned instruments often
ct of themselves the most fabulous exertions; they are impelled by
extremity of their sensitivity to intense and positive reaction. In
er words, they tend to accept the invitation of their potentialities.
od examples are offered by many different kinds of prodigies, some
whom apply their special gifts to narrow areas of applicability, while
ers rise like angels to the grace of their celestial aspiration.

Observe, for instance, in a simple field of performance, the type of
digy who has a peculiar genius for playing chess. When we compare
ease with which this type of mentality envisages the entire board
d sees in a flash every conceivable combination of moves that
ght emerge out of any specific set of conditions; when we compare
s all-embracing spontaneity of vision with the ordinary intelligence
t is obliged to plod laboriously through the successive steps of the
me's possible evolution, trying to retain in a severely strained memory
e difficult series of moves that are projected in the imagination, we
gin to understand the gap between the two minds. The one can
prehend within a moment whole chains of tactical moves which may
volve hours of time for the actual passage from inception to culmina-
n. The other is obliged to meet each position in its context and
vise as far-reaching a strategy as his more limited powers of retention

and projection permit. Time and again this latter player is likely to confronted with emergencies which are unforeseen situations. unforeseen occurrence is a rare phenomenon in the life of a c champion, likely to be produced only by an adversary of his o stature. The mathematical exactitude of a chess strategy renders infinitely more challenging to the intelligence than a military strate because a military tactic perforce deals in the maneuvering of ponderables to a certain unavoidable extent. The utmost skill in calculation and disposition of forces may still be upset by unpredicta elements of chance or of morale. Whereas, within the precise fra work of unalterable functions and magnitudes, the strategy of ches conducted under ideal conditions of absolute exactitude; the elem of fortuity is eliminated. This is the particular fascination of the ga And this too constitutes the difference between playing chess living life.

In life one deals with many unknowns which exert immeasura and unforetellable influence on its unfolding. Only such a transcende vision as is attributed to the Deity might conceivably embrace all happenings at once. For even though in the ultimate analysis illusional life of extended duration and complicated eventfulness w to be summarily comprehended as all of an instantaneous spontane still, what human mind from within the vortex of being could possi encompass the bewildering fluctuations of the human will as calcula elements in an absolute design? No, the game of chess may be analog to the ultimate pattern of being as the intuition sees it, but the ga of cards called bridge is much closer to the process of life as interpre by the realistic intelligence. In this card game there is a blending of forces of shrewdness and chance; the latter is a constant challenge the former and renders absolute certainty of maneuver impossi The most that can be said for the effectiveness of skill in this gam that it is likely to prevail in a long test, since the law of averages sho empirically that chance distributes itself evenly in a large series trials. From the mathematical and aesthetic points of view chess offe more beautiful interplay of precisions. Its perfection is not marred the accidental.

While there is nothing moving or uplifting in the phenomenon of
the fine chess player, beyond a certain pleasurable satisfaction that any
intelligence will derive from the spectacle of logic supremely developed
and exercised, this same kind of faculty when driven by the higher
purposes of aesthetic or philosophic impulsion becomes at once a
precious instrument. In the artist, in the scientist, in the metaphysician
becomes an implement of creativity instead of remaining a talent
quandered on virtuosity. In the employ of a Mozart, a Darwin, an
Einstein we see it yielding the immense harvest of its most fruitful
disposition. For instance, as the mind of a chess player envelopes the
whole constellation of pieces and possibilities on a chess board, so does
the mind of a Mozart, by his own description, envisage the entire
architecture of a symphonic composition in its original conception
before he has written a single notation. Mozart sees his entire symphony
as spontaneously as Bergson sees his creative evolution, unarrested and
unbroken by the fallacious process of the intelligence which so habitually
conceives of all sustained movement as a series of separate, immobile
stages of being. Our feeble intelligence tends to analyze motion by
breaking it up into divisible units of itself even while our intuition tells
us that this is an untrue representation of motion in its essence and
that the mind resorts to this way of seeing because its instinct still is
to grasp tangible particles where it cannot grasp whole abstractions.
Intuitively we know that the nature of all things is an endless transition.
Yet when we wish to depict something we seize nothing more than an
instantaneous impression of this transition, an arrested version of it.
But in the musical forms of such masters as Bach, Mozart, Beethoven
and others breathes the intuitional truth. The most thrilling part of
this whole study will have to do, in succeeding chapters, with this vital
matter of eternal transition which is the real state of all things.

For the time being I shall content myself with quoting from Bergson's
Evolution Créatrice a brief passage related to our present preoccupation
with the faculty of instantaneous conception of transitional forms. It
is descriptive of the process of music itself. "There is no essential difference between passing from one state to another and remaining in
the same state. An object may very well remain the same object, I may

very well continue to look at it from the same angle, etc.; the vision
that I shall have of it at any given instant is different from that which
I just had of it the instant before, if only because my vision will have
aged by that much. My memory is there, which pushes something from
that past into this present instant. The state of my spirit, in progressing
along the path of time, expands itself continually by the experienced
duration which it gathers; it makes, in a manner of speaking, a snowball
of itself. But precisely because we close our eyes upon the incessant
variation of each psychological state, we are obliged, when the variation
has become considerable enough to impose itself upon our attention
to speak as though a new state had been juxtaposed to the preceding
one."

The artist, by revealing more perceptibly this plastic movement of
reality, may achieve for his audience the sublime habit of nevermore
isolating the present from the past. In music the achievement can be
particularly dazzling. By the durational architecture of successive notes
organized in time and spread so that a passage many minutes later
still related to all that preceded it and to all that shall follow, keeping
itself an integral part of the whole "instantaneous gesture," one perceives most clearly the indivisibility of what has been and what will be.
In the truest sense both the past and the future become associated
emanations of the present. However, for anyone who has not either
interested himself in metaphysics or enjoyed a highly developed instinct
for aesthetic values, this matter of duration and simultaneity remain
confusing until it is carefully clarified, as I shall presently attempt to
do. At the moment, it suffices to appreciate the nature of this genius
for seeing-the-whole, and gradually to understand the special advantage
that flow out of it.

It becomes easier to appreciate the magnitude of this genius when
one begins to compare to it the merely normal capacity of an ordinary
mind. The ordinary mind, for instance, cannot even hear a symphony
as a whole, far less conceive it! Try as he will, the man possessed of a
average intelligence is unable to acquire the faculty of seeing-the-whole
except by colossal discipline and constant practice in the process. He
can see whole forms that are presented to him in the three-dimension

ects to which he has become accustomed since infancy. But he can-
t easily infer whole forms when they are represented to him symboli-
ly; this requires an exercise of imagination involving a combined
ocess of retention and projection. For example, he can see a cathedral
en it is presented to his vision as a tangible edifice, but he can only
ve fragmentary glimpses of the same cathedral if it is shown to him
terms of the blueprints that are its sole reality prior to actual con-
uction. Only the trained architect could envisage the whole structure
his mind's eye; and something more than a trained architect is
quired to envisage the marvelous as opposed to the mediocre.

Similarly, the ordinary intelligence that does not happen to be tone-
af can usually grasp a simple little melody after hearing it a few
nes. It is only by becoming conscious of what the things are which
: are able to grasp easily that we can begin to understand what hap-
ns when the scope of things gets a little and a lot beyond our grasp.
hen a mind of normal capacity hears a Beethoven sonata or a Bach
rtita it may derive satisfactions and pleasures from elements of these
eat structures, but not one in a thousand persons, at the present
age of musical sensibility, grasps more than fragments of their total
blimity. In the first place, the musical idiom, once it gets beyond the
nplest modes of expression, remains esoteric to the untrained multi-
des; so do most of the art mediums, in varying degrees depending
on the extent of their abstraction from the more familiar ways of
mmunicating. If the average concertgoer, John Doe, could suddenly
dergo the miraculous experience of hearing a musical composition
rough the ears of a great composer it would not be exaggerative to
mpare the event to the sudden acquisition of eyesight by a man
itherto almost if not quite blind. A whole magical interweaving of
otives, a masterful harmony of diverse themes, a multitude of con-
ibutory elements would be discovered, and there would rise majestically
the attendant spaces of the listener's imagination a noble image of
ch architectural splendor as he had not before dreamed of. It is
bsurd to expect John Doe's experience of music to be on a level with
at of J. S. Bach; it is equally absurd to expect him to react to a poem
f John Keats the way Shelley would, or to see in a situation on a

chessboard what Alekhine would see. But it is not absurd to expe
that he will develop an appetite for further tastes of the intimatio
that he will have detected in these experiences of his. Even his earli
intimations lift him appreciably out of apathy or mediocrity toward
light that he may learn to love.

Thus, until a man grasps the full form of an exalted work as al
as he grasps the full form of an obvious, commonplace work, he
having only a partial experience, receiving sensory stimulations whi
arouse but a fraction of the emotional and intellectual response whi
they invite. Most of us are still vague when it comes to acknowledgi
the shortcomings of our sensibilities and are readier to recognize the
in others than to concede them in ourselves. The unhappy truth in
its ramifications is still more complex than we have yet indicated.

For we find that even those human beings endowed with gre
genius in some one field of being are often painfully limited in othe
so that they may be relatively insensitive to communication that do
not come to them in their own special idiom. We have learned fro
long experience not to expect from any individual a capacity for eith
creation or appreciation in all the categories of art and philosophy
once. We have come to take it for granted that a Rembrandt may n
be expected to compose songs like a Schubert, nor Shakespeare to pai
a Holbein. And we know also that it is probable that Rembran
would have been a feeble music critic, Schubert a feeble critic of pai
ing, and Shakespeare a feeble critic of both. All these men would,
course, have started out with a vast potential of appreciation whi
might have penetrated to the heights of any attainment capable
drawing their interest; but such is the nature of man's present inte
lectual and emotional constitution that he is likely to exploit a speci
faculty with which he may be generously endowed and feel never th
slightest serious temptation to employ a second or third faculty. Eve
where there have been extraordinary exceptions to this generalizatio
a man's major contribution has generally been confined to the mediu
of his highest talent, as for instance in the case of Leonardo da Vin
whose foremost genius still speaks to us out of the serene spirituali

his paintings although, in his time, he displayed a wide diversity of
ent for engineering and allied arts.

It would seem, in the main, that the human spirit achieves its highest
pirations along the path of its best ability, reluctant to dissipate its
ergies in the cultivation of more than any one necessary medium of
tion and communication. What more could Rembrandt have dis-
vered to himself or to us by endeavoring to write sonatas and
mphonies? What need had Dante for practicing the other arts so
preme in his own period? The dilettante pursues several arts for his
nusement and self-gratification; the artist consecrates himself lovingly
the most direct pursuit of the good, the true, the beautiful.

Perhaps the greater problem of aesthetics, as of all creative process,
:s on the side of receptivity rather than in the realm of creativity.
he creators have their spontaneous genius for creativity, which ensures
eir productivity. Their powers may, of course, be nurtured and
.creased along the various lines of purification that we are studying;
it essentially they are less of a problem to themselves, creatively at
ast, than the less creative human beings who seek the best ways of
igmenting those sensibilities which measure their capacity both to
ve and to receive. Are they to be expected to develop an infinite
usceptibility to the stimuli of all the communicative arts and sciences,
r are they to find their way to some specific medium whence they may
e best suited to draw their nourishment and inspiration? Should John
Joe hope to be in equally elevated and productive rapport with the
ofty spirits of every variety of genius? Should his life be a feverish
ushing about from art gallery to concert hall to theater to dance recital
o philosophic discourse to readings of poetry ad infinitum?

It is a tantalizing thing for a John Doe whose tastes begin to grow
o that he senses the abundant treasures awaiting him along many beck-
ning paths; it is hard for him to make selections and rejections, every-
hing looks so good! It is only later, when he will have grown wiser with
ccumulated experience, that he will probably discover some further
nportant truths which will help him to resolve this difficulty. If he is
ortunate he will learn that many great and different arts and artists all
idiate in their own peculiarly individual fashions the vibratory messages

of a great ultimate similarity. If it were possible to measure the relativ
intensities and qualities of ideas and emotions, he might find that Jame
Roe has an experience looking at Fra Angelico frescoes very similar to hi
when listening to the music of Palestrina. Yet, because James Roe ha
developed his particular receptivity to the language of painting and John
Doe may have tended to favor the language of music, Roe cannot ge
nearly so much out of Palestrina's communication when he tries to liste
to it, and Doe is unable to see more than a poor superficiality o
Angelico's saintly Annunciation. And still, the messages inherent in th
creativity of Fra Angelico and Palestrina are both laden with illimitabl
love and spiritual import. Both of these rare spirits hold out their arm
in tender fellowship to anyone who shall perceive them with responsiv
grace. So also are John Doe and James Roe eager to respond and to b
in as close a communion with such spirits as their natures will permi
They have vague and growing apprehensions of the forces resident in th
works of these humble servants and masters of their arts, and they year
to make themselves more and more sensitive to the infrangible totalit
that is the essence of those works. They may approach it here, there an
elsewhere, catching intimations as best they can from whatever worl
come within their ken. But, pragmatically speaking, they will penetrat
nearest to the quintessential nucleus by narrowing and concentratin
the force of their own efforts. As a rule this happens gradually in a rel
tively unconscious manner because of a natural tendency of most in
dividuals to derive more comfortable and greater stimulation from on
particular medium than from many. It is not usually so in early chil
hood, which is a most interesting period to observe the formation o
personal tastes and tendencies.

Thus far we have only been approaching the vital matter of exalte
sensibility. We have not yet examined descriptive details and, of cours
in the attempt to do so we shall be obliged to limit ourselves to a min
mum of citation of personalities because the subject is as vast as th
whole biographical catalogue of human genius. A brief excursion into th
temperamental atmosphere of human nature at its more creative leve
will have to suffice, with our principal objective confined to a summa
understanding of whatever quantitative and qualitative differences ma

found in mentalities at those levels. Then, when we shall have noted ose differences sufficiently to provide us with a clear idea of what sort mind has the furthest-reaching vision, there will be a final need to rn an attentive ear to Schopenhauer's penetrating analysis of what is quired to assure this mind of its highest functional fulfillment.

In the urgent prefatory pages of his *World as Will and Idea*, Schopen- uer stipulates as essential to the understanding of his work "an ac- aintance with the most important phenomenon that has appeared in ilosophy for two thousand years: I mean the principal writings of nt. It seems to me, in fact, as indeed has already been said by others, at the effect these writings produce in the mind to which they truly eak is very like that of the operation for cataract on a blind man; and we wish to pursue the simile further, the aim of my own work may described by saying that I have sought to put into the hands of those on whom that operation has been successfully performed a pair of ectacles suitable to eyes that have recovered their sight—spectacles of hose use that operation is the absolutely necessary condition. . . . For ant's teaching produces in the mind of everyone who has compre- ended it a fundamental change which is so great that it may be regarded an intellectual new-birth. . . . But if, besides this, the reader has ngered in the school of the divine Plato, he will be so much the better repared to hear me, and susceptible to what I say. And if, indeed, in ddition to this he is a partaker of the benefit conferred by the Vedas, e access to which, opened to us through the Upanishads, is in my eyes he greatest advantage which this still young century enjoys over previous nes, because I believe that the influence of the Sanskrit literature will enetrate not less deeply than did the revival of Greek literature in the fteenth century: if, I say, the reader has also received and assimilated he sacred, primitive Indian wisdom, then is he best of all prepared to ear what I have to say to him."

And just as Schopenhauer says that a reading of him is absurd without previous understanding of Kant, so must a knowledge of Schopen- auer's Will and Idea be presupposed in any serious contemporary con- ideration of aesthetics.

Chapter VII

HYPERAESTHESIA IN CREATIVE INDIVIDUALS

IT IS in the works of men of genius that we find the final eviden
of their special powers. But where we are not always ourselv
equipped to see all that there is to be seen in their works, we m
learn much from special and general characteristics of their psychologic
make-up. One has to be almost a genius oneself to infer solely from th
productions of an artist, all the physical, mental and moral activity th
has contrived to effect these productions. If it were possible complete
to know the creator by his creations, we would never have had th
enormous literature that has grown up around the lives of our disti
guished artistic producers. It is not only curiosity that has impelle
biographical study as a literary and scientific procedure. It is a healtl
intellectual appetite for knowing as much as there is to be known abo
the process of creation. Indeed, the art of biography has on occasio
been carried to such heights of descriptive verisimilitude that it h
served in a useful and stirring fashion to re-create genius which in certa
instances has in every other, tangible sense been lost to the world.

I am thinking particularly of the tantalizing case of the classical an
earlier Greek painters, and specifically of Apelles whose work has bee
described by his contemporaries in such terms as to challenge the achiev
ment of all succeeding ages. Not a shred of the murals of Apelles h
survived to our times; there were not even any fragments available to th
scholars of Rome, as far as we can learn. Yet, according to the viv
accounts of the critics of his day, Apelles was a draftsman surpassing
the nobility of his talent all other genius of which Greece was then
prolific. These accounts, in themselves works of art of no mean propo
tion, take the greatest pains to convey by every possible channel
expression and by all demonstrable evidence the well-nigh superhuma
grace that imbued every gesture of this extraordinary man. The mo

ugitive line that he drew seemed to arouse those who appreciated him
o unusual emotions of admiration and delight. However much we may
assume by the relativity of all values that perhaps Apelles was no more
o his age than some of our masters are to ours, and that perhaps to us his
creations might even have seemed overrated, nevertheless it is remarkable that we should have such vivid images of him and of his work
projected to us over the centuries by the enthusiasm of his admirers.
Furthermore, it is probable in the case of Apelles and a few of his fellow
painters that their genius was not exaggerated, because they were ex-
olled and their painting celebrated far beyond the sculptors of the same
age, and we are fully acquainted with the eminent qualities of Greek
culpture, archaic and classical!

However, it has not been our privilege to know a great deal about
he lives and mental workings of artists until fairly recently. Earlier
biographers and historians concerned themselves principally with the
ives of those leaders who seemed to wield the most direct influence on
human affairs, the political and military figures. And their commentaries
were in the major part confined to the narration of actions, with no
deeply analytical insight into underlying characters and motivations.
Only toward the Renaissance period do we begin to have more detailed
and sensitive attention given to the personalities of artists and thinkers.
Vasari made an ardent effort to delineate the various genius types that
surrounded him, and his *Lives of the Painters, Sculptors and Architects*
represents one of the earliest contributions to the art of serious
biographical study. Then, somewhat later, the great mentality of Goethe
made initial essays into threshold areas of autobiography, though it was
Jean Jacques Rousseau who made the first tremendous pioneer gesture
of writing a completely autobiographical work in minute and candid
detail. This self-descriptive masterpiece, the *Confessions*, inaugurated a
whole new era of self-awareness that gradually acquired literary momentum. But it needed the well-nigh psychotic insistence of Rousseau upon
the most unrestrained self-revelation to shock the world into recognition
of the amazingly complicated and stupendous role that the ego plays,
and often plays so blindly, in the social constellations. Rousseau provides
us with the modern awakening to that most revelatory self-awareness of

all times which has flowered from literary to psychological, medical and sociological inquiry.

The results have yielded us formidable advancement in the understanding of ourselves, of the elaborate subliminal forces which govern so great a part of our behavior and which, when successfully liberated and directed into positive function, propel us into healthy states of well being and productivity. However, in all the rich literature of biographical and autobiographical material, nothing is so instructive as the more systematic and penetrating analysis that is now furnished to us by the medical sciences.

Dating from the late nineteenth century, when the school of Nancy produced the psychiatric researches of Liebault and Bernheim and when Charcot and others were equally productive in Paris, there arose a science of psychotherapy that in many ways is as contributive to the psychology of aesthetics as it is directly applicable to psychopathology. The advent of Sigmund Freud brought to the world a new profundity of understanding and opened up perspectives leading toward further horizons of mental integration. The psychoanalytic technique introduced a methodology for piercing veils of the subconscious and unmasking the cunningly disguised impostures that the different phases of individuality impose upon the struggling personality. Dr. Ernest Jones suggests that there is still inadequate appreciation of "the extent to which psychoanalysis has already been applied to sociology, to the study of racial development, and above all, to the psychology of the normal man." G. S. Hall remarks how few "especially in this country, realize that while Freudian themes have rarely found a place on the programs of the American Psychological Association, they have attracted great and growing attention and found frequent elaboration by students of literature, history, biography, sociology, morals and aesthetics, anthropology, education and religion. They have given the world a new conception of both infancy and adolescence, and shed much new light upon characterology, given us a new and clearer view of sleep, dreams, reveries, and revealed hitherto unknown mental mechanisms common to normal and pathological states and processes, showing that the law of causation extends to the most incoherent acts and even verbigerations in insanity; gone far clear up the terra incognita of hysteria; taught us to recognize morbid mptoms, often neurotic and psychotic in their germ; revealed the erations of the primitive mind so overlaid and repressed that we had most lost sight of them; fashioned and used the key of symbolism to lock many mysticisms of the past; and in addition to all this, effected ousands of cures, established a new prophylaxis, and suggested new sts for character, disposition, and ability, in all combining the practical d theoretic to a degree salutary as it is rare."

I should like to be able now to refer the reader to study of the lives d analyses of men of genius so that he might see for himself the full gnificance of what we might call the constructive abnormality that oclaims itself in practically all such personalities. The more thoroughly e looks into authentic records of the men who have contributed the eat treasures of artistic, religious, scientific achievement to the world, e more completely convinced one becomes that no one of these impressive figures is without greater or lesser characteristics of mental normity. Since this is not a work devoted to psychological and sychiatric analysis of the creator mentality, and yet since it is necessary r us to give at least an indication of certain special facts pertaining to eative cerebration, I shall present the minimum of what seems essenal to the progress of our thought. And since, further, it would be impracticable to embark upon any consecutive and systematic study of lives the form of case histories, I shall mention almost haphazardly and ith scant detail a few suggestive examples, which are literally a mere inuscule quota of the immense totality of available material. I cannot frain from urging the interested reader, however, to enlarge upon this nsatisfactory nibbling at the edges of so rich and vast a subject by ndertaking further researches on his own initiative. He will be rewarded ot only in the sense of augmenting his understanding of ethical and etaphysical connotations of the aesthetic force, but he is bound to rofit psychologically from the empathic experience of absorbing from galaxy of spiritual giants some of the essence, some of the life-and-soul lood of their exalted grace. If I tend to overuse the word "grace," subtituting it for "genius" or "beauty" or any other word that implies oodness, I do so entirely deliberately in order to accentuate by this

iteration the broadest implications of "grace" as established in Chapt
Two.

Schopenhauer, who suffered all his life the tormenting consequenc
of the hypersensitivity which at the same time provided him with suc
trenchant intuitional powers, and who became a desperately unhapp
victim of many neurotic delusions and obsessional fears, has this to s;
of himself and his kindred spirits: "People of genius are not only u
pleasant in practical life, but weak in moral sense and wicked. Suc
men can have but few friends; solitude reigns on the summits . .
genius is closer to madness than to ordinary intelligence. The lives
men of genius show how often, like lunatics, they are in a state of co
tinual agitation. Genius is solitary." He was subject to fits of deepe
melancholy and morbid rage, accompanied by ideas of persecution. Eve
the casual noises of the street provoked him to fury, and he wrote th;
"to be sensitive to noise is one of the numerous misfortunes which di
count the privilege of genius." On an occasion when he was annoyed b
hearing his landlady talking outside his apartment, he burst forth an
shook her so violently that he broke her arm and was sued for damage
He was aware of the fact that during the time that he was writing h
World as Will and Idea he was frequently so abnormal in his person;
appearance and behavior that he attracted much attention and w;
dreaded as a madman. He became convinced that he was inspired b
spirits outside himself. He expressed surprise and even astonishmen
retrospectively at the works which he had produced, feeling that the
must have been created by another person. In recognition of his inspir;
tional nature he said: "When my intelligence had touched its apoge
and was, under favourable conditions, at its point of greatest tension,
was capable of embracing anything; it could suddenly bring forth rev
lations and give birth to chains of thought well worthy of preservation.
In his more depressed moods he had little enthusiasm for his fello
men, and his bitterness was similar to that of Nietzsche who had a clos
feeling of kinship to Schopenhauer. "If I could only satisfy my desire t
look upon this race of toads and vipers as my equals, it would be a con
solation to me." He suffered hallucinations of a prophetic nature fore
telling his imminent death, and his chief concern was then to bestov

on the rare men of spiritual insight and goodness his revelatory
message. He asserted that he was driven not merely by scientific and
philosophic urgency but as though impelled by a demoniacal force.
'Beneath my hand, and still more in my head, a work, a philosophy,
ripening, which will be at once an ethic and a metaphysic, hitherto so
unreasonably separated, just as man has been divided into body and
soul. The work grows, and gradually becomes concrete, like the foetus in
a mother's womb. I do not know what will appear at last. I recognize a
member, an organ, one part after another. I write without seeking results,
for I know that it all stands on the same foundation and will thus compose a vital and organic whole. I do not understand the system of the
work, just as a mother does not understand the foetus that develops in
her bowels, but she feels it tremble within her. My mind draws its food
from the world by the medium of intelligence and thought; this nourishment gives body to my work and yet I do not know why it should
happen in me and not in others who receive the same food. O Chance!
Sovereign of this world, let me live in peace for a few years yet, for I love
my work as a mother loves her child. When it is ripe and brought to the
light, then exercise your rights, and claim interest for the delay. But if,
in this iron century, I succumb before that hour, may these unripened
principles and studies be received by the world as they are, until perhaps
some related mind appears who will collect and unite the members."
When Schopenhauer, at the age of nineteen, wished to visit his mother
at Weimar, she wrote to him: "I have always told you that it would be
very difficult for me to live with you; the more nearly I observe you, the
more this difficulty increases, so far at least as I am concerned. I do
not hide from you that, so long as you remain what you are now, I would
support any sacrifice rather than submit to it. I do not misunderstand
the foundation of goodness in you; what separates me from you is not
your heart, not your inner, but your outer self, your views, your judgments, your manner of behaving; in short, I cannot harmonize with you
in anything that concerns your external self. Even your ill-humour, your
lamentations over the inevitable, your sombre face, your extravagant
opinions which you give forth like oracles, and tolerate no opposition to,
oppress me, shock my serenity, and are no use to yourself. Your dis-

agreeable discussions, your lamentations over the stupidity of the wo
and human misery, give me wretched nights and bad dreams."

Of course, he recognized in himself many of the qualities of which
was so bitterly contemptuous in others; his contempt was self-inclusi
just as was his alternative exultancy. "Just as the most beautiful bod
he wrote, "contains within it faecal and mephitic gases, so the nobl
character offers traits of badness, and the greatest genius presents trac
of pettiness and excessive pride." He was obsessed by myriads of t
neurotic fears that are so familiar nowadays to our psychiatric clinics.

To mention just a few as enumerated by Lombroso:[1] "The invasion
cholera, at the beginning of 1831, completed his troubles. On the l
night of 1830 he had already had a dream, which he looked upon as
prophecy, foretelling his death in the new year. 'This dream,' he wro
in his Cogitata, 'influenced me in my departure from Berlin immediate
the cholera began in 1831. I had scarcely reached Frankfort on the Ma
when I had a very distinct vision of spirits. They were, as I think, n
ancestors, and they announced to me that I should survive my moth
at that time still living. My father, who was dead, carried a light
his hand.' That this hallucination was accompanied by real brain affe
tion is indicated by the fact that at that time he 'fell into deep mela
choly, not speaking to anyone for weeks together.' The doctors we
alarmed, and induced him to go to Mannheim for change of scen
More than a year later he returned to Frankfort when the acute peric
of his illness had apparently passed. Signs of it remained, however,
his peculiar bearing, his habit of gesticulating and talking aloud to hi
self as he walked through the streets of the city, or sat at table in tl
restaurant, and in his fury against 'such philosophasters as Heg
Schleiermacher and similar charlatans, who shine like so many stars
the firmament of philosophy, and rule the philosophic market.' F
accused them of depriving him of the praise and fame he deserved l
deliberately keeping silence concerning his work. This was a fixed id
with him, like the idea of his own infallibility, even after he seemed
return to a relatively normal condition, thanks to the fame which, aft
a delay of thirty years, at length crowned his name and his works."

[1] Quotations from *Men of Genius*, by Cesare Lombroso.

"He lived on the first storey, in case of fire; would not trust himself to
barber; hid gold in the ink-pot, and letters of change beneath the
d-clothes. 'When I have no troubles,' he said, 'it is then that I am most
aid.' He feared to touch a razor; a glass that was not his own might
mmunicate some disease; he wrote business documents in Greek or
tin or Sanskrit, and disseminated them in books to prevent unforeseen
d impossible curiosity, which would have been much easier avoided
    simple lock and key. Though he regarded himself as the victim of a
st conspiracy of professors of philosophy, concerted at Gotha, to pre-
rve silence concerning his books, he yet dreaded lest they should speak
    them; 'I would rather that worms should gnaw my body than that
ofessors should gnaw my philosophy.'"
I have dwelt on these manifestations of Schopenhauer because he
presents so vivid a picture of the man of genius exalted and oppressed
hypersensibility and neurosis. And the list is endless.
William James, himself a victim at stages of his career of profound
:urasthenia, contributed to his own reintegration by the philosophic
ojectification of some of his neurotic trouble. His Gifford Lectures on
e Varieties of Religious Experience present with the deepest insight
    modern times the human hunger for religious and philosophic con-
ction. He too was sensitive as was Schopenhauer to the melancholy
pect of what he calls the "pain-threshold." And he concludes that
norbid-mindedness ranges over the wider scale of experience. The
ormal process of life contains moments as bad as any of those which
isane melancholy is filled with, moments in which radical evil gets its
inings and takes its solid turn. The lunatic's visions of horror are all
rawn from the material of daily fact. Our civilization is founded on the
hambles, and every individual existence goes out in a lonely spasm of
elpless agony. If you protest, my friend, wait till you arrive there your-
·lf!"
"How can things so insecure as the successful experiences of this
·orld afford a stable anchorage? A chain is no stronger than its weakest
nk, and life is after all a chain. In the healthiest and most prosperous
xistence, how many links of illness, danger and disaster are always inter-
osed? Unsuspectedly from the bottom of every fountain of pleasure, as

the old poet said, something bitter rises up: a touch of nausea, a falli
dead of the delight, a whiff of melancholy, things that sound a kne
When such a conquering optimist as Goethe can express himself in tl
wise, how must it be with less successful men?

" 'I will say nothing' writes Goethe in 1824, 'against the course of 1
existence. But at bottom it has been nothing but pain and burden, a
I can affirm that during the whole of my 75 years, I have not had fc
weeks of genuine well-being. It is but the perpetual rolling of a rock tl
must be raised up again forever.'

"What single-handed man was ever on the whole as successful
Luther?" continues James. "Yet when he had grown old, he looked ba
on his life as if it were an absolute failure. Failure then, failure! So t
world stamps us at every turn. We strew it with our blunders, our m
deeds, our lost opportunities, with all the memorials of our inadequa
to our vocation. And with what a damning emphasis does it then bl
us out! No easy fine, no mere apology or formal expiation, will satis
the world's demands, but every pound of flesh exacted is soaked with :
its blood. The subtlest forms of suffering known to man are connecte
with the poisonous humiliations incidental to these results. 'There
indeed one element in human destiny,' Robert Louis Stevenson write
'that not blindness itself can controvert. Whatever else we are intend
to do, we are not intended to succeed: failure is the fate allotted.' A1
our nature being thus rooted in failure, is it any wonder that theologia
should have held it to be essential, and thought that only through tl
personal experience of humiliation which it engenders, the deeper sen
of life's significance is reached?

"But this is only the first stage of the world-sickness. Make the hum:
being's sensitiveness a little greater, carry him a little farther over tl
misery-threshold, and the good quality of the successful moments ther
selves when they occur is spoiled and vitiated. All natural goods peris
Riches take wings; fame is a breath; love is a cheat; youth and heal
and pleasure vanish. Can things whose end is always dust and disappoin
ment be the real goods which our souls require? Back of everything
the great spectre of universal death, the all-encompassing blackness. 1
short, life and its negation are beaten up inextricably together. But

e life be good, the negation of it must be bad. Yet the two are equally
entital facts of existence; and all natural happiness thus seems infected
th a contradiction. The breath of the sepulchre surrounds it." Thus
eaks James.

Robert Burns wrote in a letter: "My constitution and frame were
origine blasted with a deep incurable taint of melancholia which
isons my existence." Aristotle remarked that men of genius are of
elancholic temperament. Flaubert wrote: "I am not made for enjoy-
ent." Goethe stated that "every increase of knowledge is an increase
sorrow."

It is not surprising that some of the greatest comic writers were melan-
oliacs. Lombroso cites the interesting incident of a patient who pre-
nted himself one day to Dr. Abernathy; after careful examination the
stinguished practitioner said, "You need amusement; go and hear
rimaldi; he will make you laugh and that will be better for you than
y drugs." "My God," exclaimed the invalid, "but I am Grimaldi!"
ebureau had the same experience. And Giordano Bruno said of him-
lf: "In hilaritate tristis, in tristitia hilaris."

However, this blanket of melancholy is not the most sensational
mptom of the sensitive mind. It is rather the mood of long duration,
oth reactive to the more positive phases of creativity, and depressive
om inner conflict involving self-condemnatory dissatisfactions. I shall
ot resist the temptation to quote James once more by way of closing
is phase of the discussion of sensitivity. "In all of us, however consti-
ated, but to a degree the greater in proportion as we are intense and
ensitive and subject to diversified temptations, and to the greatest pos-
ble degree if we are decidedly psychopathic, does the normal evolution
f character chiefly consist in the straightening out and unifying of the
ner self. The higher and the lower feelings, the useful and the erring
npulses, begin by being a comparative chaos within us—they must end
y forming a stable system of functions in right subordination. Un-
appiness is apt to characterize the period of order-making and struggle.
f the individual be of tender conscience and religiously quickened, the
nhappiness will take the form of moral remorse and compunction, of
eeling inwardly vile and wrong, and of standing in false relations to the

author of one's being and appointer of one's spiritual fate. This is t
religious melancholy, and 'conviction of sin' that have played so larg
part in the history of Protestant Christianity. The man's interior is
battle-ground for what he feels to be two deadly hostile selves, o
actual, the other ideal. As Victor Hugo makes his Mahomet say:—

> Je suis le champ vil des sublimes combats:
> Tantot l'homme d'en haut, et tantot l'homme d'en bas;
> Et le mal dans ma bouche avec le bien alterne,
> Comme dans le désert le sable et la citerne.

Wrong living, impotent aspirations; 'What I would, that do I not; b
what I hate, that do I,' as Saint Paul says; self-loathing, self-despair;
unintelligible and intolerable burden to which one is mysteriously t
heir."

Of course, William James would have been profoundly interested
the analytical interpretations of these divided selves which have be
since formulated in the schools of Sigmund Freud. The schizoid ty
of personality is somewhat more systematically understood today. T
interplay of the conscious and the subconscious has been so illuminat
that we can deal with it more efficaciously than formerly. We are able
see in a depressive neurosis that there is increasing weight of the su
conscious forces and impeded functioning of the effective powers of t
conscious. Mencius felt this intuitively when he said that "he w
attends to his greater self becomes a great man, and he who attends
his smaller self becomes a small man."

We come now to some examples of hyperaesthesia which show t
exquisite heights to which sensibility in great artists may rise. The
reactions both to nature and to aesthetic experience when confront
with accomplished works of art or even works of philosophic and scie
tific character are beyond the widest margins of the normal person
reaction. Imagine while reading these active and reactive extremities
what a pitch these same sensibilities are employed when directed in
the concentrated act of creating. One then begins to have some idea
how and why a great work of art contains so much that is poignant ar
compulsive.

Malibran, on first hearing Beethoven's Symphony in C Minor had convulsive attack and had to be taken from the hall. Berlioz has scribed his emotions on hearing beautiful music as: first a sensation of luptuous ecstasy, immediately followed by general agitation with lpitation, oppression, sobbing, trembling, sometimes terminating with ind of fainting fit (hysterical syncope). Urquiza fainted on breathing e odor of a rose. Only a mild element in Baudelaire's extensive cata-gue of quirks was his very delicate sense of smell, too; he said that he uld not live in Belgium because the trees had no fragrance. Byron had convulsive attack on seeing Kean act. The painter Francia is said to ve died of the emotion of joy on seeing one of Raphael's pictures. ewton was so affected on discovering the solution to a problem that was unable to continue his work. "It is this exaggerated sensibility of en of genius, found in lesser degree in men of talent also," says Lom-oso, "which causes great part of their real or imaginary misfortunes." This precious gift," writes Mantegazza, "this rare privilege of genius, ings in its train a morbid reaction to the smallest trouble from with-t; the slightest breeze, the faintest breath of the dog-days, becomes r these sensitive persons the rumpled rose-petal which will not let the ifortunate sybarite sleep."

Charles Lamb in early life had an attack of insanity and wrote of it Coleridge as follows: "At some future time I will amuse you with an count, as full as my memory will permit, of the strange turns my enzy took. I look back upon it at times with a gloomy kind of envy, r, while it lasted, I had many, many, hours of pure happiness. Dream ot, Coleridge, of having tasted all the grandeur and wildness of fancy ll you have gone mad. All now seems to me vapid, or comparatively so." oleridge produced his celebrated *Kubla Khan*, considered by some udite people to be among the greatest poetic lines of our literature, in -health, during a profound sleep induced by opiates. He was able to call only fifty-four lines. Because of the frustrations of his powers of ill, his abuse of alcoholic stimulant and opium, Coleridge never suc-eeded in executing any of the gigantic projects he formulated.

Interesting instances of normal persons acquiring heightened sensibili-es during stages of mental illness have been recorded by Esquiros who

relates "the history of a patient in the Bicetre who, during his mala
had shown a remarkable talent for writing, though when in good hea
he would have been quite incapable of doing as much. 'I am not qu
cured,' he said to the physician, who thought him convalescent. 'I
still too clever for that. When I am well, I take a week to write a lett
In my natural condition I am stupid; wait 'til I become so again.' "
also reports the case of "a merchant whose affairs were in danger. D
ing his illness, this man found means to re-establish them; the result
each of his attacks was the perfecting of some mechanism, or the inv
tion of some means for facilitating his industry; and at the end of t
invaluable insanity, he was found to have recovered both his reason a
his fortune." Of course, more modern analysis of such cases wou
probably disclose revealing etiologies to such maladies.

Diderot said: "If nature has ever made a sensitive soul it is mine. M
tiply sensitive souls and you will augment good and evil actions." Alfi
Sterne, Rousseau, George Sand conclude that "there is nothing wh
agitates the soul with such unconquerable force as musical sound
Musset, Goncourt, Flaubert, Carlyle, Schopenhauer and countless oth
had so delicate a perception of sounds that the noise of the streets, a
even bells, were insupportable to them; they were constantly changi
their abodes to avoid these sounds, and at last fled in despair to t
country.

Elements of swollen egotism, sadism and brutality are incessan
occurring. Donizetti was savagely brutal to his family. It was after a
of wild anger, in which he had beaten his wife, that he sobbingly co
posed his celebrated aria "Tu che a Dio spiegasti l'ali." Hobhouse wr
that Byron was possessed of a diseased egoism and that even when
loved his wife he refused to dine with her in order not to give up l
old habits. He treated her so badly that finally she was driven to cons
specialists as to his mental condition. Bulwer-Lytton, according
Lombroso, ill-treated his wife by biting and insulting her, so that t
courier who accompanied them on their honeymoon refused to proce
to the end. Later Lytton confessed to the wrong he had done her, b
wrote to her that a common life was insupportable, and that he m
live in liberty. Pursuing Lombroso's apt biographical studies a litt

ther, we find that "Carlyle's wife, a most intelligent and cultivated man, though capable of becoming (as she had hoped and been ured) her husband's fellow-worker, was compelled to be his servant. e idea of travelling in a carriage with his wife seemed to him out of question; he must have his brother with him; he neglected her for er women, and pretended that she was indifferent. Her chief duty was preserve him from the most remote noises: the second was to make bread, for he detested that of bakers; he obliged her to travel for es on horseback as his messenger, only saw her at meal-time, and for eks together never addressed a word to her, although his prolonged nce caused her agony. It was only after her death, accelerated by his iduct, that, in a literary form, he showed his repentance, and nar-ed her history in affecting language, but, as his biographer adds, if e had been still alive would have tormented her afresh."

Grimm tells us that Voltaire, despite all his shrewdness and sharp :, was hypochondriacal to an agonizing degree. "With respect to my dy, it is moribund. I anticipate dropsy. There is no appearance of it, t you know that there is nothing so dry as a dropsical person. Diseases ore cruel even than kings, are persecuting me. Doctors only are needed finish me." Grimm comments that, despite all the travels and pleasures which he indulged, "this did not prevent him from saying that he is dead or dying; he was even very angry when one dared to assure n that he was still full of strength and life." Concerning the want of derstanding with which the general run of people persecuted genius, oltaire said that "the history of human intellect is the history of human pidity."

From Lombroso and George Sand we learn that "Chopin during the t years of his life was possessed by a melancholy which went far ward insanity. An abandoned convent in Spain filled his imagination th phantoms and terrors. One day George Sand and her son were late returning from a walk. Chopin began to imagine, and finally believed, at they were dead; then he saw himself dead, drowned in a lake, and ops of frozen water fell on his breast. They were real drops of rain lling upon him from the roof of a ruin, but he did not perceive this, en when George Sand pointed it out. Some trifling annoyance affected

him more than a great and real misfortune. A crumpled petal, a fly, ma
him weep."

Molière suffered from melancholia, and convulsions hindered h
from doing his work for weeks at a time. Paganini, Mozart, Schill
Dostoevski, Mahomet and innumerable greater and lesser figures w
seized with convulsions of epileptic and other causes. Chateaubria
was subject for a long time to convulsive movements of the ar
Napoleon, besides a great many other curious manifestations, had hat
ual spasms of the right shoulder and of the lips. Pascal endur
paroxysms for days at a time. He wrote in his famous *Pensées*, with pr
ably himself in mind: "Extreme genius is close to extreme folly, a
men are so mad that he who should not be so would be a madman o
new kind. Men of genius have their heads higher but their feet low
than the rest of us; they are all on the same level, and stand in the sar
clay as ourselves, children, and brutes."

Tasso wrote in a letter: "I do not deny that I am mad but I belie
that my madness is caused by intoxication and love, for I know that
drink too much. . . . So great is my grief that I am considered
others and by myself as mad, when, powerless to keep my sorrowf
thoughts hidden, I give myself up to long conversations with myse
My troubles are at once human and diabolical; the human are cries
men and especially of women, and also the laughter of beasts; the d
bolical are songs, etc. When I take into my hands a book to gi
myself up to study, I hear voices sounding in my ear, and distingui
the name of Paul Fulvius." In *Aminta*, he wrote (translated from t
Italian poetic form): "I shall live in the midst of my torments, a
among the cares that are my just furies, wild and wandering; I shall fe
dark and solitary shades, which will bring before me my first fault; a
I shall hold in horror and disgust the face of the sun which discover
my misfortunes: I shall fear myself, and, forever fleeing from myself,
shall never escape." Under some hallucinatory influence, or in son
sort of maniacal attack, he drew a knife upon a servingman who enter
the ducal chamber; he was imprisoned, we are told by a Tuscan a
bassador, more to cure than to punish him. To the physician Cavallaro
complained: "I am always troubled by sad and wearisome thoughts,

res and phantoms; also by a great weakness of memory." He wrote to ttaneo: "I have here much more need of the exorcist than of the sician, for my trouble is caused by magic art. I will tell you about my lin. The little thief has robbed me of many crowns; he puts all my ks upside down, opens my chests, hides my keys, so that I do not w how to protect myself against him. I am always unhappy but ecially at night. When I am awake I seem to see lights sparkling in air; sometimes my eyes are inflamed so that I fear I may lose my ht. At other times I hear horrible noises, hissings, and tinklings, the nd of bells, as it were, clocks all striking the hour at the same time. hen I am asleep I seem to see a horseman throwing himself on me d casting me to the earth, or else I imagine that I am covered by filthy sts. All my joints feel it; my head becomes heavy and in the midst of many pains and terrors sometimes there appears to me the image of Virgin, beautiful and young, with her Son, and crowned with a rain-w." I mention these few details of Tasso's long catalogue of complaints cause to the modern ear they comprise practically a stereotype clinical ture.

The musician Handel had attacks of furious and epileptic rage; npère burnt a treatise on the future of chemistry because he believed had written it by satanic suggestion. Newton, Swift, Browning and any others were subject to vertigo. Mahomet after prophesying fell to states of "imbecility" which were probably epileptoid. Swift died complete dementia, and predicted in his early youth that he would e insane. Walking one day in a garden, he saw an elm tree almost mpletely devoid of foliage at the summit. "Like that Tree," he said, shall die at the top." He became a difficult character, humiliated, and sulted cabinet ministers, and wrote to a duchess who expressed a sire to make his acquaintance that the greater the persons were, the wer must they bow before him. Beethoven in his absent-mindedness ed to appear in public in such states of deshabille that he was arrested one occasion for vagabondage and only released from prison when entified by friends. Everyone acquainted with Boswell's Johnson has owledge of that extraordinary man's sensitivities and peculiarities. pe thought he saw arms protruding from walls; Goethe acknowledges

that he once saw his own image coming to meet him. Oliver Cromw
under an extreme fatigue which prevented his sleeping, had a vision
his bed curtain opening and a woman of gigantic proportions appea
and announcing that he would be the greatest man in England. Did
was known to forget the hour, the day, the month, the person to wh
he might be talking, so that he would carry on in long monologues
a somnambulist. He would forget cabs he had hired, leaving them
stand before his door for a whole day at a time so that he had to m
large payments to the coachmen. Ampère once wrote an import
formula on the back of a cab so that when it drew away he had to h
off in wild pursuit of it. When he saw the magnificent shores of Ge
and the Italian Riviera for the first time he said he thought he wo
die of happiness.

The reader of Rousseau can gather from his *Confessions, Dialog*
and *Reveries* what deep sensitivity there was in this poetic and fo
ful thinker; toward the last years of his difficult life he became a tra
victim of the persecutory ideas emanating from his maladaptation to
society in which he lived. But during the greater part of his career t
hypersensitivity, as in the cases of all the persons whom we ha
sketchily mentioned, served to drive him to all the more intense me
tation and creative activity. "My imagination," he writes in his *C*
fessions, "has never been so cheerful as when I have been suffering. I
mind cannot beautify the really pleasant things that happen to me, o
the imaginary ones. If I wish to describe Spring well, it must be
Winter. . . . There are times in which I am so little like myself t
I might be taken for a man of quite different character. In repose I a
indolence and timidity itself, and do not know how to express myse
but if I become excited I immediately know what to say." The trem
dous efforts Rousseau made, not only in his intellectual labors but
way of maintaining himself, since he was without independent mea
gradually increased the strain on his naturally hypochondriac dispositi
and precipitated him ultimately into profound melancholy and psycho
manifestations. "My agitations and anger affected me so calamitou
that I passed ten years in delirium, and am only calm today." Howev
his agitations began later to take the form of imaginary enemies w

ied and misinterpreted all his acts; if he read a newspaper they said
was conspiring; if he smelled the perfume of a rose they suspected he
s concocting a poison. No visitor came to him whom they had not
judiced against him. They corrupted his hairdresser, his coffee-
rchant, his green grocer, his landlord; the shoeblack had no more
cking when he needed him; the boatman had no boats when he
hed to cross the Seine. A publisher whom he did not even know was
own into the Bastille and he concluded that this was done in order
tematically to deprive him of the press."

Finally he was driven by this persecutory obsession to write his
alogues sur Rousseau Jugé par Rousseau, in which he sought to placate
enemies and defend himself. It was dedicated to "all Frenchmen
o still love justice and truth." He sought to distribute copies of this
per to all passers-by whose countenances seemed to reveal that they
d not yet been prejudiced against him by his sinister persecutors. He
o placed a copy of the Dialogues, along with a final entreaty in the
m of a letter addressed to God, on the altar of Notre Dame Cathedral
Paris. And when he found the railing before the altar closed, he
pected that the conspiracy against him extended to the very portals
Heaven. In his Confessions he wrote: "I have very ardent passions,
d while under their influence, my impetuosity knows no bounds; I
ink only of the object which occupies me; the entire universe besides
nothing to me; but this only lasts a moment, and the moment which
lows throws me into a state of prostration. A single sheet of fine paper
npts me more than the money to buy a ream of it. I see the thing and
tempted, if only I see the means of acquiring it I am not tempted.
en now, if I see anything that tempts me, I prefer taking it to asking
it." Apropos of this hint of kleptomania, he confessed a moving
isode during one of his sojourns in Paris. A friend invited him to a
rformance at the Opera, and after buying the tickets, handed one of
em to Rousseau lest they be separated by the commotion of the large
dience in the already darkened house. Rousseau purposely allowed
mself to be jostled until he slipped out of sight of his host, and then
stened to the box office where he turned in his ticket for the hand-
me price paid but a moment before.

In such men as these there is a constant accumulation of seeth
meditations and sensations which, rarified by a naturally exquisite s
sibility and actuated by a strong volitional emotion, bursts forth s
modically into conceptions of fine quality and high import. Though
process may be a continual one, a sort of persistent unconscious cere
tion, the moments at which it emerges into explosive creativity se
inexplicable and as though the author were but a medium for so
mysterious inspirational force from the outside. The inspiration has b
described as a "sweet and seductive fever, during which thought becon
rapidly and involuntarily fruitful, and bursts forth like the flame o
lighted torch." Dante expressed himself this way:

> I mi son un che, quando
> Amore spira, noto ed in quel modo
> Che detta dentro vo significando.

("I am one who, when love inspires, attends, and according as he spe
within me, so I express myself.")

In Goethe, Ariosto, and many others, creation was frequently of
apparently instantaneous nature, even being produced on awaken
from sleep. Many men claim they have elaborated solutions to proble
during their sleep which they had been unable to solve in waking ho
Bettinelli wrote: "Poetry may almost be called a dream that is acco
plished in the presence of reason, which floats above it with open eye

As an example of the lengths to which a fanatical thinker may go
give full value to his thesis, a young German philosopher of the l
century named Mainlander wrote *Die Philosophie der Erlosung*, whi
achieved no slight fame at the time. In order to conform to his o
theories as literally as possible, he imposed upon himself a rule of ab
lute chastity and, on the day of publication of his book, hanged hims
in order to confirm a passage in it which read: "In order that man m
be redeemed it is necessary that he should recognize the value of n
being, and desire intensely not to be." Leibnitz was so susceptible to t
hypersensitivity of his imagination that on numerous occasions, wh
he thought of the idea of death, he fainted.

In Morris Cox's valuable *Genetic Studies of Genius*, edited by T

n, Leibnitz is credited with a hypothetical intelligence quotient of
, second only to John Stuart Mill's 195. The ratings are based on a
efully elaborated analysis of the early mental traits of three hundred
ld-acknowledged geniuses, selected from Cattell's objectively deter-
ied list of a "thousand eminent individuals of history." This care-
study has produced some forceful conclusions in the effort to identify
special traits of creative talent, and particularly in its concentration
on precocity. A sound effort has been made in this work to avoid
ne of the bias which tempted Lombroso in his earlier period of inquiry
draw some challengeable and rather sensational conclusions. Lom-
so had something of the impetuosity of genius himself, and while
biographical embrace of the problem was large, he had not the
antages of later, more systematic and less intuitional scholars, such
Galton, Toulouse, Odin, Ostwald and others, advantages of far
ater statistical records and considerable advancement in the technique
personality analysis. Lewis Terman concludes from Dr. Cox's studies
t "geniuses, so called, are not only characterized in childhood by a
erior IQ, but also by traits of interest, energy, will and character that
eshadow later performance. The ancient saying that 'The child is
her to the man' probably expresses a truth far more profound than
one has hitherto suspected . . . the traits which make for prodigious
formance in manhood are probably in evidence as budding capacities
the child." And the three foremost traits found to be most generally
aracteristic are profoundness of apprehension, consistency of action
ulting from deliberate volition, and originality of idea. In other
rds, sensibility, will and idea. The precocities of most of the world's
liant figures are well enough known to require no enumeration here;
t it is important to mention in passing that precociousness, while in-
ative of much, is neither an invariable characteristic of genius nor by
y means a guarantee of it.

I shall make brief mention, before closing this particular subject, of a
v of the interesting habit patterns formed by productive personalities
their conscious and subconscious efforts to attain the maximum
tensity of creative power. The "fine frenzy" of poetic inspiration is a
l phenomenon in many instances, and some of the descriptions of the

appearance and state of genius types when immersed in moods of m
tation and acts of creation resemble Sappho's enduringly famous, v
nigh clinical picture of manifestations of the love passion. According
an account by Reveille-Parise, the man of genius frequently "exhibi
small contracted pulse, pale, cold skin, a hot, feverish head, brilli
wild, injected eyes." After the moment of composition it often happ
that the author no longer understands how he has come to his h
point of achievement. In their quest for the summit of their pow
some well-known figures have resorted to the following little idios
crasies: Leibnitz found that he was able to do his best thinking i
horizontal position, and consequently he made it a rule to medit
horizontally on all possible occasions. This habit was common t
great many persons. Descartes buried his head in a sofa. Cujas wor
lying prone on the floor, which Shelley always loved to do also, p
ticularly when he could find a hearthrug that he placed in such a v
as to have his head close to a good, hot log fire. Rousseau liked to me
tate with his head exposed to the full glare of the sun; Bonnet sou,
for himself a cold room and wrapped his head in hot compresses. Mil
composed with his head leaning down over his chair. Schiller plung
his feet into pails of ice. Paisiello composed in bed, covered with mo
tains of blankets. Most of these apparent oddities were instinct
methods for increasing cerebral circulation and of shutting out possib
ties of diversion. Many sought the added impetus of rhythmic incitati
the influence of rhythm upon mental and emotional processes is
course enormous. From the *Life and Letters of Charles Darwin* we le
that Darwin was greatly interested in the subtle forces of rhythm
nature, and that his intuition led him into investigations which
termed "fool's experiments" because they often seemed so remote fr
scientific procedure. One of his researches took the form of having
bassoon played in proximity to the cotyledons of a plant. The rhythm
poetry is capable of providing both release and expression to men
excitation far beyond that of prose. Byron considered poetry to be "t
expression of passion under excitement, which grows in vigour a
effectiveness as the excitement increases." An explosive definition
what poetic rhythm can mean to an agonizingly unbalanced mind

ted from the diary of Manicomio of Pesaro, by way of a mental
ient's own explanation of why he wrote verse: "Poetry is a spon-
eous emanation from the mind . . . poetry is the cry of the soul
rced by a thousand griefs." The totality of impression that one gains
m all these intensified modes of behavior provides us at least with an
imation of how specially "stepped up" is the working of the human
nd when under the strain of rising to its highest powers.

Chapter VIII

NUANCE

〰〰〰

THE moment one imagines high sensibility combined in person with the other attributes of artistic drive, one begin envisage some of the fruitful results that may be expected t forthcoming. The major reason for laying so much stress upon element of sensibility is no esoteric one. The simple fact is that with it the human spirit labors under handicaps tantamount to blindn deafness or general anesthesia. For at the stage of spiritual and aesth experience to which mankind has brought itself over long ages of p ress, all further growth and all further appreciation must inevitably accomplished by way of the most delicate and barely perceived val Ineffable, these values have been frequently termed, because their s tlety lies beyond the descriptive capacity of words, much as mod theoretical physics which presents us with such concepts as that of quantum, approachable only by way of mathematical abstraction. other words, we have advanced beyond the relative crudities of primitive capacities and achievement, and we have come to that ep of our development wherein the nuance plays an immense role. To insensitive mind, nuance has little or no meaning, and yet it has co to constitute a veritable sine qua non of all advanced artistry, a thought and feeling. A proof of this significant truth may be found in scientific effort of modern semantics to surmount the obstacle of c grown, misapplied, and insufficient language medium. Words tend become an inadequate means of expression as they fall behind in onward flow of our progress into realms of nuance. William James w so far as to say that "language is the most imperfect and expensive me yet discovered for communicating thought." It is as though each time begin to reach high altitudes the rarity of the atmosphere threatens be beyond our equipment for breathing. And we are stopped unless

88

project our inquiring feelers further than our thwarted selves. That
␣hy we have constant and ever-increasing recourse to our various
␣and sciences.

␣Ve are, too, driven on by a religious urge. As our minds have become
␣her illuminated by grace of the enormous progress in scientific and
␣eral enlightenment, we do not any longer find complete comfort or
␣enance in the creeds of a religious past which are no longer credible
␣nspiring. Faith cannot survive its own creeping suspicions of being
␣quated; it too must maintain a sense of spontaneous coherence with
␣here and now. Consequently, there is an enormous desire on the
␣: of all sensitive minds for spiritual fortification. Despite the for-
␣lable achievement of man's advance in the clarifying of nature's
␣ifold workings, there still lie upon him the baffling and stupendous
␣ghts of unsolved problems. However brightly he may have illuminated
␣process of his living, man is still oppressed by the remorseless threat
␣xtinction at death. He has penetrated no further into the darkness of
␣greatest obstacle to his final optimism. Indeed, as his understanding
␣reases, his former faith in the immature hopes and promises of his
␣ient creeds diminishes, leaving him perhaps more bereft than ever in
␣history of any substantial comfort or assurance as to the permanence
␣his being. Hence we have the spectacle of an advancing humanity,
␣hing ever-higher altitudes of sensitivity and spiritual vitality, and
␣sequently at a poignant stage of bleak bewilderment. As its knowledge
␣ws, its judgment becomes more exacting, leaving less and less room
␣credulity. None of the old props suffice. Yet somewhere in the
␣itive glimmerings that emerge from our peristent searchings, there
␣s a new hope. This hope is founded upon renewed delicacies of
␣erception. It becomes increasingly apparent that all structure, all
␣ng, is ultimately immaterial, and that to understand it is to cultivate
␣nsitivity to the nuances which relate it to our corporeal nature.

␣ince it has become scientifically and philosophically so evident to
␣that ultimate reality in every phase presentable to our consciousness
␣essentially unsubstantial and primarily kinetic, we find that we are
␣e to accustom ourselves to this concept through various channels of
␣roach. Each art and each science seems, by its own system of logic, to

traverse the chains of nuance peculiar to its particular domain, lead
us most wonderfully in every instance toward the same kind of enlig
enment. The experience of this enlightenment is an important funct
in the subsistence of our spirituality. Indeed, it is the primary purp
of this book to seek this enlightenment by a study of the specific ar
painting, an art which increasingly engages the interest, the fascinat
and the love of more and more persons. From this point I shall pur
the investigation in terms of plastic form as envisaged, imagined,
realized or implied by the artist-painter.

The art of painting has played a vigorous and influential role in hum
affairs. At different periods it has exerted different influences, both
degree and in kind. I shall presume a modicum of familiarity with
history of the fine arts and shall refrain from looking backward in
great detail. I believe we shall make better headway if we plunge i
the subject from a fairly contemporary point of departure, evoking me
ings from the past only when they relate directly to whatever thou
we may be developing at a given moment.

As already shown, it cannot be expected that any individual, un
he happen to be of a genius type, will be able to absorb the en
message contained in a work of art until he shall have cultivated a m
than superficial familiarity with its particular idiom and acquired
steadfast effort a comprehension of its whole nature and significan
It seems particularly regrettable that an art so apparently "visible"
that of painting should remain one of the most esoteric of the mediu
of expression. Even music, subtle though it has become in the fine cou
of its development, and abstract though it be in the architecture of
audible patterns, exerts more of a compulsion at least upon the emotio
nature of an undeveloped discernment than do the plastic arts of pai
ing and sculpture. Yet some of the world's noblest spirits, endowed w
genius of the highest order, have spoken to their fellow men via th
pigments brushed upon canvas. And it is high time that we make
effort to bring this, and indeed all the arts, nearer to the multitudes
people who would love them if they could but know them. It is rep
nant to the alert mentality of today that any of the arts should contir
to be shrouded in a kind of august mystery penetrable only by

:sthetic élite. Most of all, it is a source of great anxiety to the artist imself, who realizes so poignantly how limited his audience is and how allow the understanding of most of that small audience. Artist and yman alike are increasingly eager to get nearer to each other. They e aware, as never before, of how much good can come out of true utual understanding and sympathy. The artist yearns to reach more an a few cultivated "amateurs"; he wants to spread the exuberance of s feeling and his insight widely enough to delight and uplift not a few t many, not many but all. This is a healthy, vitalizing instinct, and would be exceedingly pessimistic to believe that we cannot encourage d facilitate a widening appreciation by clarifying some of the obscure lues involved. We have come to a point in time and cerebral expe- nce where it might almost be said that we have new mentalities de- anding fresh resources and wider communion.

Alfred North Whitehead says this emphatically when he writes that he quiet growth of science has practically recoloured our mentality so at modes of thought which in former times were exceptional, are now oadly spread through the educated world. This new colouring of ways thought had been proceeding slowly for many ages in the European oples. At last it issued in the rapid development of science; and has ereby strengthened itself by its most obvious application. *The new entality is more important even than the new science and the new chnology.* It has altered the metaphysical presuppositions and the aginative contents of our minds; so that now the old stimuli provoke new response. Perhaps my metaphor of a new color is too strong. hat I mean is just that slightest change of tone which makes all the fference."[1]

In that last sentence we have a clear indication of how great a role ay be played in contemporary thought by a slight nuance, a discreet ading of meaning. Whitehead also wrote that "the science of Pure athematics, in its modern developments, may claim to be the most iginal creation of the human spirit. Another claimant for this position music. . . . While the harmony of logic lies upon the universe as an n necessity, the aesthetic harmony stands before it as a living ideal

[1] *Process and Reality*, by Alfred North Whitehead. The Macmillan Co., 1930.

moulding the general flux in its broken progress towards finer, sub issues."

Whitehead's attribution of such importance to mathematics is plained by what we had to say briefly about the quantum theory the general hypothesis that we now have of the immateriality of ultin being. "So long as you are dealing with pure mathematics, you are in realm of complete and absolute abstraction." If the ultimate element matter are in their essence vibratory (the Quantum Theory bases it upon the hypothesis that existence is essentially vibratory radiation wave systems of energy emerging from the atom), then mathema would indeed seem to provide the nearest intellectual medium approach to a logical apprehension of so abstract a process of being. as Whitehead himself proceeds to point out, aesthetic harmony j the harmony of logic as systems for approaching these abstractions. a contemporary understanding of the aesthetics of the art of paint should provide a significant contribution to the general trend of dea with the abstract. The art of painting is perhaps even more suscept to analysis and explanation than that of music, since the latter rem the more intangible medium, more closely related to the nature pure mathematics. Whereas painting deals a little more concretely w abstraction, representing symbolically as it does many of the tang aspects of reality and dissolving them by implication into the rhyth flow of essential ideation. Painting deals with the appearance of thi which is perhaps closest, after touch, to man's instinctive mode perception. It deals most literally with appearance, and at its subt level of achievement it dissolves all the illusions of appearance reveals some of the underlying reality. The physicist tells us and "sho us mathematically that a chair is no more substantial than the compon vibratory waves of energy that compose its atomic nature. The pair relates his experience of a chair to his experience of the spaces apparent substances around it, and then, by maintaining the rhyth flow of nuance radiating in every direction, relates the whole experie to himself as originating source of the entire apperception. Howe rather than attempt to describe such an experience briefly, which impossible, we shall proceed now to examine the purposes and mean

e disposal of the modern painter, and we shall hope to define the new
orizons which lie before the creator and the lover of this great and
owing art.

But we shall interject this further brief thought before embarking upon
ar main theme. It is most important not to confuse the ways of an art
th the ways of a science, and especially nowadays when it requires the
ost strenuous efforts of scientists to preserve humanized aspects of their
gorously abstract reductions of nature. A. S. Eddington sees the whole
oblem when he writes that "the external world of physics has become
world of shadows. In removing our illusions we have removed the
bstance, for indeed we have seen that substance is one of the greatest
our illusions. The frank realization that physical science is concerned
th a world of shadows is one of the most significant of recent advances.
. The materialist who is convinced that all phenomena arise from
e electrons and quanta and the like, controlled by mathematical
rmulae, must presumably hold the belief that his wife is a rather
iborate differential equation; but he is probably tactful enough not to
trude this opinion in domestice life. . . . We have not yet reached the
actice of the Laputans, who 'if they would, for example, praise the
auty of a woman, or any other animal, they describe it by rhombs,
cles, parallelograms, ellipses, and other geometrical terms' . . . If this
ıd of scientific dissection is felt to be inadequate and irrelevant in
dinary personal relationships, it is surely out of place in the most
rsonal relationship of all—that of the human soul to a divine spirit."[2]
One way the artist-painter reveals his intuition of this "illusory nature
substance" is by eliminating the static contours of objects which
ınkind had come to accept automatically as true. The fluidity char-
:eristic of good painting creates a sensation of interpenetrant fusion
tween matter and space. Apples on a table as seen by the layman and
the artist present a world of difference in concept. The layman cata-
gues in his mind the several shapes in their association to each other
d to the table, retaining a sense of separate identities whose only
ıtionship is one of nearness or even contiguity. A whole multitude of
 thinking habits formed throughout the history of man's develop-

The Nature of the Physical World, by A. S. Eddington. The Macmillan Co., 1929.

ment prevents all but the most intuitional mentality from seeing bette
seeing more truly. But now, at last, owing to the intelligible process (
science, which has discovered that the solidest-appearing of solid objec
is in reality as unsubstantial in its ultimacy as the airiest vapors, all me
of knowledge will gradually recognize at least intellectually the fallac
that has dominated their visual processes. If a hard stone is now know
to consist of whirling constellations of electrical charges gyrating throug
space in certain clusters that are not even conforming to any apparer
laws of being or behavior, then it becomes easier to understand that a
the apparently separate items we see around us may likewise participa
in a totality, even as the so-called electrons and the vast spaces with
which they circulate make up what we see to be, and call, a stone. Thu
if we were to reduce an artist's concept of several apples on a table
verbal terms in which he may never have consciously thought of ther
we might say that he recognizes the apples, the space in which the
dwell, and the table on which they rest, all to consist ultimately of tl
same sort of immaterial electrical impulses. Hence he conceives of
these shapes as illusions as long as they seem to remain separate. F
realizes that there is no such thing as an actual line which circumscrib
any one of these apples, isolating it. He also realizes that within his ov
experience, which to him is the most real awareness available, the
apples fluctuate in the intensity of their apparent reality, dependi
entirely upon his eye and sense of touch. If he looks at apple A, the
apples B, C and D retire into secondary perceptibility. Intellectua
he continues to attribute equal reality to all of them. But plastically th
advance and recede in importance, in "realness," as they approach
draw away from the attention of the beholder.

The final impression of a fully realized picture is similar to the i
pression that a mathematical mind has when it contemplates visions
totality as apprehended via limited constellations of parts. No conte
porary mind of any maturity can fail to respond to the beauty of mode
physics, which, like all other approaches to the mysterious truths, con
tutes a wonderful poetry in mathematical idiom. Even those to whc
the idiom itself is elusive must sense with delight the resultant conce
as they are translated into the impure but nevertheless challenging l

ıge of words. But, as Eddington points out, there is a natural tendency
be bewildered by what is being revealed. Because when we discover
ıt "substance is one of our greatest illusions" we find ourselves split
tween two ways of looking at things. Our intelligence now insists, on
ꞓ basis of our logical physical inquiry, that everything is ultimately the
ne thing—a sort of electrical energy acting in packets of élan. The
ʀticular configuration of the packets determines the apparent forms of
tities. One constellation may constitute a grain of sand, another an
ular nerve cell. A vast mathematically formulated agglomeration of
ch constellations produces what we call a man, among trillions of other
ings. And yet our intelligence cannot long abide the literal concept of
ırselves and our romantic world as merely mathematically predicated
ıanta of motive energies. We are more interesting to ourselves, and
ꞓ world is more interesting to us, when we also play the game of life
cording to less rigidly physical rules. Our intuition asserts its passionate
ꞓnviction that the mystery behind all this electrical phenomenon
volves us intimately in a spiritual necessity. And that is precisely what
ıe vision of the artist asserts plastically. Behind all the physical phe-
ɔmena as viewed by the human eye, he senses an ultimate mystery
ɪvolving him in a spiritual necessity. Just as Eddington rejects mere
ımmateriality as the final concept, just as we abhor the reduction of a
ɔman to "a rather elaborate differential equation," so does the artist
ɪnscend the fallacy of merely seeing the world as separate shapes
ɪvided by distances, but rather sees an all-embracing entirety, self-
ıclusive.

Let us now study some of the knowledge at the disposition of a
ɔntemporary artist that was not even within "guessing" distance of the
ırlier man. Much of what the older masters did apprehend intuitively
ɔ a limited degree is now become common knowledge. The caterpillar
ıode of progress pertains in art as in ethics or in science. The leaders
t the head of the grande bête humaine make their moves, and the rest
f humanity follows or gets pulled along, exerting no slight drag on the
training leaders. All along the way, if we are curious enough to take
ccount of the stages of progress, we can note important differences in
ɦe qualities and capacities of succeeding generations. And, most par-

ticularly as we approach modern times, these differences become strik
because of the radical speed-up in the general process of human
genuity and scientific proficiency. Even during the period of
Renaissance there were transitions from one brief period to anot
that made huge differences in the style and content of the artists
those days. And the influence of those artists upon the general tre
of their times was enormous. In every one of these periods genius fou
its own more or less limited ways of expressing itself and accomplish
its feats of beauty according to its lights. In Siena, Masaccio and all
stood for was still unthought-of; Duccio could no more have painte
three-dimensional figure such as appeared only a hundred years later
the walls of the Brancacci Chapel of the Carmine at Florence than co
Galileo have employed Newtonian laws of physics in his calculatio
Because Duccio and Simone Martini and all their religiously inspi
Sienese school were deeply immersed in the Byzantine tradition. T
great change leading toward Masaccio, and beyond, came not so mu
as a result of evolution within the process of painting itself, but, as
often is the case, as a result of the immense social and philosophi
innovation in the person of St. Francis of Assisi!

St. Francis represented a momentous departure from medieval
ligiosity. He and his followers in the Franciscan order opened the eyes
their contemporaries to the immediate wonders of nature, and start
a healthy cult of spontaneous adoration of the beauty to be found in
things at all times. It is impossible to overestimate the importance
this innovation. Its repercussions spread into the realms of religion a
aesthetics, the latter being of course, at that time, an entirely unse
conscious emanation of the former. Eventually science too emerged fro
its prolonged lethargy and began to enjoy a reawakened vitality such
men had given it in the age of Aristotle. The social repercussion w
enormous; the whole culture and political organization of Floren
flowered and spread its fragrance far and wide over the Europe of t
fourteenth and fifteenth centuries. And instead of painting devotiona
in the restricted symbolisms of the church, the artists began to fi
once again, as they had found centuries before, a mood of worship
many of the intimate details of their daily lives. The perfection

rugino's space composition and Leonardo's spirituality through his
ightened mastery of tactility were still only a suspected potentiality of
int to Masaccio, though he himself was the initiator of these accom-
ishments. To Perugino, Raphael, Piero della Francesca, Leonardo,
d others, such aerial composing as was achieved by Paul Cézanne was
ll an unexpressed and undeveloped part of their understanding of
rm. Sensitivity to the vast function of nuance in space remained in-
itional for centuries. It is only recently that it has become somewhat
tellectualized, which is not necessarily to its advantage at the moment.

Bernard Berenson says, apropos this sense of nuance in space: "Believe
e, if you have no native feeling for space, not all the science, not all
ie labor in the world will give it to you. And yet without this feeling
iere can be no perfect landscape. In spite of the exquisite modelling
f Cézanne, who gives the sky its tactile values as perfectly as Michel-
ngelo has given them to the human figure, in spite of all Monet's
ommunication of the very pulse-beat of the sun's warmth over fields
nd trees, we are still waiting for a real art of landscape. And this will
ome only when some artist, modelling skies like Cézanne's, able to
ommunicate light and heat as Monet does, will have a feeling for
pace rivalling Perugino's or even Raphael's."[3]

Until Tintoretto, followed by El Greco, there were only the merest
ntimations of such vibrant spontaneity as found a temporary culmina-
ion in the gestures of Hals and Rubens. And the explosive immediacy
f a Van Gogh is only a recent attainment. It would now be a fairly
ertain impossibility, and at any rate unnecessary, to outdo the achieve-
nents of past artists in point of skillful, descriptive representation.
Religious subject matter, portraiture, figure, genre, landscape, still life,
ll have been mastered technically in many idioms and styles. The
landscape painting of the Chinese in the T'ang and Sung dynasties,
brushed in the meager medium of black ink, represents perhaps as high
a spiritual expression as can be envisaged in the graphic arts. Today's
fresh genius lies in a fresh spontaneity of vision, which is inevitably
and eternally new. No poet of today can see with the eyes of yesterday.
If he will but paint with his own eyes, thinking with his own brain,

[3] *Florentine Painters of the Renaissance*, by B. B. Berenson.

he will have much to say. Actually mankind could never paint the sar
picture two days in succession, much less two generations or tw
centuries. It is impossible. The experience of yesterday must ma
today's picture by that much different. It is only when the huma
spirit complicates itself by growing self-conscious and seeking to 1
original by contriving novelties of expression, instead of having fai
in the authentic spontaneity of its inherent individuality, that we beg
to get devitalized, ostentatious displays instead of direct artistic expre
sion. If every individual were to give forth his impression of the wor
simply and faithfully, according to the images formed by his ow
personal sensibilities, there would be no two versions alike. Eve
person would present the valuable evidence of his own peculiarly uniqu
reaction. These reactions would differ in quality and intensity in dire
relationship to the sensitivity of the mentality involved. "Dans
peinture, il y deux choses," says Cézanne, "l'œil et le cerveau."

The truly original genius never has to give a thought to originalit
nor ever has to fear the impairment or dissolution of his "fire," h
force, his uniqueness, by any outside influence of training or acquain
ance with and love for tradition and older masters. The true artist ca
not see uninterestingly or uncreatively, because he cannot be a duplic:
tion, in his experience, of any other artist or person. A great sensibili
will reveal the world to him through the nerve endings of his ow
peculiar system. A Van Gogh adored the skillful mediocrities of man
inferior spirits who were superior craftsmen in his day, because h
appreciated and needed and envied the craftsmanship that he instin
tively knew to be of inestimable value in the production of his ow
feverish and exquisite vision of nature. It would have been utterl
impossible for Van Gogh to have been "imitative" and equally impo:
sible for any other living soul to have painted Van Goghs.

Furthermore, it is most important to understand the causes of th
phenomenon of "influence" and to dismiss the stigma attaching t
instances of it in artistic production. Fully to understand it is fully t
accept it as an inevitable happening in the vast experience of life an
art. There is no shame attached to a would-be artist who "copies" th
style of another. The explanation of his behavior is simply that he love

e other's vision of nature more than anything he himself sees in ture through his own eyes. He is under no obligation to maintain e integrity of his own vision. His communications may lack interest d significance to others, and if this is so we shall simply say that he a lover of art rather than an artist, and let it go at that. And if his tivity stems only from the vulgar drive of pretension to artistry, that happy fact will proclaim itself at the first glance of a sincere artist. here is nothing in all the immensity of creation that stands out so amefully and so blatantly as any false gesture in the pure atmosphere genuine art. However awkward the effort, so long as it springs truly om the earnestness of love, it will carry conviction and make a humble ontribution to the totality of creative accomplishment. The gentlest hisper of the true artist carries clearly into distances of time and space which the ambitious shoutings of the spiritual fraud or artistic umbug never penetrate as anything more than noxious noise.

The man who gives his life to painting today knows that he is not ntering into an enterprise of lucrative promise, but is rather with-rawing from a practical life, not into a retreat but into a meditative nd creative fervor for which he is willing to sacrifice all the comforts nd pleasures that might be expected of a more normal existence. This an unusual state of affairs—peculiar to this and the past century. The pheavals of the French Revolution and of the Industrial Revolution recipitated vast changes in the political, social, economic and cultural spects of our existence. The new ideals of liberty, equality, fraternity ave birth to new and liberalized forms of government, which in turn roduced opportunities for the lower and middle classes to play a arger part in, and to exercise greater control over, the functioning of nodern life. This supplanting of the hitherto all-powerful aristocracy esulted in many upsets of tradition, both economic and cultural. And he final impact of enormous and rapid scientific advance, resulting n an industrial ferment and productivity undreamt of during the long ges of handicraft, created a condition of mixed bounty and social ncertainty. The pressures of rugged individualism and the increasingly competitive nature of all enterprise fomented a state of ever-shifting values and powers. Furthermore, scientific thinking led to critical

research and ultimately to Darwinism, which initiated modern schoc
of biology, psychology and philosophy that inevitably affected tl
traditional religious beliefs of earlier centuries. The influence of bo
church and state were thus subjected to considerable further moderatio
The social status of individuals fluctuated rudely, and the genera
rapid, uncertain tempi of personal and national destinies render
economic and cultural stability uncertain.

One of the net effects of these radical changes was to alter the fun
tion of the artist in contemporary society. Where he had former
occupied a definite place in the economic structure, he now found hir
self thrown upon his own resources, obliged to seek purchasers of h
productions and never sure of a constant market. Formerly he ha
been apprenticed to masters of large and busy ateliers until ready f
independent creativity; later he had been a member of an organiz
and protective guild, or had been assured of the enduring patrona
of church, state, royalty, nobility, merchant prince. There was a stea
demand for works of art, and a systematic arrangement for supplyi
what was required to the mutual benefit of artist and amateur. Whe
this fine adjustment was gradually disrupted and finally shattered t
the disappearance of the institutions that had been art's most natur
patrons and clients, there appeared certain state authorities, such a
most pre-eminently, the French Academy, which sought, often fc
political reasons, to establish official standards to be imposed upo
practicing artists, and initiated the custom of exhibiting works of a
in temporary and permanent salons where artists were encouraged t
vie for popular and critical favor, honors and support. This competitiv
struggle for recognition, upon which the artist depended for actu
survival, tended to divert his creative instinct from pure spontaneity c
expression to various ambitious strivings for the bourgeois market. Th
public market, lacking the widely developed taste and appetite for th
arts that existed among the people of Florence in the Renaissanc
period, for instance, does not always stimulate the best efforts of cor
temporary artisans. But fortunately, we can always rely upon the u
alterable integrity of the highest spirits, and hence we continue, unde
these new circumstances to have artists who consecrate themselves hear

d soul to that never-changing ultimate principle of living and painting cording to their deepest intuition.

Even though art has long since ceased to draw its main inspiration om the formal structure of religious faith, it does not require much aping of the surface to reveal that its major impulse stems from an notion essentially religious. Somehow or other, the more we examine e underlying motivations of many recent great painters the more we nd them to be basically imbued with an ardent love for the same rt of transcendent loftiness that animated the earlier, more ceremonial d highly formularized forms of worship. This important fact will recur ain and again in our dealings with modern creativity. In a manner speaking, we might apply a psychoanalytic technique to the process this creativity, and I believe we should disclose at the bottom of ie artistic urge a very godly energy. It is hard to imagine beauty far om godliness at any time. Certainly an unbeautiful person will never roduce a beautiful work. And though the age we live in may seem by s material prepossession with worldly vanities to reject the gentle rtues, there are a thousand proofs to the contrary, and in the deepest eart of man an eternal longing for the serenity of grace.

Pierre Auguste Renoir, despite the exultantly sensual vibration of is magnificent art, entertained a shrewd suspicion of contemporary nortcomings and a devout hope for a regenerated spiritual ardor. He as always insistent that craftsmanship be maintained as the founda- on of sound artistry, but he mourned the apparent diminution of the eligious feeling which he found to be the supreme attribute of the lder masters. To Ambroise Vollard he spoke regretfully of "that erenity one never wearies of" in the old masters. "Serenity was within hemselves; it came not only from the nature of their simple and tran- uil lives, but from their religious faith. They were conscious of their railty, and in their triumphs as well as in their failures they associated he spirit of divinity with all they did. For them, God was always resent; man did not count. . . Their works have that aspect of gentle erenity which gives them their profound charm and makes them mmortal. But man, in his modern pride, has chosen to reject this partnership, because it belittles him in his own eyes. He has drive out God and, in so doing, he has driven out happiness too."[4]

There is a profound sadness in the plaint of so fine a master as Reno when he becomes depressed enough with the materialism of the tim to ask: "Will we ever see a return to tradition? We must hope for but not count on it too much. Since the whirlwind of the Revolutio passed and withered everything, we have no more pottery-makers n joiners nor foundrymen, nor architects nor sculptors. By the mere chance there are a few painters left: they are like seeds scattered chance in an abandoned field; they take root in spite of everything

Of course, this longing for a revival of moral fervor is in the hear of all deeply sensitive men, and it is even coupled with the convictio that intellectual progress must soon wait also upon such a reviva "Religious emotion, stripped of corruption . . . may presently blo through life again like a great wind," writes H. G. Wells, "bursting th doors and flinging open the shutters of the individual life, and makin many things possible and easy that in these present days of exhaustio seem almost too difficult to desire."[5]

The tremendous diversification of effort in the modern world painting, while it may seem to stem from the chaotic conditions the times, represents something more than mere turmoil and bewilde ment. More important than the negative signs of discontinuity, mor and intellectual perplexity, and egotistical impetuosity is the quiet bu steadfast earnestness with which countless resolute artists pursue thei inner vision of what is beautiful. The one magnificent characteristic c man at his best seems never to alter its quality or diminish its intensit His need to spread the beautiful truth that is within him as widely a he can among his fellow men provides an everlasting assurance that th best in man is most likely to survive. We may take this fact a little to much for granted unless we remind ourselves from time to time of th incalculable fortitude with which man at his best endures the desperat trials that attend him in his creative life. He makes the most formidabl

[4] *Renoir*, by Ambroise Vollard.
[5] *The Fate of Man*, by H. G. Wells.

acrifices in his determination to share himself with his brothers; it has
een called the sort of love that surpasseth understanding.

What is this excruciating urge to communicate one's intuition to
thers? It would be so heavenly a peace to be able to dwell quietly alone
a thought. Is it merely vanity that keeps impelling one to explain oneself
ad one's peculiarly personal findings to others? Even the tranquil
Oriental thinkers who rid themselves of so large a part of natural
appetite and ambition, who settled themselves resolutely into states of
entle resignation and day-to-day contemplation of life's sufficiently
absorbing display, nevertheless succumbed to the need of expressing
neir philosophy to others. They exerted themselves greatly to persuade
nankind of the wisdom of their findings, and it was as though the
ategrity of their own lives was blemished until all men were brought
nto the serenity of their sublimation.

Thus the poet and the painter cry out to their fellow men their
ager message that the wind in the trees is no mere wind in mere trees,
or the apple on the table simply an apple on a table, nor man on the
arth merely mortal on a planet, nor life a mere moment of stir from
blivion. They yearn to share with us a growing intuition that oblivion
a human corruption of infinity.

The skeptic, always scorning what he terms intellectual analysis,
ants to know why it is important for us to make penetrating inquiries,
ad why being merely mortal on a planet with oblivion in the offing
not good enough to be let alone. The beginning of an answer lies
the simple fact that for some minds there is as compelling an affinity
etween themselves and the unknown as between male and female.
he quest for truth, for ultimate understanding, is as real a human
ppetite as hunger itself, and infinitely more absorbing, more chal-
nging, since it is far less easily satisfied. And perhaps the cynic will
better placated if he is shown, too, how even this apparently rarified
ppetite stems from more fundamental ones and, indeed, bears promis-
g possibility of enhancing their satisfaction. Because, at bottom, the
arning for full comprehension is no mere intellectual curiosity with
solution as its unique reward. At least, speaking for myself (and it is
sentially from oneself that all such reasoning must flow), a primary

urge of all these searchings is to find tangible assurance of immortality. Just as appetite for love in civilized man surpasses in many ways his hunger for food, so in more civilized man does hunger for truth surpass all.

Now the artist has grown more and more aware of his appetite for the beauty that he finds in truth, and at the present stage of his activities he approaches his métier with perhaps more scrupulous and breathless zeal than for many centuries. He has renewed his recognition of the spiritual nature of his art and the extent of the reward to which he may aspire by addressing himself devotedly to his labors. He has added sufficiently to the delicacy of his own powers of discernment to catch now the nuance of a nuance. He no longer supplies a programmatic demand for pictures of a propagandistic content, such as was required for many generations by church and state. He is more entirely "on his own" now, less permeated with any philosophic or religious influence from outside agencies, more of an eclectic. He is free to lavish his love anywhere and everywhere, to find beauty in God or God in beauty; he is intellectually equipped to see the macrocosm in the microcosm and to detect the harmonies that underlie the universal surface. He reads the structure of his own soul according to the pattern and principle of his aesthetic integrity.

Chapter IX

SPONTANEITY, THE AESTHETIC IMPERATIVE

N THE preceding chapter we introduced the subject of nuance and
began to discuss the more obvious differences between the mental
outlook of today's artist and that of his ancestors. It is important
er to lose sight of the fact that what is practically "second nature"
v was once upon a time acquired only by dint of intense study and
lication.

ne should perceive the long history behind such illusory naïveté
that of a Van Gogh. It does not do to be too readily misled by the
arent awkwardness of his impetuosity. It is plain to any perceptive
dent that a Van Gogh painting bears within it the vast insight and
erience which are the heritage of centuries of effort. With all the
mingly primitive qualities of his emotion, it does not require a great
l of thought to realize that there is much in his art which could not
sibly have issued from the brushes of a similar temperament at an
lier period. Besides, it is doubly impressive to remind oneself that
n Gogh's dominant motivation in painting pictures was to fulfill
burning instinct for godliness. He had started out by deserting the
urgeois role to which his family and circumstances tended to tie him,
l had gone into the poverty-stricken homes of coal miners with the
pe of alleviating their desperate plight. He was consumed by a
erish passion of sympathy and love. When he finally resorted to
ntbrushes it was primarily because, in the extremity of his emotion,
wished to express everything that he felt for the struggling souls of a
ely pressed humanity. His adoration for the heroism of his peasants
athed from his coarse-grained canvases with no less ardor than Fra
gelico's luminous beatitudes from the quiet walls of monastic cells
San Marco. It was not long before Van Gogh revealed his saintliness
every aspect of his aesthetic vision. His pictures were like graphic

transcriptions of the epistles of St. Theresa, palpitating with excessiv
passionate suffering and adoration. The beauty of everything inflic
upon his hypersensitivity such painful ecstasy as no human being
long endure without collapsing. In plain fact, the life and works of s
a man as this, even though his art certainly did not attain to the ser
perfection of some more monumental spirits, reveal to us the stagger
fact that such rare men as are gifted with the sensitivity to see and
feel a little more of the divine radiance than they are at present equip
to withstand must burn brightly but briefly in this unready world.
a Van Gogh the aesthetic drive operated like incessant electrical sho
he represents to an extreme degree the experience of all creative arti
Aesthetically he was so pure, so released from all spiritual frustration
repression, that every instant of seeing was fraught with intense exp
ence of beauty. His vision was perpetually bursting with spontane

It is the Van Gogh and the Cézanne type of mentality that is m
typical of the subtle advance that has been made in the art aura
modern times, and yields highest promise of things to come. This
the type of mind most alive to the nuance as we are now seeking
understand it, and this is the state of mind most capable of prodigi
creativity. What Van Gogh exemplifies in spontaneity Cézanne rep
sents in rare sensitivity to the architecture of space and all that
connotes. It may well be that these are not necessarily the most exqui
artists of their time; comparison of merit in art is a nonsensical af
anyhow. It is vain indeed to speak of degrees of beauty. However
is true that some men are innovators while others produce works
art at once contemporary and yet so well within the rhythmic flow
tradition that they remain delightful experiences without supply
any outstandingly vital impact upon their times. It still remains true t
every gesture of beauty is a precious contribution to the totality of l
But we cannot avoid paying attention to instances of specially inte
experience. Therefore, while it is possible to think of many manifes
tions of genius in the world of recent painters, it is of particular inter
at this moment to remark upon an aspect of that genius which is
tinguished in Van Gogh. It is the aspect of his peculiarly promin
gift of spontaneity. It is upon this gift that much of our future acco

hment will probably be based. The whole atmosphere of contem-
ary psychology, philosophy and science indicates it. A regenerated
gious emotion will most certainly spring forth from the soul of
manity in much the same way as Van Gogh's pictures sprang with a
lence of love from his tormented psyche.

Nobody can fully realize until he has given great thought to the
tter just what it is to see and to feel spontaneously. The whole
umulation of experience in seeing and feeling is such a gradual and
mulative one that a person is unaware of the patterns of habit into
ich he falls during the process. Most of us lose much interest in
at we see as soon as we think we have a familiarity with it. Some of
so mismanage and abuse this inestimable privilege of vision that we
ght almost be said to allow a spiritual atrophy to set in. We find
rselves confessing to a boredom with our surroundings much as we
mplain of too dull a diet, and we seek a "change of scene" with a
easure similar to that of dining out for the gratification of a different
isine. Perhaps the average person gets a little sense of this fact on
rtain rare occasions when circumstances shock him into more than
ual awareness. For instance, when a man has passed a week or two
 sea with no sight of land to break the continuity of ocean, his first
urs on shore are likely to find his vision somewhat freshened for the
hts of mother earth. Or, at a time of some great spiritual catharsis,
 particular instance of which has often been known to occur when
 person has miraculously survived a perilous accident, man looks about
m with a strange feeling of seeing things for "another first time"
th something like hysterical enthusiasm. These occasional freshenings
 perception are suggestive, but only suggestive, of the artist's per-
tually unspoiled receptivity.

It is instructive to keep ourselves under observation in this matter
 seeing. One way to judge ourselves is to note those special occasions
 which we seem to see with greater than casual pleasure. If, being
ccidentals, we voyage to the Orient, we usually find a heightened
imulation in the appearance of exotic landscape. If a sunset suffuses
aven and earth with unusually glowing color, we are moved. We
e stirred by almost anything that we call spectacular, involving a dis-

play of more that habitual visual incitation. Almost anything that
were to see for the first time in our lives would certainly arouse e:
interest.

And yet, in the extremely sensitive make-up of the artist type th
is such a continuous renewal of susceptibility that the artist sees
every instant of living as though he were seeing for the first ti·
Nothing is a repetition for him, nothing stays the same in appeara·
or in feeling. Besides, the everlastingly busy mentality of such a per
is, in a creative way, gifted with a faculty for forgetting. It has
instinctive aversion to encumbering itself with the impedimenta
past experience. It nourishes itself upon its experience and grows uį
it, but it meets the dawn of each new minute ready and disengag
Perhaps this explains why Renoir's daily prayer was that he mi·
remain always a child in spirit. He dreaded the occlusion of adult h·
and progressive apathy.

This explains, too, why, out of the rich catalogue of recent artist
have singled Van Gogh at this time for special attention. He ·
possessed to a unique degree of that happy faculty of spontaneity
developed with practice to such a pitch that every visual experie·
became for him something akin to a miraculous revelation. He had
to look at a field and he became filled with an emotion of tremend·
consequence to himself and to the world with which he communica·
by his painting. The beauty in all things was so intensely visible to k
that he suffered from an almost convulsive urgency to show it to
fellow men. Where this sort of experience may be frequent with m·
genius, in the case of Van Gogh it was well-nigh incessant, and
course it turned out to be more than the mortal frame could bear.

The reaction of an average man to the Van Gogh attitude is lik
to be one of bewilderment, skepticism and caution. Only the fact t
art has gained a foothold of respectability protects a man whose te·
perament is as challenging as that of a Van Gogh from a destiny e·
more tragic than was his. The intensity of his response to the m·
apparently casual aspects of nature and of mankind seemed so ex·
gerated, compared to the normal person's reactions, that he was ine·
tably looked upon as a strange and frenzied creature. Perhaps had

ıode of communication been different, had he poured forth his fervent
ıessages in terms of passionate sermons preached from conventional
ulpits, he would have been better understood. But then probably his
ıfluence would have been restricted to the few within hearing of his
oice, whereas his pictures project his unique vision down the years.
urthermore, it is not at all pertinent to make suppositions based upon
lternative modes of expression. The unalterable fact is that Van Gogh,
fter surveying the horizons of his possible pathways, followed the com-
ulsive direction of what was most probably his greatest talent. It was
ı the beautiful that he found the utmost meaning and the most
anscendent promise. I think it can be said not unreverentially that
ıch a man represented a highly aestheticized version of the Christ
ıaracter. And since, indeed, the major emotion of his social atom was
rofound grief at the world's miserable failure to embrace any of the
hristian philosophy, his own religious impulse turned to a more
ıodern outlet and a more modern hope. His instinct, and a growing
orld instinct, led him from a despair of human ethic to a hopefulness
ı human aesthetic. Since thousands of years, and especially the last
vo thousand, have indicated that one cannot expect much more than
ɔ service to the highest incentive of human wisdom, perhaps a more
ersuasive inspiration might be evoked by a cultivation of man's grow-
ıg love of the beautiful. If the world will not respond to God's truth
expounded by the Son of man, there is still the hope that it may
spond to beauty. God is evidently patient and resourceful, and appears
ı many forms. He speaks to us through many voices, and it is our
ıramount duty to learn to hear and to understand, so that we may
ırticipate in the grace of fully loving him.

In his devout study of Dutch painters, called *Maitres d'autrefois*,
romentin perceived the increasing power of beauty over the spiritual
ogress of man. He was prophetic of the advent of such a painter as
an Gogh and of such an age as ours. "Where belongs our gratitude?"
ɛ asks. "To what is worthiest, to what is truest? No. To what is greatest?
ɔmetimes. To what is most beautiful? Always. What then is the beauti-
l,—this great lever, this powerful moving spring, this mighty magnet,
ıat may almost be called the sole attraction of history? Is it nearer

than any ideal on which in spite of himelf man has cast his eyes
the great (heroic) so seductive only because it is more easy to confo
it with the beautiful? It is necessary to be very advanced in morals
very learned in metaphysics, to say of a good action or of a truth
it is beautiful. The simplest man says it of a grand deed. At bottom
naturally love only what is beautiful. Imagination turns thither, se
bility is excited by it, all hearts precipitate themselves toward it. If
seek carefully for what the mass of mankind loves most voluntarily
may be seen that it is not what touches it, nor what convinces,
what edifies it; it is what charms and excites its wonder."

What does a Van Gogh's spontaneous vision reveal to him
remains unseen by other men? Why, if we could look successi
through the eyes of a thousand men, in the thousand variant exp
ences we should undergo . . . why, when we came to seeing thro
the eyes of Van Gogh would we be suddenly electrified into a quicke
and a heightened awareness? Since, obviously, it is not a matter
greater anatomical perspicacity, since Van Gogh's ocular powers
not unusual and therefore do not enable him to see any further actua
than usual, we must surmise that the uniqueness of his experience n
lie somewhere within the bounds of what is visible to all of us if
would but notice.

Within the bounds of what is visible to all of us occurs the en
miracle of the artist's experience. And if it be objected that some
of it lies in the realm of the imagination, the true artist will be
first to affirm that no image that he can envision stirs him as mucl
what he sees in nature, the basis of all his imaginings. For the per
who has not even given a great deal of thought to the process of see
much must be explained. Indeed, it is fascinating for an intellig
person suddenly to discover how blind he has been to the signific
elements of all that he has been looking at during his lifetime. W
he undertakes to re-educate himself in his seeing habits, a whole
visual logic becomes available, and suddenly he finds himself thri
with a new ability to embrace the quality of things, just as when
acquires the logic of mathematics he is enabled to embrace the qu
tities. For there is a logic in the behavior of light and darkness, in

)earances of edges and surfaces, in the transformations of near to
, in every infinitesimal facet of visible form. We even forget the
stence of the most elementary rules of this logic because we are so
ustomed to apply them at every instant of seeing; the application of
s logic for all practical purposes has become automatic. Let us examine
 mode of operation a moment and reawaken ourselves to the indis-
sability of it to our dailiest activity. We shall then further see how
dispensable this same logic is in its appliance to the more subtle proc-
of seeing beyond our routine vision.

We take as much for granted now in our seeing as we do, for instance,
 our walking. We certainly tend to forget how laboriously we had to
rn how to walk, and what a drawn-out process it was. And yet the
 of seeing was an infinitely longer and more complicated process of
velopment, and, unlike walking, is never perfected. In our infancy
r eyes did not tell us much, and we had to make constant investiga-
ons with our hands to verify and to expand upon the evidence of our
ght. Only after many years of accumulated auxiliary information were
 gradually enabled to draw accurate conclusions about things from
eir visual appearance alone. In the beginning we certainly could not
ess from the appearances of things just how near and how far away
rious objects were. It was only by our reaching and our crawling
ross intervening spaces that we slowly acquired an ability to judge
stance from appearance. To an infant, an orange five feet away, a
air twenty feet away, a house five hundred yards away and a mountain
n miles away are all so far out of its immediate orbit of experience
at they are simply more or less remote in feeling, and offer no sen-
tion of measured relativity of space. A view out of a window to an
fant is different from the same view to an adult. To the child the
rious evidences of distance, such as the diminution of texture as
rfaces recede, and the laws of perspective, do not yet furnish him
ith a knowldege of the actuality. In his earliest window-gazing we
ight almost say that the scene would as readily seem to him to be
ainted on the glass, and that the lamppost a hundred yards away is
pparently to him on no different plane from that only fifty yards away
ut simply looks like a shorter and narrower shape. Similarly, if he could

talk to us, he would reveal himself to be laboring under multitudes illusions. A man walking down an avenue in a direction that takes rapidly toward the child's visual horizon will not be understood a man receding into space but as a man who simply changes his posit in relation to objects around him and grows progressively smaller volume. A small house five hundred yards away and a huge mans two miles away might appear to be the same size, and therefore, only way their respective situations in space could be identified wo be by a recognition of perspectival and atmospheric appearances. other words, and in order not to lavish too much time on this import: but fairly simple matter which needs less explaining than reminding, reader has but to lend himself to a simple experiment by which he n refresh his understanding of elementary vision.

Let the reader fix his attention on any scene that happens at moment to confront him. Let him then clear his mind of all automa assumptions and begin to analyze his understanding of the scene bef him. How much actual truth would his eyes alone tell him about t things he is looking at if he were to eradicate all the auxiliary knowled of his past experience which rushes to contribute its synchronous te mony to the visible evidence? His eyes alone, without benefit secondary information, present him with a two-dimensional impressi of varying colors and tones. Even the so-called edges, where one m; terminates and some other aspect of substance or space neighbors do not signify more than an abrupt change. Nor do textures rev themselves by anything more than their tonal aspects. Every furth knowledge has had to be acquired by a slow process of inquiry utilizi; the other available senses, particularly the sense of touch and the expe ence of traversing extended spaces involving passage of time, which one of the important measures of space. Gradually the reader shou come to understand that every visual experience is only initiated by t experience of his eyes and is then qualified by a synchronized cerebratic which utilizes the whole multitude of data which has been assembl in the conscious and subconscious reservoir.

A simple instance may be shown in the appearance of a book lying c a table. If the beholder happens to sit with his eye level just a litt

ner than the surface of the table, then a careful observation will
ow the book to appear considerably thicker than its width. Also the
th of the table will seem to be considerably less in area than, let
ay, the depth of the drawer facing the beholder. And yet this person
immediately say, if describing the book and the table he is looking
that the book is certainly, like practically all books, wider than it is
ck, and that the table is certainly wider in area than the drawer is
p. This is all implied to him by the perspectives that he uncon-
ously records in his reaction to the appearance not only of the book
l table but of all other objects within the scope of his vision. Hence
s that almost invariably when an untrained person makes an attempt
draw such a book lying on the table, he draws far more in the dimen-
ns of what he knows about the book and table than what he literally
s. The result is a confusion between concept and percept, wherein
ch destroys the validity of the other. There are, of course, stages in
e evolution of graphic arts in various cultures where this sort of mixed
presentation has been utilized with discretion and has yielded certain,
nited decorative design. But since the aesthetic we are studying dwells
an age of four-dimensional comprehension, it is most unlikely that
o-dimensional art idioms will have much to say to the hypersensitive
entality of the future.

One more point that we tend to overlook among the elementary
ctors of our seeing faculty is the matter of what is technically known
the focal center, or point of vision. We shall have occasion to refer
it frequently as this study progresses; it will suffice for the time being
remind the reader how completely different this particular factor
akes the process of seeing from the process of photography. In fact,
we shall see later, this slight difference between the retinal and
mera lens functioning renders the whole futile controversy between
ine art" and "photographic" enthusiasts utterly nonsensical. Briefly,
e camera lens registers every portion of the area with equal intensity
the panoramic or two-dimensional sense. For instance, if there were
picket fence traversing the foreground of a camera representation,
very piece of wood in that fence, from the extreme left across to the
treme right of the picture, would be recorded with unvarying fidelity,

no part or portion seen with any less accuracy or intensity than a
other part. Whereas the human view is vitally different. By the natu
of our eyes we can center our vision at only one point of a given ar
at any one instant, and every other point within the area of vision
seen secondarily, and with decreasing clarity as it is more remote fro
that particular point of focus. In the case of the picket fence, if th
eyes were fixed on one of the posts, then that post would be seen
great detail, and the posts on either side of it would be progressive
less clearly seen as they receded from the focal one. Their appearan
would alter progressively in many different ways, which we shall
into further along in our study, for these alterations have an immen
bearing upon aesthetic experience. Furthermore, because the fence
in the foreground of a view, the camera will always show it clearly; th
lens cannot focus its range with the nuanced discretion of a human ey
Whereas, if a man happens to fix his eye upon a distant mountai
then the fence, even though very near to him, will have a vaguer an
utterly different aspect from what it would have if the eyes happend
to be focused at another point nearer the fence. Thus, if one be
sensitive as one should be to all the nuance involved, one could crea
many different pictures of the same scene simply by directing the ey
at different focal points for each experience. This sort of thing ha
been done with interesting results; results, indeed, often more startli
and revelatory even than Monet's variations on the theme of changi
light.

Of course, these elementary truths are well-known to every intellige
person who gives such matters any thought. But it is astonishing
find that there is an enormous resistance to them, in almost every cas
when people attempt to express themselves graphically. The experien
of what we might call pure seeing is impaired by the volume of pr
judgment which we inflict upon most of our vision, and impaired to suc
an extent that we are often astonished at the ease with which a
observant craftsman can successfully represent appearances which
the confused layman seem so elusive to reproduction. The capacity
reproduce an appearance successfully has little to do with aestheti
as an end, but as a means it is extremely important. And it entails litt

e than the exercise of unadulterated perceptive logic. So often the
teur student of painting seems bewildered at the task of representing
appearance, for instance, of transparencies, such as a glass of water.
s difficult for him to understand that transparency reveals itself by
same logical laws of light and darkness as opacity. He is confused
really by what he sees in the glass of water but only by what he
ws about it. He knows so many qualities of liquid and of glass
t differentiate them from other substances that he feels they must
necessity be less amenable to representation. But the moment he is
suaded to forget his ideas about these qualities and simply to repro-
e each value of tone and color in its context, he finds that a glass
water is rendered on his canvas as automatically as a carefully observed
ck of wood or piece of paper. In the last analysis, every substance and
m in nature translates itself into appearance by the same direct mode
light-behavior. If we look upon any object or assemblage of objects
though it were a pattern of varying minute tonal values, and if we
roduce these tiny areas of relative lights and darks in their proper
ationships, as in a mosaic, we shall always achieve a resemblance to
things perceived.

Another great fallacy in the ordinary attempt to see purely comes
m an anatomical ocular habit of which most people are unaware
til it is pointed out to them, and even then they are not quick to
sp the enormous consequence. It is the involuntary act of incessantly
fting the focal point during the process of seeing. This is done so
nstantly and to such good purpose in casual observing, that it has
come an unconscious function. If the reader is not aware of this
portant phenomenon, he can easily verify it by a careful observation of
own manner of looking at things, and also by watching the activity
other persons' eyes. The latter is a surer test because, in attempting
observe one's own process of beholding, the self-consciousness of the
ort may disturb the normal function and produce a fixed stare, which
not at all the usual way of seeing. What happens in the ordinary
holding of a landscape or a view of things is that the eyes dance about
perceptibly within the orbit of what they are observing, never staying
ed upon any particular point of the whole scene. In this way they

achieve a more thorough grasp of that which is under observatio
they were to remain fixed at a particular point, they would ha
satisfactory vision of that point, but their grasp of the rest of the s
would diminish in direct proportion to the distance of details
from that specific point. For instance, if one were looking o
window at some houses on the farther side of a river, as long as
eyes fixed themselves upon those distant houses they would ha
clearer perception of the houses than of the sky or of some trees on
near side of the river or even of the balcony immediately outside
window. But as a matter of fact, the eyes do not stay fixed upon
houses; it is not their habitual manner of seeing. They handle
situation quite differently. They center for an instant on the ho
then they may center on a road near the houses, then on the lumi
horizon, then on a tree trunk standing between themselves and
river, then upon the balcony or a boat in the river or a flying bird
infinitum. The fact is that as they constantly shift their focus
still take in the whole scene.

But different elements of the scene become secondary all the ti
The focus shifts both latitudinally and in depth from near to far.
result is really a succession of different experiences, a continual varia
of the form of space observed. For if the eyes are fixed on the white
of smoke of a railroad train passing along the near bank of the r
the whole spatial form of the scene is utterly different than when
eyes are fixed on the distant houses. The eyes, it is true, may be se
all the many things mentioned as well as a lot more that is wit
range, all at the same time, but in respect to the infinite relations
of all these details making up a total spatial form, they change e
time the eyes shift their focus.

From all this we can gather that the ordinary experience of se
really consists of a sort of cataloguing of separate items until the m
holds within its memory a collection of impressions yielding a t
image. This is true even in the case of less extended visions than
of a landscape. Observe, for instance, a face. One may focus one's att
tion on the eyes of that face and in so doing may have an impress
of the whole expression as displayed by the rest of the features.

process of observing that face satisfactorily will inevitably expand
a cataloguing of the aspects of the whole area, the nose, the mouth,
the various lines around the eyes and in the cheeks which reveal
racter and feeling, the chin, etc. Were a person to refrain from this
d of seeing, his vision staying fixed upon the first point that it may
ounter, his experience would differ vastly from the normal, and he
ild dwell in a succession of semihypnotic states. But for the purposes
aesthetic comprehension, one must understand this basic principle
eeing. One must realize that practical, everyday seeing is characterized
a process of successive, intermingling impressions, which is certainly
most useful mode of acquiring knowledge of the visual facts; but
lispels all apprehension of ultimate form. Ultimate form must be
n spontaneously, at any one, but at one, aspect of its many-faceted
nifestation.

This fallacy of pure seeing is one of the major elements in unsuccessful
nting, and accounts for the reason why such multitudes of paintings
not pictures at all but merely arrangements of groups of painted
ects. For no matter how skillfully the painter may arrange objects
order to create a design, and no matter how deftly he may render
m on his canvas, he will not have made a work of plastic significance
long as he has ignored this basic law. The trouble stems from the
t that the painter usually shifts his visual focus as he covers the
a of his canvas, eying each object and each part of each object as
paints it. No matter how perfectly he may thus give descriptions
the appearance of things, he is still only describing separated objects,
n statically; he has been blind to the intrinsic current of indivisibility
ining through all substance and space. His pictures fail not because
has lavished each detail with loving "realism," but because he has
arated each detail from all possibility of functioning in the total
m; he has looked at each part separately when he should have kept
eye always at any one same visual center and seen all other detail
it appeared to him while his eyes remained focused at the focal
int. In Bergsonian terms, he has shattered the continuity of the élan
al. Bergson frequently sees this problem in terms of breaking up an
livisible movement by superposing a mosaic pattern. "Let us sup-

pose," he says "that an artist of genius has painted a figure on can
We shall be able to copy, or to see, his picture in terms of multi-colo
squares of mosaic. And we shall be able to reproduce the curves ;
nuances of the picture better and better as our squares will be smal
more numerous, more varied in tone. But it will require an infinity
infinitely small elements, providing an infinity of nuance, in ordei
obtain the exact equivalent of the figure conceived by the artist
a simple thing that he has wished to transpose as a unified conc
upon canvas, and which is the more perfected the more it appears
be the projection of an indivisible intuition. Now, suppose our e
to be so constructed that they cannot see this master's work as ot
than an effect of mosaic. Or supposing that our intelligence is so forn
that it cannot understand or explain the appearance of the figure
canvas except as a work of mosaic. We would then simply speak of
picture in terms of an assemblage of little squares, and we would
dealing in a mechanical hypothesis. . . . But we would not be appr
mating the real process by which the artist created his figure, in wh
there were actually no squares of mosaic assembled at all. Thus it
the picture, that is to say . . . the simple act projected onto canv
which, by the mere fact of entering our perception, is decomposed
our eyes into thousands and thousands of small squares which prese
when reassembled in our minds, an admirable arrangement."[1] So Bergs
sees the reality, the artist's gesture, as an "indivisible intuition" whe
integrity has been broken up by the complicating eye and the falteri
intelligence into an untrue assemblage of particles.

The same intellectual blunder occurs in the analysis of any simp
motion. If I move my hand in the simplest gesture from one spot
a table to another, the movement is susceptible to two interpretatio
Felt from within, it is a pure, indivisible act; analyzed from the o
side, it is envisaged as the path of a certain curve that my hand b
traveled from A to B. Within that curved line the intelligence insi
upon distinguishing a number of successive positions that my ha
has occupied in its voyage from point to point, and the line itself
defined as a certain co-ordination of these separate positions. And y

---

[1] *L'Évolution Créatrice*, by Henri Bergson. Librairie Félix Alcan.

know, intuitively, that movement is something more than a series
successive positions in an ordered direction. It is our limited and
ctory intelligence that deprives the essential truth of its intrinsic
taneity. And it is the pure intuition of the artist that restores that
taneity.

ow, when the artist looks at nature, with his hypersensitivity to
ace and his instinct for maintaining the focal center of vision which
res his seeing the essential form in every visual experience, he
unters a fresh adventure and a reactive emotion at every instant.
fact that he does not break up everything that he beholds into
rately scrutinized details fills his life with an awareness of rhythmic
1, that may remain forever invisible to other men. The habit of
ng fragmentarily, taking in the parts of an object or a scene in a
ulative survey, blinds the seer to all plastic apprehension. It is
lar to hearing the successive parts of a symphonic work as a group
eparate melodic and harmonic episodes with no sense of the tran-
ident architectural motive that involves every portion of the work
ssolubly with every other portion. Separate, individual sounds have
e to say, but when a current of rhythmic and tonal relationships
rs into their performance they immediately acquire suggestive form.
n separate colors, despite many illusions to the contrary, have little
ay. If all things in our world happened to be of the one same color,
re would, of course, be no awareness of color at all. Though we are
n not aware of it, our reaction to any single color really depends
n our consciousness of other colors in relationship to it.

Ve may, for instance, see a certain blue which we call a beautiful
e. Its blueness would be meaningless if everything in our world were
red with that particular blue. Actually it is only able to please us
its harmony with and contrast to all other color in our experience.
thermore, we quickly learn that such blueness, or any other color,
no absolute and permanent meaning for us at all. We can make
t particular blue seem a distasteful color to us simply by surrounding
with certain other colors which tend to evoke a disagreeable clash
qualities. More often than we realize, our judgment of a detail is
ch influenced by other details to which it is related. The more

sensitive we are to the interplay of values the more eternally fresh
new is all our experience. For it is inescapably so that the more
regard nature in isolated morsels of detail the more we have impressi
of sameness and invariability. Whereas, the more we behold nat
in its harmonic aspects, details forever blending into contexts, the m
we see that no value is ever really the same for us, but consta
playing a different role in relationship to its momentary configurati
Hence, in the infinite variety of combinations within which all nua
of detail will occur, to the sensitive eye no visual experience is e
exactly the same as any other.

The student who begins his experience with painting pictures
intimations of this important fact to a greater or lesser extent, depend
upon his sensitivity, as soon as he starts to observe plastically. Sim
examples of his failure to do so are available, of course, in number
canvases that are not pictures at all in any true sense of the word.
us envisage for a moment some simple little object around which
shall build a picture. Suppose it to be a red candle standing in a cop
candleholder, on a polished mahogany table. The average layman
sit before such a subject and within a few minutes of looking
probably have seen ten or fifteen pictures, and then, when he st
to work, may paint no picture at all. For he will have seen the pictu
without being conscious of them. Each "sight" will have been
instantaneous affair. First he will most probably have looked dire
at the candle, seeing all else secondarily and incidentally. But it e
matters at what part of the candle he fixed his eyes, because if
looked at the top of it, it will appear to him quite different than if
looked at the bottom end of it. In one case it will look shorter a
fatter; in the other case, longer and thinner, depending also on his
level. His next "sight" might have its focal center on the candlehol
so that the candle itself will have become secondary. Or he might h
centered his vision on the reflection of the copper holder in the tal
or the reflection of the candle. Or he might have looked at the w
behind the candle. In the abstract, there are as many possible vis
centers as there are points in the area beheld, thus providing us w
an infinite variety of theoretical plastic experiences. However, as so

our painter begins to paint he is likely to make the unpardonable
or in aesthetic seeing of which we have been speaking. That is, he
y look directly at the gray wall while he paints the wall, at the candle
ile he paints the candle, at the copper holder while he paints that,
., until all detail has been completed. If he does so, then he will
ve produced a group of objects, but not a work of art in any significant
se. And to anyone looking at it, his work could not possibly convey
ything more than a sense of some objects, perhaps realistically
resented, but suggesting nothing further. If he wished to produce
nething more significant he must reveal all these details in their
fluential relationship to each other when seen as form and not as
arate shapes. Under such circumstances, every area in the picture
comes tinged with the influence of every other area and no detail is
affected. The gray wall will seem greenish near the candle if the eye
directed at the candle. If the eye is directed at the wall, then the
ndle will seem a less brilliant red. The copper color will be influenced
the red candle, by the gray wall, by the mahogany, and all these
jects are themselves modified by their neighbors. So are the spaces,
e intervals between objects, modified. If the eye is directed at the
ll, then the wall will seem near; whereas, if the eye fixes itself upon
e candle, the wall will seem a little more remote. If the eye is fixed
on the front edge of the table, then the candle will seem to have
ss space between it and the wall than when the eye is directly upon
e candle. However, since these spaces and values vary with the mov-
g of the eye, it becomes obvious that, unless the eye maintains one
nsistent point of view, we shall have a series of totally unrelated,
nsignificant variations indicated on the canvas. We shall find our-
lves giving a lot of puckers and curvatures to space from a lot of
fferent points of view, with the result a hodgepodge of objects which,
ven though they may have some relationship to each other, will have
o quality of what Berenson calls "life-enhancement" to the beholder.

is due to the common ignorance of this factor of focal consistency
at we often hear such misleading talk about the necessity for artists
"eliminate" all but essentials from their canvases. This is the result
a reasoning backward by unenlightened critics, who assume from the

Chapter X

SELF AND NONSELF

〜〜〜

N APPROACHING the subject of identification of self with that
which lies outside the self, it must of course be understood that some
persons are psychologically so constituted as to grasp immediately its
found implications, while others are almost congenitally incapable of
n imagining what it is all about. A sense of separation between the
er self and that self's perception of the outer world develops grad-
ly, during the first two years of life. Within a period of the first few
nths of existence there is practically no sense of separation what-
ver; whatever comes within the sensual experience of the infant is
ply and uncomplicatedly accepted as a part of being. Instant by
tant whatever is encountered is so accepted; memory does not play a
scious role. As the infant lies in brilliant sunlight with birds twitter-
about, then as far as the infant is concerned all its being is the
ghtness, warmth and twittering of that moment. Of course, it is
ays extremely sensitive to the nearness or farness of its mother, and
the sensations of support with which it is always inevitably in contact.
t in so far as experience of objective things which happen into its
it is concerned, all such experience might just as well be a dream,
ving no more genuine objectivity for the infantile mind. Things within
ching and touching distance supersede everything else by their tan-
ility and apparent immanency. Things remote are practically non-
stent; and indeed, if something at a distance happens to attract an
ant's attention, the first reaction, provided it is not a frightening thing,
a desire to reach out and touch it—to make the thing part of the
ant's world of being. It is only by the most gradual accumulation of
perience that the infant discovers an extensiveness to the world which
etches realistically out in all directions away from itself as center.
slowly perceives that there are things just as real and solid and touch-

able ten yards away, or around a corner out of sight, as the things i
playing with in its crib. It discovers that when it seizes or touches it
at any time there is always an answering sensation, a feeling of one j
of the self being touched by another part of the self, but that whe
touches a rattle, or a rubber doll, the sensation of touching remains
in the fingers with no self-involved responsive feeling coming from
rattle or the doll. It also discovers, as its memory begins to play a
in the learning process, that the doll is just as real and existent whe
lies on the other side of the room on the window sill as when i
directly at hand; it learns this by repeated experiences of holding
doll, then seeing it being taken away, and later having it back ag
It learns more along the same line as it begins to crawl. Then it fi
wider and wider areas to explore and more remote horizons to ver
It assures itself of the tangible reality of many things farther and fart
away from and outside itself. And it is in this gradual fashion tha
child begins to form an assumption of a world quite independent
itself. On the basis of its experience it reaches the stage where it gra
as much reality to remote things that it only knows about as it does
things within its tactual and perceptual field. And this, in turn, le
toward what we might call a cooling-off tendency in the reaction
immediate stimuli. Since the growing person's consciousness becon
filled with more and more stored-up knowledge, and his attention
comes divided between wider diversities of interest, each little individ
experience of seeing becomes less eventful, and tends to fall into pl
as just another little moment in a great passage of events. And mu
of each little experience that was once vast to the infant while it last
now evaporates into something scarcely noticed, because it has be
repeatedly experienced until it is taken for granted. For instance, imag
the difference in reaction to an orange of an infant and of a child of t
To the infant, sufficiently developed to sense the various qualities,
orange held up before it is a great adventure of roundness and wa
color and fragrance—something that it would be most exciting to tou
and to hold and to feel. As long as the interest in it lasts, it is an inter
of large dimension and intensity. All the infant's being is momentar
wrapped up in that orange; it experiences nothing but orange until it

d of orange or until it craves feeding, etc. Certainly its visual expe-
ice is enormous in its aesthetic implications. Whereas the child of ten
o sees an orange is just seeing another of many, many oranges that it
  seen and known before; the orange is merely one form and color
ong myriads of others. In appearance it has neither novelty nor any
ticularly arresting quality. Probably its greatest significance is its
tatory potentiality. It might stimulate the child's appetite for it. But,
thetically, it is certain that the infant's experience will have been
ead over a wider expanse of reaction. In terms of impact upon a
ality of consciousness, the experience of an orange has been far
re eventful for the infant than for the child of ten. But again, to the
st, that orange returns to its powerful role; it acts upon the conscious-
s of the sensitive artist with all the impact that it exerts upon dawning
sciousness, and with certain greater forces that are the consequence
  more matured intuition. Without necessarily being aware of it, the
ist returns to his earliest sensations of seeing; the purity of his im-
ssions is not vitiated by familiarity. In fact, to the exquisite sensitivity
the artist-mind, familiarity is merely an illusion. To him no object can
ssibly remain in the state of sameness; it evolves along with the time
d space in which it has its being, and it must also change in the eyes
  the artist as he himself progresses through time and thought. A man
y pass a tree every day for years. Or, rather, let us say he passes a
ck, which to mortal eye is unchanging, and the more sensitive the man
e less possibility is there of his ever having two identical feelings about
vision of that rock. Furthermore, if any man should look at that rock
five minutes at a time, he would be seeing a different thing during
e last minute from what he was seeing in the first minute. Every
stant of looking adds its nuance to the totality of impression; every
ental or physical change of focus throws the rock into a new context,
okes a new form.

Now, in this matter of estimating the nature of self-participation and
entification with the objects and spaces that surround us, we have to
k questions that at first hearing may seem elementary; and yet we shall
iickly find that they only seem easy to answer because we have taken
great deal for granted without ever having really thought much about

these things. For instance, we are accustomed to consider ourselves mo
closely involved with what is nearest to us and more detached fro
things farther away in space. My dictionary lying here at my elbow o
the table seems more a part of my experience at this instant than t
same edition of it lying fifteen feet away on the window sill. It occupi
more space in my retinal image of all that confronts me; it has mo
perceptible texture and apparent weight, and it is within reach of r
hand, which is an element that never fails to play a large role in spa
judgments. And yet, if I fix my eyes upon the farther dictionary ar
keep them there, then the nearer one is seen only in the radial out
edge of my field of vision; I am then only aware of the nearer one, b
see more distinctly the farther one. But still the awareness of somethir
near somehow seems to implicate itself in my intimate sense of t
present instant more inescapably than anything farther away. And
explain why this is so, why our innermost sensations associate themselv
so adheringly to the near, is to explain a great deal of our physical ar
psychological make-up. We shall find the explanation involving n
only spatial considerations, but the factor of time also. Psychologically v
project into any view of distant things a feeling of remoteness, due
intervening space which separates ourselves from the faraway, and a
automatic mental reservation of a time projection too. What is neare
to us seems to partake more of the absolutely present instant than wh
we may see five miles away across a wide expanse of land; we envisar
the space partially as something that takes time to traverse, and thoug
in the purest sense of visual experience we may see the horizon eve
more clearly as horizon, looking directly at it, than we see the shado
on the lawn just in front of us, still that shadow is imminent in feelir
and bears a profound influence on the instant's actuality. The ne
seems more actual than the far.

However, psychologically we can obtain reversals of this aesthet
phenomenon. As soon as something distant enters our consciousne
something bearing potentialities of great and instant concern to us, the
it swiftly overwhelms our usual measures of imminency. A threatenir
storm cloud may seem closer than many nearer things. In other words,
would seem that whatever has properties directly affecting us physical

imminently likely to do so, has special claim on our attention. A
siological and psychological tension relates us to all near forces that
upon us. The ground we stand upon supports us, while ground
her away is only theoretical ground. The ground underfoot is an
uality that can scarcely be denied; it affirms its substantial relationship
our self by its very function of sustaining our weight. By standing
on it we experience it almost as reliably as we do other things that
touch and hold in our hands. We substantiate the ground underfoot.
erything in the here-and-now category of being elicits more response
n our instinctive sensibilities than anything of the yonder. As infants,
whole security lay in the sense of sure support directly under and
mediately around our body. Were this security to become the least
shaky, disturbed, or dubious, the infantile reaction would be instant
l intense. Nothing in the world of infancy is more productive of a
se of ill-being than any threatened failure of support. And nothing
s real and satisfying as the reachable and touchable. It is probable that
ich of the mature reaction to visual experience is intimately related to
s early conditioning. Part of the aesthetic satisfaction that we take in
qualities of stability and inherent balance must stem from this early,
tinctual yearning for secure equilibrium. Our own poise associates
lf empathically with the equipoise of nature and of art. In Goethe's
ters from Italy there is an interesting allusion to this phenomenon
en he describes the discomfort arising within him at the mere sight
some window sills out of alignment: " . . . the window-sills in these
ttages," he writes, "are, without exception, oblique, and lean to one
le or the other, so as to offend and violate all sense of the level and
pendicular, which are so indispensable in the human mind, and form
e foundation of all architectural propriety."
We find in the great artist such an intense identification of himself
th the nature of which he is a part that his stature seems to take on
ich of the monumental stability of that nature, while he imparts to his
presentations of it some of the further grace of his own genius. I once
ked an artist, who is one of Europe's great figures in the field of
inting today, at what stage of his life it began to be indicated that his
ergies would be directed to painting. I was somewhat astounded when

he answered that it was probably around the beginning of his secon
year, if not earlier! The explanation is full of rich significance, especiall
when one bears in mind the power of this early sensation which carrie
itself over as a memory into mature years. He explained that wheneve
his mother left him all alone in his room he was inconsolable unles
she left the shade high enough for him to be able to see some leaves o
the branch of a tree just outside his window. As long as these leave
were there for him to see, there was no dreadful sense of loneliness; the
seemed to fill his being with what was needed in the absence of hi
mother.

Since the formation of the ego proceeds along the path of contac
with external reality, it is always challenging to clarify the confusio
which naturally characterize attempts to establish borderlines betwee
the "integral" self and that which lies outside the self. What is left c
the self when it is isolated from all external stimulation? As a totalit
of course, this experience is not possible. How much is external reali
inevitably flavored by the personality of the observing ego? What, the
is left of reality when it is isolated from the self? To a certain extent, th
intense artist is something of a solipsist; to his special sensitivity, it
exceedingly difficult to divorce any reality which he experiences from a
empathic involvement and identification with himself.

It stands to reason that the more of such identification we have takin
place in an individual the more self-revelatory that individual will be i
any description he may make of external reality. The degree of his ow
energy, sensitivity and love will ensure a degree of originality to h
expression. And, all too often, an individual's lack of faith in the suf
ciency of such originality leads him to a corruption of his most valuab
assets by seeking to imagine and invent something richer than the natur
product of his perception. He may fail there to realize that even h
imagination is incapable of producing any novelty or beauty beyond tl
capacity of his own psyche, and that in seeking to transcend the imag
evoked by his own immediate experience he will most often bring for
the fiasco of unspontaneous artifice. This spiritual fallacy and its relate
fear, so prevalent in these times that original creativity must be revol
tionary to maintain its dynamism and avoid mere repetitiveness, w

gage our attention later; it has great bearing upon the crucial matter
spontaneous as opposed to factitious, "voulue" creativity. The wonder-
len dream of life itself is an unending miracle of inspiration to the
ıly creative spirit; to feel the need of concocting dreams within the
eam can only indicate the rêveur trop éveillé.

Let us now explore the realms of reality into which the ego of the
inter projects itself, and the manner in which it does so. This will
plain in large part what it is in his most wonderful works that em-
wers the artist to involve the beholder of his creations so empathically
d compellingly in his own spiritual intuition. Let us begin with the
perience of envisioning a picture by this sort of projection.

I shall stand in the middle of a meadow and analyze the scope of my
ctorial vision. At first I may have a feeling of general exuberance, as a
sult not of any specific aspect of the scene encountered, but flowing
ɔm the totality of impression. After all, I am ultimately an agglomera-
ɔn of electrons and protons whirling through their spatial immensities
thin the confines of that particular systemic constellation comprising
[e. This agglomeration is sensitive to the conditions, the atmospheres,
 which it may be subjected. It will be as though, being there in the
eadow, I represent a system of potential responses to stimulation. The
ılaxy of stimulating influences out in that meadow, just as anywhere
se under the heavens, is enormous. But by the unhappy limitations of
y own scarcely awakened senses, I respond only partially to the small
ɔrtion of stimuli that I am able to receive. And so, my experience in
ıe beginning consists of an awareness of certain quantities and qualities
 stimuli which may seem wonderfully manifold to me, even though,
ıtellectually, I know them to represent only a minuscule part of all
ıat is there. Within an instant my being is invaded by sensations of
armth or coolness, luminosity, color, fragrance, sounds, pressures, from
ass-carpeted ground underfoot and perhaps the varying touches of the
ɪoving air. My feeling of delight will come from all these and many
ther contributing factors. I yield myself to their power, or, as Isadora
ɪuncan used to say, I "tune in" on them so that their magical waves
em to play upon me as an instrument. The point I wish to make is
ɪat long before I may become absorbed by some specific aspect of this

continuing experience, I am inevitably propelled by a great variety o
causes into a mood, a state of mind and being responsive to this wid
set of influences.

One of the most emphatic characteristics of that mood is a sensatio
of complete absorption in the instantaneous circumstances. As I fa
deeper and deeper into the spell of that which is all around me I becom
increasingly detached from preoccupations, from thoughts connecte
with the infinite aspects of existence other than here and now; and, a
the totality of my consciousness becomes more focused upon this presen
instant, there is activated a higher and higher pitch of response. Whi
some persons warm up to this intensity of absorption only slowly, i
frequently and incompletely, others do so rapidly, often and consum
mately. So much depends upon the extent to which a person is able t
yield himself to the atmosphere of any given moment. The vast majorit
do not even realize how little of their total psyche is ever released upo
a particular here and now. The common experience of man is to e
counter whatever presents itself to him with only a part of his capaci
and attention. So much happens within any instant to which we clo
ourselves, either because we are directing the greater part of our atte
tion elsewhere or because, all too often, we have not developed the a
of opening ourselves to wider areas of ambiance. Recall the well-know
comparison of what the native American Indian could read in a fore
setting which conveyed practically nothing to the blunted senses an
experience of the white man. Test yourself at this moment, even as
test myself. How much is happening within sensible range of your pe
ception as you sit quietly in your chair? Are you really taking everythir
in? As you grow more aware, is there not really enough to provide gre
stimulation and a sense of harmonious eventfulness? From what h
occurred within range of my chair here by the window I could elabora
a Proustian chapter.

But certainly not if half my mind is occupied with thoughts of ho
badly the grass just below needs to be cut, and many another preoccup
tion that could so easily invade my field of attention and destroy tl
consonance of the many things that are the fruit of this unique insta
at my window—an instant that will never again occur in all the eterni

fore us exactly as it has just occurred. Within the summer mood of a buzzing along the ceiling, birds twittering above and below the rise d fall of wind sounds in the foliage all around the house, I hear foot-ps on the quiet road beyond the lawn, which say one thing to me fore I look, and something else when I see that it is a young high-iool girl plodding up the hill carrying her violin, all in the heat and grance of midafternoon. I have now mentioned only a tiny particle all that I have noticed at that particular instant, for the mind indeed ɔves fast and can record much if it is resolved so to do. And yet the tle I have written will have given the reader a deeper insight into this re and now of mine than he will have had before the description tered the stage. This is what I mean by yielding oneself to the atmos-ıere of any given moment. This very room in which I so often sit ndly before my desk is as full of visual adventure for me as any other ot on earth, though I must remind myself, as the reader will remind ımself, that, were I to be away from my home for a few months and en return to these familiar premises, there would be a temporarily agic appearance of novelty to the place, even though not a thing had ıanged except a freshening of my own responses. And yet I would aintain that the richest experiences come to me here not when I am ljusting myself after an absence but rather when I am so completely home to every detail of my surroundings that I dwell within the vast ıra of endlessly varying nuance. The breeze that stirs my white paper ;ainst a slightly grayer desk, the beam of sunlight that narrows and idens on the cover of my dictionary as the window shade seems to :eathe with the slightly moving air, even the fortuitous architecture of ıe books before me on their shelves, each a different height and color ıan its neighbor, like the houses along the banks of the Arno which ere legally required to be so built by the good taste of the Florentines ıd the Pisans—these few and a host of other casual conditions combine ɔ keep me in a constant state of stimulation. The same sort of thing ıay be pointed out in the matter of larger aspects of nature; I am more ıoved aesthetically by the enchanting nuance to be found at every ıstant of random walking through a quiet countryside than by the ɔectacular and the esoteric.

But now let us return to the meadow where I was falling into a mo
that was leading us toward picture-making. As I dwell within t
experience of being in the meadow I gradually become accustomed,
least a little bit, to what was, of course, an utterly new vision to me
the moment first encountered. I do not think that the "artist type" e
shifts his eye from one focal point to another without feeling each tin
that he is seeing what he has never seen before. As the sense of nove
wears off, a profounder emotion sets in—a sense of one's inner self l
coming absorbed into and identified with that which he beholds. F
persons ever permit themselves to sink quite so deeply into the proc
of aesthetic seeing. Even people of great intelligence delight themsel
as a general rule with the apparent qualities of a gracious landscap
much as they enjoy the surface melodies and tonalities of music witho
grasping the form of the internal structure. To approach any real app
ciation of what it is that your artist sees, it is necessary to "dwell with
the experience of being in the meadow" until you become hypnotize
as it were, to such an extent that at last what you are seeing seems to
the all of everywhere and the now of eternity. I suppose it is what v
call the essence behind the appearance.

At this stage of seeing, the gracious or ungracious shape of a tree, t
color of grass or flowers, or sky, the dramatic or undramatic arrangeme
of hills mean little in themselves. They are all assimilated into the gre
ensemble of space and time. Color becomes color of the ensembl
shapes abandon their literal intransigence to melt into the fluid imm
teriality of form. And the artist too is drawn into the compelling flux
his own intuition. I notice, in my meadow, that, geometrically, n
vision of the "picture" is best described by the projection of two arcs
180 degrees each; one longitudinal from my feet forward to the horizc
and back up to the sky over my head; the other latitudinal, starting i
the space somewhere left of my ear and going forward to the horizc
and back to the latitude of my right ear. But still this does not altogeth
envisage the important factor of the most imminent space close-at-ey
There is that vastly significant visibility out-of-the-corner-of-the-eye
with its conveyance of the most immediate presences, as well as th
extension downward to the feet and a little behind, plus the dome

overhead and receding behind. Some of this vital area is felt rather than seen. And here lies the immense significance of Bergson's concept the grace of continuity, measured duration and extension. For, out of e remote horizon, on a flat-surface representation such as a picture, ust advance toward the self, or toward the horizon must recede from e self, a measured perspective which, on reaching the two-dimennal boundaries of the canvas surface, will continue their function to e completion of my latitudinal and longitudinal arcs, thus enveloping e seer to the full extent of his absorption. Without either the material presentation or the symbolic implication of the full 180 degrees, there lost that whole vast sense of the self as origin. And the fact is that, st as in music or the dance, or in an architectural edifice of any medium, e ego aspires to become implicated in and associated with the serene erfection and noble ease that characterize the breathing of a pure, hieved harmonic form. And so, when a satisfactory representation of easured recession is achieved, having its nascent form originating out and at the immediate self, and receding in full cadence to the infinitely mote, then the self is projected into and absorbed into and inherited to its own fullest habitation, for it becomes extended by empathic ovement into the whole self-including movement.

The simplest manner of illustrating this first concept is in the image f one's own body as seen by oneself, recumbent. The first immediate ass (after the nose, which is sometimes seen by the eyes incidentally) ill be the upper torso, thence along to the feet, and then out into ace, the first departure from the idea of absolute self. Though, in fact, e body is as unrelated, except by habit and sensory, physical connecon, to the spirit, as is the space beyond and around it—and as related. f this sense of immediacy be excluded, a picture can only attain a more less mobile panoramic concept, utterly dissociated from involvement f the self, and, at most, a gracious display of harmonics with all the leasing orchestral effects, as fruitful to the eye as much music is to the ar, but as void of significance to the spirit as all sound save that of usic. So, if I cut out, as so great a proportion of "picture-makers" do, portion of the broad scene that confronts me, failing to include all its mplicated perspectives, if I "frame it off" as a segment of space detached

from myself, I at once sever the life-cord between It and Me and c
only achieve that small modicum of loveliness which is for the eye aloı
and in which no poet has ever found the Beautiful. The omission of tł
all-important space between myself and that which is remote from ɩ
is quite as "impossible" in terms of Truth as to eliminate the ba
structure of any edifice, leaving the upper portion suspended in air.

And so, much haphazard speculation as to the difference betwe
photographic representation and plastic, pictural expression is at oɪ
clarified by this element of extension. However, the matter is tł
only begun, since the whole long gamut of color and tonal perspectiᵥ
in their finest nuance is involved to a degree beyond the discretion a
sensitivity of a camera lens. In fact, whereas a photographed version
an object is greatly reduced in sensitivity as compared to even the mɪ
"ordinary" human eye, and whereas a poet's picture achieves that rɪ
significance· of rendition which is a revelation to the "ordinary" eᵥ
still, to the dull, rather apathetic average vision, the one is about
inert and inexpressive as the other. And yet, there is in every moɪ
that sense of touch by which from first infancy the sense of extendᵥ
space and scope is developed, which invades the field of vision and
forever afterward confused into a behavioristic function, much
Watson's mice respond to conditioned stimuli like the ringing bɛ
In other words, Berenson's tactile quality, which is to be found in aɪ
absolutely essential to the pictures by the few greatest masters, rendᵥ
the whole vast aura of spatial extension, succession, quality, by meaɪ
of arousing through the integrity of visual rendition that primal recɪ
nition of masses and associations through the sense of touch. Noᵥ
what is this tactility, this illusion of touch; and what is touch, tł
important auxiliary to perception? We began a consideration of t`
subject in Chapter Two. By this sense we not only ascertain the qualɪ
of objects in respect to their surfaces, but we apprise ourselves of thᵥ
shape and dimension. And it is evident, if one eliminates the "knoᵥ
edge" acquired since birth by that combined experience of touch aɪ
sight, that with sight alone there can be only the most ephemeral sɪ
of recognition and measurement of objects extended in space. For tł
main measure lies in our apprehension of their relative "duration

tudinally and longitudinally in relation to ourselves. We want to
ow about an object how far it extends from its (our) left to right,
w far it reaches (recedes) from its front to rear, how far away it is
m ourself, from other objects around it, from the horizon or farthest
rceptible object. Thus, too, we measure its weight, its tangibility.
And it is uniquely in terms of these external objects that we define the
ality and quantity of our self as a body also existing dimensionally
space, since we cannot ever apprehend or comprehend ourselves
jectively, being beyond possibility of entire scrutiny. Thus we con-
ive ourselves as extensions, durations in timed-space, only through
e logic afforded us by our judgments of objects and intervals external
us.

Our ever-present though often subconscious sense of time begins to
nction in the developing analysis of our experience in the meadow.
tween the near and the far, the nearest and the farthest, lies a succes-
n of objects and intervals, shapes and spaces, which, like a passing
events in time, seems to possess a measured quality of duration. Of
urse, it is my own mentality that projects its particular nature of
ythmic susceptibility into what the cold intellect might call the
phazard disposition of things in space. An ordered mind will take
ordered view of nature; a disorderly mind is more likely to see
aotically. The stature of a mentality imposes its proportions upon
e field of its vision, and the stature of a mentality will most certainly
veal itself in the pictures it paints, the poems it writes, the dances
dances. But since these objects and intervals seem to recede from
e near to the far, an almost automatic psychological transposition
ccurs which associates nearness to the concept of Now, and the far-
ff to a more remote time. And as, from the actual Now there recedes
ato the remembered past its succession of events and into the antici-
ated future its imminent and remote inevitabilities, so from the actual
Iere of the self there recedes a succession of plastic experience in all
isible and apprehensive directions into the distant, remote. Remote
akes on a "time" significance and a sense of being "alien," removed
ar from the self.

An interesting example of the confusion which the mind imposes

upon space and time lies in the instance of a man on his way to
destination, walking along a road. He instinctively regards the persp
tive of road-space ahead of him as extended into the future, and th
road which he has traversed, behind him, as receded into the past. I
let him suddenly change his purpose, alter his destination to the pla
whence he has come, and he faces about, confronting that which
moment before lay stretched behind him as an endured past, no
suddenly transformed to as real a "future" as had been his initial desti
tion now rejected and behind him.

So, as I stand confronting a landscape, do I feel the recession
objects and intervals not only before me but radiating in an infin
of directions within the compass of 360 degrees of which my self
the inevitable center. And finally my intuition begins to assert its
and to negate some of the intellectual fallacies that have become t
habitual encumbrance of pure thinking and pure seeing. My vision of t
meadow returns to a phase of uncomplicated sensation resembling th
of childhood. All my accumulated habits of practical perception, i
automatic space judgments derived from long practice in combini
the testimony of my eyes with that of other forms of experience, retr
before the higher authority of this final insight. I am released of t
impediments of everyday methods of looking at things, methods whi
have been skillfully developed for every practical purpose except th
of seeing creatively into the truth, which is so beautiful.

No longer do the distances across my meadow and beyond into t
final horizon of my vision translate themselves into muscular sensatio
of tension adapted to ideas of my own reaching or walking into the
Seeing the landscape before me aesthetically is an experience far remov
from that of seeing it in more usual and more casual terms. I co
sciously and unconsciously demolish everything "practical" in th
process of observation until at last seeing becomes for me little mo
than being, or, shall we say, little less. I do not move my eyes abo
from here to there in the panorama, as ordinarily one might, to mal
the myriad little and large comparisons of textures, colors, tones, shape
sizes, directions. I no longer investigate charming details; all the min
delights of the roving gaze and the wandering attention are sacrifice

re the experience to be explained in terms of the process of thought,
ould say that even the exercises of logical reasoning are abandoned
this final stage of awareness, and the conception crystallizes into a
mentous impression of instantaneity—an instantaneity that en-
ops all the duration and extension which by the intellect is always
ken up into successive parts, and which is only revealed in the
ffable integrity of its ultimacy by the spontaneity of aesthetic in-
tion. There is a certain dreamlike quality to this ultimate type of
on, partaking as it does of some of the characteristics of the dream
enomenon. The narrowing and narrowing down of the attention,
e elimination of distracting preoccupations until the entire psyche is
iquely engrossed in the one act of perception, these are the con-
ions which, in dreams as in creative seeing, intensify the apprehensive
oacity and heighten the emotional response.

This quality of instantaneity, enveloping all the duration and exten-
n that ordinarily characterize our response to most aspects of being,
ems to draw all matter and space within range of my focused vision
o a oneness, an indivisible continuity. Objects, the shapes of objects,
longer seem to stop at their edges, things no longer seem to exist
static juxtaposition, areas from left to right and from near to far
longer seem to neighbor each other; there seems to be a merging
all separateness, a continuing flow and interpenetration of being. At
earlier epoch of human thought it might have been considered that
is representation was the rather stirring illusion of a poetic mind
ger to satisfy its own longings for timeless integration by discovering
ch virtues in nature. But now, as so often before has happened in the
quence of intuition and scientific verification, we find metaphysics
d aesthetics and physics happily in a joie d'accord. The plastic
alities inherent in the thinking and the seeing and the painting of
ch masters as Leonardo, some of the great Chinese, Rembrandt,
ezanne, others, were evidence of the prescient genius of these spirits.
or our physical understanding is now tending to corroborate that
hich we have spiritually long hoped and long suspected. This con-
nuity of which I speak may be further explained in terms of an easily
omprehended gesture, such as, for instance, the movement that your

hand may make if you lift it from one spot on a table to another sp
It is a simple, spontaneous act, a motion from here to there. And y
in an intellectual analysis, this gesture becomes infinitely complicat(
The arc which the motion of your hand has described will come to
defined as a path composed of a succession of points or locations throu
which your hand has passed in a succession of instants. The simj
act is thus broken up into an infinitely divisible number of spa
fractions traversed during an infinitely divisible period of time. V
recognize a profound incompatibility between our intuitive acceptan
of the gesture as an unbroken event within the evolution of our bei
and our so-called rational, dissective analysis of it into a series of p)
gressive positions separated by intervals. The succession of juxtapos
objects and intervals in a landscape and in a picture of a landscape, «
for that matter, in any aspect of nature, may be compared to this seri
of theoretical positions. When seen creatively or aesthetically, the tr
form, which we have come to call the plastic form, is apprehended
spontaneously as the hand itself was moved. My eye, my mind, n
spirit embrace the elements of the meadow-scene as they would t)
raising of a hand, the smile of a friend. I do not break up a smile in
its component parts stretching from the moment of its incepti(
through the physical stages of its development to the climax. In t)
last analysis, there must be nothing more complicated and nothii
less spontaneous in a work of art than in a spiritual smile.

That is why I persist in drawing the analogy between creative p(
ception and the vision of a child. The important difference is large
in the fact that the creator has traversed the wide areas of experien(
between what I call first simplicity and last simplicity. He has acquir(
knowledge tempered by the wisdom to forget. As Irwin Edman has p
it: "One might say almost that it is the business of the poet to forg
much of what usually concerns us in our reactions to things. He mu
recover, where he is successful he does recover, for us the immedia(
of sensations such as a child has before it has been deprived of t)
innocence of the eye and ear and has learned to live and talk in secon(
ary formulas and relations."

Now, since I am the inevitable center from which my own visio

iates outward into the world that is presumably common to us all,
I wish to communicate my vision and my feeling to others I shall
nt my picture as much as possible in a way that will project a beholder
it into that central point of origin. I do not seek to project him into
: atmosphere of the picture, as so many critics mistakenly suppose,
t into the vibratory rhythm of my own insight. Just as there are ways
analyzing the process of a graceful gesture, faulty as we have already
)wn them to be, so there are halting ways of analyzing the process
such a projection, which should at least clarify some of the methods
d purposes of the plastic arts. This sort of projection will convey to
: observer of my realized picture that instant and simultaneous sense
experiencing my vision himself. He will be propelled, by the logic
my representation of it, into the integrity and compulsion of my
ice, time and measure. Far more completely than any worded thought
.nsmission can effect, I shall have visited my own mode of seeing
on another spirit. Regardless of my own stature, of my exalted or
:ager attributes, the achievement of such communion is vital to the
)wth of the human spirit. The mere event of seeing in a degree
proaching totality through another's eyes in momentous. Few people
ke the time and make the real effort to do so. Fewer still understand
e necessity of developing some familiarity with the idiom of nuance,
iich is so essential to the communicability of an inner experience.
'e are somewhat aware of the variations in individuals' opinions, tastes,
nsibilities, temperaments, from the testimony of their patterns of
:havior. But how deeply does one individual penetrate into the inner
orld of another's consciousness? How often does anyone have the
:uberant feeling that his inmost soul is utterly revealed and compre-
:nded, given to and loved by a fellow mortal? Only at the highest
vels of art and love do our deepest intuitions hold communion and
:alt us above the solitude of our usual futility.

One of the important factors in social relationship is that we sense
id presume in one another areas and levels of an inner life. Most of
s are fortunately introvert enough, at least occasionally, to discern
ithin ourselves certain impalpable but influential regions of conscious-
ess that do not rise easily to the social surface of our personality but

are filled with a longing to do so and to find affinity. Each one of
feels at bottom that he sees his world in the unique terms of his c
peculiar configuration, and one of the first instincts of the inner c
sciousness in pursuit of sympathy and affinity is to share the sin
larities and enthusiasms of its high moments. The child's instinct is
bring you all his pretty possessions, his dolls, his dresses, his picture bo
for you to see. Later, he will wish to show you his subtler and lof
loves, his ideas and his passions, and his truths. Finally, he yearns
give you that which most preciously consummates it all, himself.
wants you to see what he sees as he sees it. He will struggle for a l
time to show it to you if he has the emotion, conviction and incess
force of will of the artist.

That is why I must show you my meadow, or my book upon
table, or indeed anything that I see at any moment of time; for I
impelled by the highest urgency to have you see exactly the mira
that seems to me inherent in it all. And that is why I want so much
see versions of the same grace through the eyes of other fervent sel
I must have you know that in true seeing physically near things
no closer to the self than things far away; the "nearest" becomes t
upon which the attention is fixed. Pure vision is akin to a state
self-hypnosis. All the distraction of everyday, practical attentiveness
separate details of the visible world is eliminated. It cannot be ov
emphasized that sight and insight are worlds apart as ways of seei
The painter finds an architecture in everything that confronts hi
because at whatever momentary aspect of eternity his attention n
be directed he is always aware of the integral movement of the ent
context. He knows intuitively, as the scientist is coming to kn
logically, that the appearance of objective reality cannot be truthfu
divided into representations of isolated fragments, any more than t
flow of human consciousness can be soundly arrested and displayed
static portions of itself. It is the sense of continuum in the hum
psyche that lifts it above vegetative and lower animal modes of existen
and that sense is still in its infancy. The philosophers seek by ev
means within their genius to nurture and amplify it. As Irwin Edm
points out in his essay on *Arts and the Man*, "philosophers as differe
as the absolutist Bradley and the empiricist Dewey admit or insist t

philosophy is discourse about what (call it experience or call it the
solute) is inscrutable or indescribable." That is why he develops the
at truth that the philosopher at the summit of his powers is an
st, and the artist is a philosopher. Both seek to substantiate their
uitions. The one who is not something of the other is not much of
er.

The philosopher Bergson has constant recourse to the art of painting
his effort to substantiate his concept of the equivalence of duration
l simultaneity in the process of creative evolution. "If I paste an
age on a piece of cardboard and then cut it up into fragments I shall
able by properly assembling the little pieces to reproduce the image.
d the child who works in this way with parts of a jig-saw puzzle,
taposing fragments of an image and finally obtaining a beautiful
ored picture, no doubt imagines that he has produced drawing and
or. However, the act of drawing and painting bears no relationship
that of assembling fragments of a picture already drawn, already
inted. Similarly, in assembling amongst themselves the simplest
ults of the evolutionary process, you may imitate most faithfully the
parent steps in the most complex effects; but in no manner will you
ve retraced the true genesis, and this addition or juxtaposition of
agment to fragment, stage to stage, will not at all resemble the pure
olutionary movement. The ordinary artifice (of the Spencerian
ethod) consists of reconstructing evolution by assembling fragments
that which has evolved . . . Instead of involving ourselves in the
ternal happening of things, we habitually place ourselves on the out-
le and recompose their process artificially. We take a series of quasi-
stantaneous views of the reality that flows by. Such is the artifice of
e motion picture machine; such is the artifice of our cerebration."[1]
Ve must rid ourselves of this cinematographic method of seeing. Berg-
n has made a tremendous contribution in his clarification of this
oblem; he has placed a momentous finger upon a crucial flaw in the
eration of human reasoning, a flaw that has impeded the progress of
ought. "There is something more to movement than the series of
ccessive positions attributed to that which moves, more in the process
becoming than in the separate forms traversed one after the other,

[1] *L'Évolution Créatrice*, by Henri Bergson. Librairie Félix Alcan.

more in the evolution of form itself than shapes perceived one a⁞
the other. Eternity no longer floats transcendent above time, like
abstraction; it is the actual substance and reality of being."²

It is difficult for us to accept these Bergsonian generalizations. ⹀
are so accustomed to a mechanical train of thought and so overwhelm⹀
with the apparent complexity of ourselves and our world in its "sl⹀
tortuous" evolution from the "simple" to the "complex." It is mai⹀
our sense of time that frustrates our understanding. We are perh⹀
overimpressed with what seem to us the indescribably baffling intrica⹀
of nature, weaving and contriving whole universes of inexplicable ti⹀
substances and space. If we could see it all as one spontaneous gest⹀
instead of breaking it up in our imagination into aeons of juxtapo⹀
states, positions and stages, we should be on our way to a closer app⹀
hension of the reality. After all, our sense of relativity is faulty at b⹀
extremes of judging magnitudes. We accept many a finite object⹀
any given moment as a simple phenomenon which, with furt⹀
analysis, can be revealed to be composed of elements and extensions⹀
bewilderingly infinite and inexplicable within their microcosmic be⹀
as the entire macrocosm. We allow ourselves to be deceived by t⹀
degrees of apparent complexity which different aspects of being prese⹀
to our naïve view. The human eye, for instance, seems to us marvelou⹀
intricate as an achievement of nature, compared to a blade of gra⹀
The fallacy is apparent to a Bergson who has this to say of it: "Mec⹀
anism and Finalism attribute to Nature the most formidable, Hercule⹀
works by conceiving that, in evolving the simple process of vision, s⹀
has summoned forth an infinity of infinitely complicated elemen⹀
whereas in reality Nature has had no more trouble in making an e⹀
than I have in raising my hand. By the human mind her simple ⹀
is divided automatically into an infinity of elements which will⹀
found to be coordinated to a single idea, just as the movement of ⹀
hand seems to have let fall outside of its essential spontaneity ⹀
infinity of points along its trajectory to satisfy a similar equation."³

² Ibid.
³ Essai sur les Données immédiates de la Conscience, by Henri Bergson. Librai⹀
Félix Alcan.

Now, the moment that, in a picture, there is primary consciousness of
separate objects to be observed one after the other, juxtaposed, the
metaphorical function of that picture is corrupted. The integrity of
movement is gone. The picture does not evoke our intuition of ultimate
grace. I shall use a final illustration of Bergson's view of pure form.
That which is pure continuity excludes all idea of juxtaposition, of
reciprocal exteriority, and of extension. Let us imagine, rather, an elastic,
infinitely small, contracted, if it were possible, into a mathematical
point. Let us then pull on it progressively in such a manner as to cause
to emerge from the point a line which will continually develop. Let
us fix our attention not upon the line in its quality of line but upon
the action which traces it. Let us consider that this action, in spite of
its sustained duration, is indivisible in the sense that it occurs without
any stops; that if one were to intercalate a stop one would be effecting
two actions instead of one and that each of these actions would be
indivisible. Then it is not the moving action itself which can ever be
divisible, but the immobile line which the action deposits beneath itself
like a tracing in space. We must detach ourselves finally from the space
which sustains the movement in order to be aware only of the movement itself, of the act of tension or extension, that is, of pure mobility.
In this way we shall have a truer picture of our development in continuity, our process of evolution . . . Intellectual analysis operates upon
the immobile, whereas intuition places itself within the motion, or,
what amounts to the same thing, within the continuity. That is where
we have the precise line of demarcation between intuition and analysis.
One recognizes the real, the lived, the actuality as being the very
essence of variability. One recognizes the separate element as static.
And it is static by definition, being a schema, a simplified reconstruc-
tion, often a mere symbol, never more than a snapshot of the flow of
reality. From intuition one may go into analysis, but never from analysis
to the intuitive."

The artist of highest sensitivity senses, and for many ages has sensed,
his continuity in all things. It is beautiful to see the modern physicist
the idiom of quanta and vibratory energies arrive intellectually,
scientifically, at a similar approximation of the true state of affairs. It

is no longer a philosopher's dream to envisage material reality as ult
mately immaterial. And since, within one atom we now know tha
there are proton and electron entities not even a billionth part of th
size of the atom that they comprise, and that the spaces separatin
them from each other and the velocities of their movements are c
magnitudes relatively as breathtaking as those of our universe whic
they also comprise, it becomes clear to the intelligence that the univers
of our own particular dimension may be no more than a molecul
itself in the all of everything. It therefore also becomes easier for th
intelligence to perceive the scope of many of its age-old errors in i
ways of estimating the measure of its environment. It is now easier t
grasp the thought that what seem to be vastly elongated millennium
of lifetimes in the history of human beings may be no more than a
instantaneous flash of being in the ultimate vastitude. Minds that a
incapable of, or unprepared for, the astronomical range of such co
clusions frequently catch similar glimpses of these truths from homeli
relativities, such as comparing the ants' or the bees' sense of the spac
and time of their world to our sense of ours.

Or take the Ephemeridae whose adult lives, ephemeral indeed to u
may last but a brief hour in a nighttime, never to see the light of da
and yet, had these May flies a faculty of memory with which to estima
their life span, and further faculties to judge of ours, no doubt the
would present quite a complex of duration to them and we wou
seem monsters of longevity. And, indeed, is not the May fly in its tu
a monster of longevity compared to other lives we might imagin
Now, then, ourselves? Where do we actually stand in this incor
mensurable affair of being, which to our intelligence can seem at o
end and moment of relativity so infinitely vast beyond all bounds
thought, and at the other end so bewilderingly infinitesimal? We sta
at last at a point of intelligence which tends to accept our intuitic
that the whole affair is a timeless and sizeless one, as simple and integr
as the thought of a gesture, of a Smile. An act of Grace! You ca
analyze it intellectually, scientifically, "realistically" (which is a drea
ful misnomer!) into concatenations of elements, stages, causal ar
effectual processes within processes, physiochemical attractions ar

lsions, tropisms, electrodynamics, quanta; you can fragmentize it
billionth parts of seconds or millennial periods to suit the purposes
ur limited faculties, ad infinitum. But you have come to know, at
: last, this is playing a game according to rules that your better sense
gnizes as obsolete, that you are breaking up into artificial hypo-
ical fractions and periods what is essentially inviolate to such make-
t tactics, that over and above the temporal fallacy of our circum-
ed minds is a transcendent Truth which must be approached in
s of that very Grace that is its essence. It is a truth and grace of
ntaneity and must so be understood. We are within its light. To
it we must Spontaneously See. Is not God a Spontaneity? The
ntaneity.

Chapter XI

ORIGINALITY AND FABRICATION

"WE ARE such stuff as dreams are made on." We know i
fact how, in our dreams, we can undergo the illusion c
extended experience and thought and emotion whic
actually occupy but an instant of dreaming. The solipsist asks himse
how much more than a similar sort of instant in transcendent time th
actual dream of life need occupy. We are indeed such stuff as dream
are made on. So must be our truest works of art.

When we think of the strange twists and shadings that characteri:
our dreams, and the difficulty we should have in resurrecting the
descriptively with any degree of fidelity, we begin to understand son
of the differences between individual minds and feelings. It is obvio
that in the realm of dreams we are not likely to be plagiarists. We
we able to dream all the dreams of other dreamers we would ha
wonderful insight into the nuance of human variability. And yet th
night life of our semisleeping minds draws all its breath from the i
spiration of human experience and the expiration of human temper
ment. It is a semblance of reality conjured up by a mind that has bee
in every instance specially and uniquely conditioned by the patte
of its own peculiar experience of reality. The only reason that the drea
reveals more strikingly these subtle differences between us is that t
dormant mind evokes more vivid images, employs more radical symbo
and generally steps up to higher intensification the substances and mea
ings of life situations. Sometimes it acts in the powerful idiom of caric
ture, sometimes it is melodramatic to the point of frenzy, sometim
it is more subtle than the rarest lyric.

However, we should not need the testimony of our dream world
convince us that we are as essentially different from one another awa
as asleep. The reason that many of us do not realize this is becau

ugh our reactions to the experiences of our environment differ most
ificantly in nuance, the idiom of our wide-awake minds is only
ly rich and artful enough to express the differences. All but the
st exquisitely inventive simile and metaphor becomes gradually
led, insipid, platitudinous. There is an ever-increasing awareness of
ineptitude of most of our efforts to approximate the essence of our
is verbally. We are so limited in qualifying terminology, so hazy
diffuse in our meanings, that our semantic engineers are incessantly
y trying to fortify the language structure and implement some badly
ded precision. Hence our fervent response to the occasional poet
o expresses in resourcefully fresh and stirring language ideas and
otions profoundly familiar to our inner consciousness but which
e remained nebulous because we have lacked the creative ingenuity
raise them from the inchoate to the realized. The sorrowful fact is
t few of us are equipped to express much more than ordinary neces-
elicits from us. We simply do not cultivate the machinery we
sess for the discernment and handling of the subtleties that con-
ute a higher grace of being. We neglect our higher potentialities.
r educational process is at fault, and leaves us still in somewhat
gnant isolation from each other, with only rare communion. The
ıber effects are not confined to the world of aesthetics!
n our dreams we undergo illusions of extended experience which
ually occupy but an instant of dreaming. In our waking life we may
lergo the extended experience of listening to a great musical com-
ition, but at the end, if we have grasped it in all the purity of its
ıificant architecture, its form, then we sense the whole conception
it as an instantaneous experience, too. Listen to Mozart's own
cription of his method of composing. Before he writes a single
ail of the subject that he is developing the whole work stands com-
ted in his mind. ". . . My subject enlarges itself, becomes
thodised and defined, and the whole, though it be long, stands
ost complete and finished in my mind, so that I can survey it like
ine picture or a beautiful statue, at a glance. Nor do I hear in my
agination the parts *successively* [the italics are Mozart's] but I hear
m, as it were, all at once. What a delight this is I cannot tell! All this

inventing, this producing, takes place in a pleasing lively dream. the actual hearing of the tout ensemble is after all the best. What been thus produced I do not easily forget, and this is perhaps the gift I have my Divine Maker to thank for.

"When I proceed to write down my ideas, I take out of the ba my memory, if I may use that phrase, what has been previously lected into it in the way I have mentioned. For this reason the c mitting to paper is done quickly enough, for everything is, as I before, already finished; and it rarely differs on paper from what it in my imagination. At this occupation I can therefore suffer my to be disturbed; for whatever may be going on around me, I write, even talk, but only of fowls and geese, or of Gretel or Barbel, or s such matters. But why my productions take from my hand that ticular form and style that makes them *Mozartish*, and different fr the works of other composers, is probably owing to the same ca which renders my nose so large or so aquiline, or, in short, make Mozart's, and different from those of other people. For I really do study or aim at any originality."

Notice the final line of this revelatory description. He does contrive an originality of style or content; the integrity of his sp taneity guarantees it. The freshness of vision, the Mozartian music, the direct consequence of Mozartian sensibilities unobstructed ambition to produce anything other than the natural effulgence their own passionate response to being. They were open and attent to the fugitive sound of that grace which they transcribed into a m that you and I can hear. Such men as Mozart and Bach, and ot good men, seem to be possessed of a kind of wisdom and humi that enable them to listen to the sound of infinity successfully. many of us storm the gates of heaven with so much of the noise of own striving as to hear little else than our own din. The mighty fo and thunder of our spiritual composers issues not from self-assertiven and stormy authority, but from their love of the beautiful essence being which they have come to know only through gentle and ste fast devotional attention. The sound of silence is a great music to c who is still enough to hear. We must learn the gentle art of listen

e hope to sing more than a vocalizing song. The Voice of God is
uiet one. There must be a great stillness and attentiveness of heart
soul to apprehend it. And when it does come to you, there will be
e need of violent exertion to proclaim your communion and trans-
the sound. It will radiate through you like a wave of grace. By
I do not intend to say that great effort must not be expended by
artist or thinker to master the medium of his expression. But the
lute will power of which we have said so much in previous chapters
reliable guardian of that responsibility. The important factor is
to confuse the showmanship of a skilled technique with the
henticity of an insight. Fauconnet, in his study of the aesthetics of
openhauer, comes to the conclusion that "more talented than some,
less than others, the man of genius possesses the specific charac-
stic of willing more enduringly and more forcefully. His technique
s métier) becomes of second nature to him. He is master of it to
point of being able to forget it."

That is why I have said that it is essential to "dwell within the
erience of being in the meadow." There are those, of course, who
t no meadows to set up their easels, but paint from an inner vision.
re again we must not confuse showmanship with the authenticity
insight. Inventions of the imagination may, like dreams themselves,
se in genuine configurations flowing out of life experience. If they are
bued with the virtues of significant form, who cares whether they
conceived in daylight observation or nighttime reverie? But there
many misguided wielders of the brush today who lack confidence,
bably subconsciously, in the power of their own vision, who fear
t to paint what one sees is inevitably to paint a platitude, and that
paint with originality one must rather, above all, avoid what is
ible and "rearrange," invent, "create." These men whose sight has
t expanded into insight are of various categories. Some are philosophers
o seek to make pictures of their metaphysical intuitions, lacking
ually the aesthetic equipment for a successful communication. Others
more absorbed in the psychological convolutions of their own
entalities and, being unintegrated with the form of the world "out-
e themselves," paint images designed to reveal the atmospheres and

emotions of their inner psyche. Many are obsessed with their discov
of the subconscious, and are satisfied with their attempts to ren
pictorial versions of its manifestations. I do not say that these and ma
other pictorial essays are without virtue and modes of significance, b
I should maintain that they are primarily of psychological import a
secondarily of aesthetic. We are at a stage in our culture where t
Apollonian, or grimly intellectual, side of our nature is in the ascendar
over the Dionysian, or joyfully intuitive, and we no longer need
Nietzsche to explain the disadvantages of this state of affairs. Bei
something of a victim of it myself, I appreciate the problem. W
the balance a little more favorable, I should not be feeling impell
to express myself in the verbalized form of this essay at all. I shou
have more complete confidence in the unique communicability of t
work of art per se. But it remains the fact that multitudes of peo}
are without the means to receive what the artist has to give. By "mear
I do not intend to say that they are without the capacity, but withc
the training and adequate knowledge of the idiom. Consequently,
seems to me that a clarification of some of the higher purposes a
procedures of the artist-painter will open the eyes of many sensiti
persons to further and better seeing. They must cease to be confus
by all the isms and asseverations of contemporary cliques and clich
They must not be dazzled by empty skill, nor prejudiced by want
it. They must not mistake extravagant novelty for creative imaginatic
nor violence for power. They must understand both the functions ar
abuses of distortion, the suggestive relevancies and pretentious irre
vancies of abstraction. They must differentiate between effort ar
achievement, between desire and love. They must recognize their ov
blindnesses and the blindnesses of spurious or purblind adventu:
They must see through to what their best brothers have to give the:

Roger Fry, Clive Bell and Benedetto Croce are uniformly dubious
any wide appeal that the best art can have at this time for uninitiat
persons. Fry wrote: "In proportion as art becomes purer, the numb
of people to whom it appeals gets less. It cuts out all the roman
overtones of life which are the usual bait by which men are induced
accept a work of art. It appeals only to the aesthetic sensibility, ar

EAD OF CHRIST   Leonardo da Vinci

ANNUNCIATION   Fra Angelic

EXPULSION FROM THE TEMPLE

El Greco

PORTRAIT OF JEAN RENOIR SEWING   Renoir

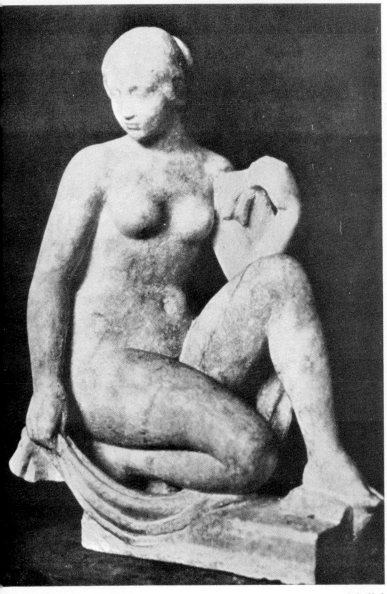

BATHER CROUCHING   Maillol

in most men is comparatively weak." The only emotion Bell con-
rs legitimate in art is that aroused by the vision of significant form.
may be a revelation, he says, of the universal "rhythm of reality."
ce writes that "the end attributed to art of directing the good and
iring horror of evil, of correcting and ameliorating customs, is a
vative of the moralistic doctrine; and so is the demand addressed
artists to collaborate in the education of 'lower classes' in the
ngthening of the national or bellicose spirit of a people, etc. These
all things that art cannot do, any more than geometry, which, how-
, does not lose any of its importance on account of its inability to
this; and one does not see why art should do this either."

he highest art, despite Croce's protestations against utilizing it as
ethical force, cannot but confer some of its own intrinsic virtue, if
y by lifting man out of his mood of narrow human exigencies and
ieties to the serene plane of enlightenment. It has no specific sermons
preach, but summons to a state of grace.

The wiser the man the more clearly he hears the summons. Aldous
xley responds to it in this way: "Suppose we stop thinking in a strictly
nan fashion; suppose we make it possible for ourselves to have direct
uitions of the non-human realities in which, so to speak, we're
bedded. The only vocabulary at our disposal is a vocabulary primarily
ended for thinking strictly human thoughts about strictly human
acerns. But the things we want to talk about are non-human realities
1 non-human ways of thinking. Hence the radical inadequacy of all
tements about our animal nature and, even more, of all statements
ut God or spirit, or eternity." Huxley's sense of a kind of separation
ween what he calls the human and the nonhuman is, of course,
nptomatic of the thought fallacy that Bergson has so brilliantly
mined. There certainly need be no such separation. But the trend
Huxley's longing, toward what he calls direct intuitions of the non-
man realities in which we're embedded, is a trend toward the serene
ne of enlightenment which I have associated with the intrinsic virtue
high art. This plane of enlightenment is the ultimate aim of a higher
ture. Whitehead, in his *Aims of Education*, defines culture as
tivity of thought and receptiveness to beauty and humane feeling

. . . What we should aim at producing is men who possess both cult
and expert knowledge in some special direction. Their expert knowle
will give them the ground to start from, and their culture will }
them as deep as philosophy and as high as art."

Let us once again return to a verdant meadow and discover some
the nuance in which an artist's vision deals and which might not
suspected by the layman. Upon the artist's perception and rendit
of these nuances depends much of the success of his picture. Inter
ingly enough, though the layman may be unaware of them as far
being able to identify them either in nature or in the picture, still
is often far more responsive to the picture possessed of them than
one devoid of them. If the artist has caught them in the full compuls
of their rhythmic force, then the layman of any moderately cultiva
sensitivity is likely to fall at least partially under their spell. Take,
instance, a spacious field of grass that stretches away from underf
into considerable distances. The naïve view of it would be simply gre
What green? Why, grass green, of course! The child usually sweep
in with water color to such an extent of flat green naïveté that
accept it as a symbolic expression of a field of grass. But the more se
tive we become to the whole experience of color the more variable
we perceive its nature to be. First of all, nearly all of us come to kn
that the appearance of the green grass directly before our eyes is so
what different from similar grass farther away. We account for
difference offhand by saying that we see near things more clearly th
far things, and that a kind of atmospheric haze alters the appearar
of things as they recede into distance. Hence the first divergence betw
fact and appearance. We know the grass a mile away to be actually
same color as the grass underfoot, but we also know that if we pa
it all into our picture the same "grass green" our pictured field will
resemble the real one at all; in fact, it will look very unreal. Nor is t
phenomenon of color perspective simply a matter of fading into distan
A good deal more is involved if we wish thoroughly to understand. T
fact is that as the waves of color vibration come to us from far av
to near they traverse fields of atmosphere which affect them. T
simplest way to envisage what occurs is as follows: Imagine a spectr

ɔe laid horizontally flat upon the field of vision between ourself and
horizon toward which we look, with the red range of the spectrum
ɪest to us. The space then between us and the horizon will divide
ɪlf into fields of color influence equivalent to the various hues of the
ctrum. The nearest area will be in the red field, receding into orange,
n yellow, green, blue and at the final distances into violet. Hence
near fields are fields of warmth and they recede into coolness. A
ɔwledge of this spectroscopic perspective helps us further to com-
hend what happens to our field of grass. The grass nearest to us,
ɪg in the red field of the spectrum, will appear to be a warm green
though suffused by the nature of the atmosphere it traverses. Farther
ɪy it will alter its appearance to a yellow-green, and then, at the
ɪdle distance where it enters into the atmosphere of its own quality,
will have the nearest semblance to what we may call "pure" green.
still greater distance it enters the cool spaces of blue and violet, and
l seem least green of all.

We must remember, too, that the color of all objects within the area
our vision is subject to this same influence, varying its quality in
ect relationship to its distance from the spectator. If we have a gray
ne wall in the foreground of our picture, it will seem a ruddy, warm
ıy as compared to the same kind of stone wall appearing at a distance
be cool. But, alas, it is not, in the final analysis, quite so simple as all
ɪs. We still must deal with color relativities. Suppose we have a
ɪster of brilliant red flowers growing in a part of our meadow. The
parent hue of the grass in immediate proximity to these flowers will be
nore intense green than elsewhere, because the eye will be stimulated
the redness of the flowers to see its complementary color more
ɪidly around it. Let us suppose, on the other hand, instead of red
wers, some brilliant shamrock green. The grass in the vicinity of the
ɪmrock green would seem pale and less green. Drop a piece of pure-
ɪite linen into the meadow, and see how relatively dark the grass
ɔund it seems in contrast. See a yellow flower against a gray wall, and
ɪe wall will seem a violet-gray; a red flower will make the same wall
ɪm greenish gray; a blue flower sends the wall into a yellowish gray.

These evocations by one color of its complementary play quite a ?
in the structure of color harmony.

It now becomes evident that unless our artist, consciously or unc
sciously, responds to these and many more kinds of nuance, he will
neglecting the subtle terms in which his poem must be painted. So
we have only scratched the surface of this vast subject. From the ma
of color, which is enormously overestimated in most people's min
we come to the far more important consideration of tonality, black ?
white, presence and absence of light. Often when the average specta
thinks he is being fascinated by the colors in a picture, or in nat
itself, he is not aware of how small a role color is actually playing in
appearance of that which is pleasing him. Indeed, were we to elimin
a great part of the intensity of color by showing him the same scene
nature through a pair of darkened glasses, he would quickly recognize
major importance of lightness and darkness. Color is undoubtedly
additional enrichment, an increase in the small vocabulary of our vis
articulation; but it is adjectival in function compared to the substan
quality of tonality. Take color away altogether and you still have
whole tremendous experience of visual form. Take away tonality a
granting that there is still somehow the light wherewith to see, you h
nothing but a formless, kaleidoscopic color mosaic. Tintoretto was c
sidered by his contemporaries to be their greatest colorist. When as
by one of his admirers to name his favorite color, he answered, "I
most beautiful of all colors is black." Ambroise Vollard recounts that
said to Renoir one day, "From the way you talk, Monsieur Renoir, o
would think that ivory black is the only color that counts, but how
you expect me to believe that you painted flesh like that with 'mud
Renoir replied, "I don't mean to compare myself with Delacroix, I
do you remember that phrase of his, 'give me some mud, and I will pa
you a woman's flesh'?"[1] And this is all from the period of the hig
colored Impressionist era.

Indeed, color is a relatively recent enhancement in the history
human vision. From the interesting investigations of such men as You
Helmholtz, Schultze, Parimaud, and the contemporary work of La

[1] *Renoir*, by Ambroise Vollard.

nklin, we are assured that color vision is now in an advanced stage
:n compared to the eras of its utter absence. In the Carboniferous
od, light impinging on the retina of living organisms gave a sensation
white only. Eventually a sensation of black developed, which was a
sation of nonstimulation, unvariable in quality except as admixtured
h varying quantities of white. This sensation of light was due to the
ction of certain elements of the visual organism, called rods. The
s of the eye were and are susceptible to whiteness only. Much later
he evolution of the visual apparatus, some of the rods developed into
e-shaped organs. These cones, merely further developed rods, are
ceptible to chromatic light, or color. But when the cones were in their
ly stage, in the Cretaceous period, they were receptive to only two
or sensations, yellow and blue. Thus there was a slow evolution from
Carboniferous period of achromatic to the Cretaceous period of
hromatic vision. In the former period there were no colored birds, no
ored flowers for a chromatic vision to operate upon. In the latter
iod, colored flowers and bees evolved. But the bees saw then, and
l see now, two colors only: yellow and blue. This dichromatic vision
plains the atavistic phenomenon of contemporary partially color-blind
lividuals in whom the color sensations of yellow and blue persist.
ially the visual apparatus of birds, most mammals, and normal human
ngs developed further. Yellow became differentiated into the two
avable portions of red and green. This brought our vision to its present
rachromatic stage. We can now understand why, when we physically
x red and green together, they revert to yellow. It is from yellow that
y originated. So also, when we mix yellow and blue, which is
uivalent to red, green and blue, they revert to the white out of which
y were developed.

We have but to see a photograph of any great painting to observe how
tle of the work's significant quality of form is lost through the absence
its coloration. This is, of course, more particularly true of older works
art, prior to the recent age of Impressionism. A Rembrandt achieves
major effects with the utmost economy of coloring. In fact, the
onomy is so discreet that where color does not occur it attains its
iximum effect by virtue of the controlled context. An overexuberant

employment of vivid hues minimizes the effectiveness of the colors
our disposal, just as a bombastic flood of loud oratory leaves little opp
tunity for subtlety or for timely accent. When we carefully exam
those pictorial experiences which seem to give us the fullest delight
the color sense, we most often find that the delight comes not from
alchemy of great quantities of pure color, but from the suggest
emergence of a colored luminosity, which is the color of an atmosph
rather than the color of component parts. If we recall the essential m
of aesthetic vision, the necessity of maintaining a focal center, then
is clear that we do not see each object and area before us in the f
coloration that they actually possess when we look at them separat
successively. Aesthetically seen, they merge into a harmony wherein ea
color is affected by all the others within the experience. They exer
mutually modulative influence upon each other.

Let us look at a bouquet of flowers from this point of view. If
eyes are fixed upon a few red roses near the center of the bouquet, th
the roses of the same color at the outer extremities of the arrangeme
nearer the periphery of our vision, will be far less clearly, and he
less vividly, seen. The outer roses will not appear to be so brightly r
If we focus on an outer rose, then those at the center of the bouq
will recede into less intense value. If we focus on a yellow flower,
roses may seem a little more purplish. If there is a bright blue w
behind the bouquet, the yellow flowers will be accented in our vis
response; if the wall is bright green, then the roses will spring forth
complementary importance. Of course, one must reiterate, time a
again, that great painting is not done, and never will be done, accord
to rules and formulae. These analytical passages are only designed
point out a few of the endless nuances upon which hangs the entire iss
of sensitized vision. The creative gesture which produces a beauti
picture is ultimately as spontaneous as the expression in the eyes o
good and wise man. Such an expression cannot, in all the subtlety of
integrity, be reproduced by recipe. But we can point out many of t
attributes of character, capacity and behavior requisite to its attainme
And therefore it is useful to understand that, in painting a bouquet
flowers, if each color of object and area is painted as vividly as, or m

idly than, it actually appears when directly and separately observed,
:n, at most, one will be painting a decoration, a series of color expe-
nces. True color must be seen in the integrity of its continuity, just
the objects and intervals of space which Bergson insists are actually
livisible. And that is why, when color is seen largely, it produces
marily a sensation of luminosity, since, in totality, colors are the
'ided elements of light.

Light is unquestionably the dominant agent of our sensory felicity.
iere is a superb logic to its behavior which never ceases to thrill the
e that discerns it. It lavishes itself upon the surfaces that face it in-
ingly, and it reaches with generous eagerness to bestow itself every-
iere that it can penetrate. The surfaces that are out of the path of its
ming, the recesses that bend away from the direction of its lightning,
ent flight, dwell in the shadows which punctuate its passage. It adapts
elf with incredible delicacy to everything it touches, caressing a
odulated surface with infinite tenderness, fading on receding forms
  imperceptible diminuendo. Take a pure-white spherical form and
serve all the indescribably gradual mutations by which the light
scribes to the human eye the graduated rotundity of a sphere. Not the
ance of a nuance will be missed by its eternally reliable behavior. If
e sphere is an exquisitely formed ivory or marble, the counterpoint of
ht and shadow will reveal every last evidence of its perfection by the
maculate smoothness with which they interpenetrate each other. If it
a crude sphere, there will be more abrupt behavior of the light wher-
er the continuing perfection of roundness is marred or interrupted.
he passage of light over a beautiful form is a gesture of continuity such
 we have ascribed to any movement of ultimate grace. Any awkward-
:ss in a sculptured form, any interruption of the plastic flow of part
 to part forming the desideratum of an indivisible whole, is immediately
:posed by the arrested grace of fluid light. That is why the Greek
ulptors loved to model their figures in the sensitive marble that was so
rtunately available to them. Marble is possessed of particularly subtle
ialities lending themselves to the fashioning of infinitely subtle forms.
/atch the passage of light over a well-preserved figure by such Renais-
nce artists as Desiderio da Settignano, Mino da Fiesole, Benedetto da

Maiano, Donatello, Verrocchio. Watch the miraculous interplay of ligˌ
and shadow in the masterly bas-reliefs of Ghiberti's bronze gates in t]
Baptistry at Florence, called by Michelangelo the gates to Paradise. T]
more perfect the form the more gloriously there seems to be an interflc
of lights into shades, shades into lights, all flowing with the unintˌ
rupted grace of fluidity such as we see clothing the pearl. Observe t]
spontaneous grace with which a free-falling garment drapes and folˌ
and see how the whole beauty of it is told by the faultless fidelity
light to the nuance it traverses. By the counterbalance of light a]
shadow we perceive the substances of our experience. In the absence
shadow we should perceive no more than light alone, and in the absenˌ
of light we should of course have only darkness. But the language
light and shadow speaks to most of us now more acutely than t]
language of our fingertips. The nuance of light and shade is more revˌ
latory of subtle form to our vision than the evidence of nuance that ˌ
might find through our sense of touch. Close your eyes and explore t]
surfaces of a sculptured marble with your hands. Try to apprehend]
total form, to estimate the degree of its beauty, the stature of the geniˌ
that went into the making of it. Then open your eyes and let it dwˌ
in the embrace of your vision. When it comes to the finest subtletiˌ
we "touch" them most understandingly and inclusively by the ligˌ
that illumines and silhouettes them.

The painter in the meadow, feeling the form of the universe inhereˌ
in the vision of what he sees before him, sees the fluent light make]
usual reliable visitation, bathing the shapes and colors which compˌ
the total form in all the nuances of its inexhaustible shadings, modulˌ
ing the extent of its presence or absence in absolute conformity with t]
undulations and convolutions of the matter being observed. Take t]
simple yellow buttercup that may be at hand. See how the light abidˌ
on all the surfaces that meet its rays, and how, where the curvaturˌ
evade its fullest touch, it gently relinquishes its empire to the darknˌ
that is its eternal counterpoise. The yellow thus lightens and darkeˌ
confluently with the shape of that which it colors. It is never quite t]
same unless it is bathed universally, at every point and from every dirˌ
tion in the same light, if such a thing were possible. And even then ˌ
would seem to vary for other reasons, some of which we have alreaˌ

iscussed. The simple story of the buttercup is in miniature the story of
l perceptible form. And so, when the artist begins to paint a picture
1at is designed to reveal the ultimate form of what he sees, his eyes
ill be caressing the rhythmical behavior of light and darkness over the
)ace of his vision, just as they would in his appreciation of a Parthenon
ieze, a Ghiberti or Rossellino angel, a Masaccio fresco. One of the
rofoundest recognitions of the revelatory magic in light and darkness
as, of course, Rembrandt's. The luminous tactility of form in his great
.chings and drawings is all achieved uniquely by the genius of his sen-
tivity to harmonious distribution of these two elements. So, too, we
ave the magnificent creations of the great Chinese painters in black
1d white; quietly they revealed the noblest proportions of their own
)uls by the wisdom with which they drew an architecture of light and
arkness into the most casual scene. Such pictures are gentle implications
r stirring revelations of ultimate grace.

Just as the appearance of color obeys various laws of perspective, and
ters in response to various psychological factors, so does the appearance
f light intensity, which we call tonality. Observe, for instance, an avenue
f receding trees. Notice that, though all the trunks may be of similar
)ne and color in separate actuality, nevertheless as they are farther
:moved from us they gradually change in quality and intensity of
)pearance. The nearest ones will seem sharply etched and dark com-
ared to those at a distance. At a very great distance they will be almost
)sorbed into the general tonality of the atmosphere that surrounds
1em. A pencil drawing by Rembrandt usually illustrates this fading of
)ne perfectly. The nearest plane will be drawn in heavy, black line, the
1iddle distance appropriately lighter, and the remote in airy delicacy.
hadows in the foreground will be accented so as to effect a much
:eater impact upon the attention of the beholder than shadows that
1ay be cast by objects farther away. In other words, the behavior of
ght and darkness will be more emphatically revealed in its deepest
)ntrasts when it is nearest to us, and will blend into softer and softer
1terplays as it dwindles into distance, rather like the impressions of a
ithdrawing sound. And, most important of all, the diminution occurs
; rhythmically as the contours of the form illumined.

Furthermore, it requires the utmost sensitivity and observational instinct to notice some of the further facts about the appearance and behavior of light. Take the familiar phenomenon of a wall of a room painted an even gray color. If this wall were to occur in some area of picture we are painting, let us say as a background to a girl's head whose portrait we are doing, it would be atrociously "inartistic" to paint the wall into our picture as the flat, even gray that we know it actually to be. Most of us sense, without knowing altogether why, the "inartistic" result of such work. The extraordinary fact is that such a gray wall observed as a background to a girl's head by truly discerning eyes will be seen at no point to be exactly the same in tone or color as at any other point of its surface. Let us say that the girl sits facing the light coming through window that is at our left; we are painting her profile. Her forehead nose and chin are mostly bathed then in strong light; her cheek as rounds back falls into gentle shadow, and her hair is quite dark at the contour of the back of her head. The wall will then seem a little darker to us in the areas neighboring her light-drenched forehead, and a little lighter in the area contiguous to her dark, shaded hair. If the color of her skin seems pink where it is illuminated, there may be a responsive suggestion of green in the darker gray wall next to it in our picture. there is a feeling of violet darkness in her hair, there may be overtones of yellow in the gray of the wall behind the hair. If she wears a brilliant white gown, will not the wall seem very dark gray in contrast? If she wears a deep black velvet, will not the wall seem correspondingly light These are a few of only the most obvious relativities which may obtain under such circumstances as described. There is simply no final ac counting for the myriad of suggestive responses and interplays that may occur to a creative and highly sensitized mentality confronting such scene. A whole, indescribably vast organization of memory patterns slowly evolved and minute attractions and repulsions, operate in the mind of each individual that beholds the simplest appearance of thing It cannot possibly ever look alike to any two out of millions of persons Naturally, the more refined the senses of the persons involved the greater will the differences of impression be. And, of course, the average laymen do not possess the verbal or alternate means of describing the

pressions accurately enough to show up the subtle differentiations
t make all the important difference!

Hence the tragic fallacy that has arisen in the mind of man and spread
poison so destructively as to inhibit the aspirations of all but the most
f-reliant. The conviction has grown up and been preached in depres-
ely incorrect self-abasement that "there is nothing new under the
n," and that whatever conceptions one may have that seem so original
d so stirringly unique to one's own experience "have all occurred
fore" in others of the billions who have lived and died. Whereas
actly the reverse of this foolish generalization comes far closer to the
ith. No one in all the deep ages of past time ever has, or in the endless
aches of the future ever will have, experienced the act-of-being in exact
plica to that of another living soul. If we could envisage the lifetime
the human race as billions of individual little bubbles rising in brief
d rapid course as in the sparkling of champagne, still a full under-
anding of each bubble would show it to be unique within the minute
ttern of its ascension. So vast is the range of the entire human tem-
rament and human experience complex that it is as though some
finite hand were to strike chords on a piano of illimitable trillions of
ys; the probability of hearing the same chord twice is remote indeed.

Now, it is objected that the average human being is so like his brothers
r all practical purposes, despite these shadings of subtle differences,
at there is precious little originality in more than a few of them. It
rtainly would appear to be so at first, second, and even third glance.
ut let the deep discernment of a penetrating spirit—a Dostoevski,
alzac, Stendhal, Chekhov—play its searching light into the caverns and
terstices of the intricate "average" soul, and you soon discover the
byrinthine nature of the simplest human psyche. That is why I accent
ie importance of equipping ourselves by training and persistence to
iarpen the superb faculties with which we are endowed, and to heighten
ie intensity of their employment. That is why I point out that with a
ttle such improvement of our faculties we could raise the level of our
ommunicative experiences to a momentous degree, and exalt the entire
ietabolism of our spiritual growth.

Chapter XII

THE FAMILIARITY COMPLEX

wwwwwwwwwwwwwwwwwwwwwwwwwwwwwwwwwwwwwwwwwwwwwwwwwwwwwwwwwwwwwwwwwwwwwwwww

GIVE a hundred individuals enough instruction and practice
the use of paints and brushes, or simply of charcoal, so that
least their hands are able to collaborate with and obey t
requirements of their minds, and then see how differently each one w
paint his picture of the same scene, the same object, the same perso
If they paint faithfully to their insight, it will be an impossibility
their pictures to be of a sameness. It is only when they succumb to t
temptation of painting in the style of someone else's insight that th
produce something of frustrated significance. The loss of spontaneity
fatal to the grace of any effort. Imagine the enormous difference of co
cept there would be in canvases painted of the same subject by su
variety of spirits as Vermeer, Van Gogh, Renoir, Fra Angelico, Mon
celli, Manet, Rembrandt, Rousseau, ad infinitum. There would not
the slightest need of signatures to their canvases. Any practiced e
would read the identity of each special genius in the merest glance at
fragment of his work. We recognize their insight as we know the sou
of familiar voices. Nor have we need of any color by which to recogni
them. Photographs of their pictures still carry the message. The subt
language of light and shade, spoken differently by each one of the
tells a new story of the same subject in every instance, a story that h
never in all history been told exactly so before, nor ever will again. N
having ever seen through these men's eyes with the slightest und
standing, will you ever lose the added virtue of their insight combine
with your own. For to experience the insight of others is to extend t
capacity of your own.

If I seem to be overemphasizing the delicacies, the subtleties, t
nuances, the nuances of nuance, in all this affair of the creative arts,
point out that they cannot be overemphasized, because they are t

y essence, substance and sine qua non of significant form. The only
son that they can seem to be overemphasized is because there are so
adequate terms by which we can successfully talk about and say
ch about them. For the most part, you have to let them talk for
mselves. That is the main purpose of this book, after all. I am en-
voring to prepare and to encourage the reader to enlarge his capacity
being receptive to them, and his capability for dealing in them. It
tainly must now be apparent that the beauty of a picture does not
in any of the superficial qualities that please the naïve and the un-
pared. If it did, then many an acknowledged masterpiece would be
ftly discredited. Think of all the pedestrian portraiture of exquisite
men and children, flowers and sunsets that fade into insignificance
side a Manet study of a lemon or a dead fish, an old discarded boot
Van Gogh's, a dilapidated hovel by Cézanne, a disreputable repre-
tation of Toulouse-Lautrec. Why, the merest trifling fragment out of
y part of a great canvas will inevitably be rich with signs of its superior
cture." The loveliest sights and manifestations that nature is capable
producing may be painted in most skillful fidelity to their ostensive
its by a well-intentioned, run-of-the-mill painter, and be utterly with-
t a trace of beauty; whereas a poetic artist without half the manual
xterity may paint a work of breath-taking beauty by setting up his easel
thin a stone's throw of his house. The picturesque has nothing to do
th a good picture. Neither has the stirring or the overwhelming.
A great artist may overwhelm with his view of what you might other-
ise have called a trivial back-porch vista or a scrubby hillside or a color-
ss frump. It is his insight into the commonplace that enlightens you,
that when you begin to share the manner of his perception, his sus-
ptibility to the nuance of which we speak so enduringly, you will find
solutely everything bathed in a universally magic light. You come to
derstand how blind you have been at any moment when things have
emed less than beautiful to you. Even the "ugly" human gestures,
ch as badly or vulgarly built houses that may be said to mar a country-
de, can be absorbed into the grace of the continuous whole. The ulti-
ate beauty with which we are so concerned primarily resides in the
ne "little gray cells" that so construe it. If the fine little gray cells are

not prepared to see in the best way of seeing, then they are blind to
transcendant. The vast majority of us rest contented with the mediocr
of what we call the pleasures of our eyesight, not even suspecting
blindness.

We must look further into this question of what is beautiful to pa
and what, if anything, is not. So many persons of even extraordin
mental endowment in other directions have a complete lack of co
prehension here. They are sometimes more aroused by the recognizab
traits of the Grand Canyon painted in all the awkward chromatics
popular verisimilitude than by the most heavenly fugues of tonality fr
the brush of an authentic artist. I have heard men question the beau
of such a picture as that in the Metropolitan Museum of the O
Woman Paring her Fingernails because they were disturbed by t
"unaesthetic" subject matter. The blindness that this connotes on t
part of excellently equipped mentalities, that have simply remain
totally unschooled in the realm of the plastic arts, is depressing a
challenging. For that matter, to illustrate how much deeper the proble
goes, I have heard relatively sensitive, creative and "successful" artis
to my baffled astonishment, call Vermeer photographic, and assert tha
since the devising of the camera, such artistry as his is thereby supplant
and obsolete! Imagine the shortsightedness or the spiritual confusic
which can fail to see and to understand the stupendous distinctio
between the dynamic of Vermeer and the static of the photograph
lens. The quietest canvas out of the spiritual serenity of a Vermeer
more possessed of all the momentous qualities of movement, of pla
ticity, than thousands upon thousands of more imperious attempts b
lesser men to sweep us off our feet by the surge and violence of muscular
wielded brushes. Is it not a shame that the sobriety of wisdom, th
hushed stillness that can surround a deep emotion, may be mistaken fc
vacuity? Of course, a great deal of such unfortunate misjudgment is ofte
due to incompatibility of temperaments. We are all acquainted wit
the heated expressions of distaste that many a superb artist has lavishe
on the works of equally gifted colleagues. The antipathy of one high
pitched temperament for another seems to be the frequent outcome c
two creative types not adjusted to each other's style of personalit

gas' acrid opinions of the landscapes of Courbet are to the point. e whole epoch of Impressionism and its long suite of schools, groups, 1 isms provide us with multitudes of examples. Naturally it is far from ing an ideal state of affairs. There may come a time, far hence, when : twists and singularities of temperament will be no obstacle to mutual derstanding and appreciation. A higher form of man may have the e ability to love other paths and goals than just his own. It is tragic to deprived of all but one's own limited aspect of the ultimates. After , how strange it is to see many of these dedicated souls pouring the most of their energies and talents into their pursuit of grace, the good, e true and the beautiful, and yet marring the purity of their course the violence of competitive vanities! We simply must learn that there : myriads of ways of speaking the same truth, but only one way of urting it, and that is with love.

There are, moreover, ways of testing the qualities of pictures. Certainly : must acknowledge that there are no fixed criteria by which we can dge the aesthetic merit of an endeavor. But there are, I would main- in, some pertinent questions that we can ask about the attributes of orks of art, and about the kind and quantity of heat that is generated * the contact of a particular spectator with a particular work. Let me ve a direct example of what I mean. A woman of considerable discern- ent, and of world renown in the field of dramatic art, was expressing eat enthusiasm for certain paintings of a radically abstract nature. I d not wish to allow my own estimation of these paintings to obtrude to an open-minded discussion of their value. But I felt from the anner of her reaction to them, or perhaps from what seemed to be issing in her reaction, that she was persuading herself intellectually to : impressed with what emotionally had not really touched her pro- undly. I found myself able to enjoy with her many of the virtues of ese abstractions, and particularly a suggestiveness of design, which, not subtle, was at least ingenious, not to say amusing. I was filled with hope that she would be able, out of her own enthusiasm, to lead me little closer to an apprehension of some of the loftier inherencies which re claimed for so many of these works, and which have evaded my ncerest efforts to appreciate. But I could not catch the contagion of

her zeal, and I continued to feel dissatisfied with the quality of her ow
emotion. At last, when we had both expended a large part of ou
vocabularies and our patience, it was clear that she continued to b
satisfied with what these works had to give her and no discontentednes
of mine could shake her from the conviction of her pleasure. Wh
should it? And yet I felt impelled to urge her to be more criticall
exacting. I knew that my final question would close the discussior
whichever way she answered. I asked her whether the impact of thes
pictures drove her into an emotion at all equivalent to what happene
to her when she saw Chartres Cathedral. If she responded affirmativel
then I was prepared to wonder about my own inadequacy, and had t
admit that probably there was more dynamic to the pictures than
could perceive. But a prolonged silence followed this query as we cor
tinued our evening stroll through the summer twilight, and then sh
stood still in the middle of the road, which seemed rather symbolic c
what had happened.

From some of the instances that I pointed out in Chapter Seven w
have an intimation of what occurs when a susceptible person comes i
contact with an exalted work of art. A formidable emotion is generatec
and discharged in various ways. But there is most emphatically a stat
of excitation that can be detected by its physical repercussions and di
tinguishes it from any milder form of stimulation. It is extreme in th
artist, and it carries over to the audience. Its forcefulness is the direc
measure of the artist's love for what he sees, and the loving impulsio
which drives him into creative fulfillment. After all, it is only the urgenc
of the artist's emotion that can precipitate him into such sustained an
soul-trying effort as is required for the successful fruition of his labor
Nothing less than fever heat is likely to brew the kind of ferment c
which we are speaking. The intensity of the artist provides the hypnoti
component that projects a beholder into the empathic experience an
emotion of that artist. Once again Bergson catches the analogy for us
"In the processes of art we shall find, in a weakened form, a refined an
in some measure spiritualized version of the processes commonly used t
induce the state of hypnosis. Thus, in music, the rhythm and measur
suspend the normal flow of our sensations and ideas by causing our atter

on to swing to and fro between fixed points, and they take hold of us
with such force that even the faintest imitation of a groan will suffice
to fill us with the utmost sadness. If musical sounds affect us more
powerfully than the sounds of nature, the reason is that nature confines
itself to *expressing* feelings, whereas music *suggests* them to us . . . The
plastic arts obtain an effect of the same kind by the fixity which they
suddenly impose upon life, and which a physical contagion carries over
to the attention of the spectator."[1]

We must observe that the hypnotic force which operates upon us
when we go to the theater to see a play is a more effective and dominat-
ing one than the same force when we merely read the play. It is not
only the form of the drama which holds us but all the artful stage effects,
timing and nuance of skillful acting, which in every tone and gesture
draw and compel our attention. The entire setting of a drama, a dance,
or a motion picture, is stripped as much as possible of all diverting elements, so that the mind of the audience is concentrated by every device
of the dramatist, the stage manager, and the director, upon the rhythm
of the performance. Hence the observer is subjected to as ideal an
atmosphere for hypnotic suggestion as the circumstances will permit.
In fact, this in great part accounts for the particularly compelling influence of the motion picture in contemporary forms of drama. In the
motion-picture theater the rapport between the dramatic action and the
spectator is more complete than anywhere else. There is not even the
sense of distance from the stage with masses of audience between oneself and the action, nor the strain of imperfect vision or hearing, nor the
sense of certain timing and spacing of events being confined to theatrical
symbolisms. One's attention is utterly absorbed into the amazing semblance of reality, and heightened reality, which transpires upon the all-
enveloping screen. This is a tremendous nearness, so powerful in its
hypnotic technique that it overcomes all the "unreal" factors of photographic instead of actual life representation.

Now, when we depart from such specially contrived atmospheres and
emerge into the everyday conditions under which we may look at
paintings, we discover that a painting's "impressiveness" labors under

[1] *La Pensée et le Mouvant*, by Henri Bergson. Librairie Félix Alcan.

great disadvantages and that, of all forms of art, it is one of the le
hypnotic. This is especially true of easel pictures, whose only setting th
serves to separate them from the distractive surroundings is a few inch
of framing. The attention can be riveted only by the power of the pictu
to command and hold it. Thus if we recall the special function of gre
painting—revelation of simultaneity of apparently successive parts
space and time, giving the spirit its unique realization of the intuiti
truth about "duration and extension," i.e., their spontaneity—we see th
to the average mentality it remains extremely difficult to grasp the fu
content, unaided by the hypnotic accessories which implement the p
suasiveness of other art forms. This accounts for some of the ineffectu
preciosities attempted by aesthetes nowadays, such as accompanying t
exhibition of a painting with music, music with kaleidoscopic colo
etc. These are all naïve concoctions for further "framing," for heighte
ing the persuasiveness of one art form by invoking the atmosphere
another. Imagine requiring a blending of "selected music" with a rea
ing of Shakespeare! No; we must build up a more general susceptibili
to the real workings and meanings of the finer arts. They must cease
be the special language of a few sensitized individuals. After all,
schools and colleges all over the world students spend years to learn t
rudiments of a few additional languages in order to broaden their mea
of linguistic communication. How vastly more important, then, to ma
the further effort of acquiring the idiom of the high arts. This is
particularly true of the plastic arts since, from earliest childhood, w
manifest an insatiable appetite for pictures. We love to see graphical
recorded images. From the fond parent's urging to "see the pretty p
ture," through the child's attempts to scribble them himself, and on in
the graphic employment of them far and wide throughout the civiliz
world as advertising media for the highest ideas to the lowliest co
mercial products, we recognize the great picture-potential. The di
culty commences when its function graduates from merely reproducti
delineation of shapes to intimations of absolute form. That is the tra
sition which so few persons are equipped to follow. The great majori
of people who look at pictures see shapes and successions of shap
separated by intervals of space. When the rare artist interweaves the

arent details into the integrated form of his insight, immaterializing
es and contours by the fluency with which his light resolves their
sory finitude and caresses their interpenetrant mutuality, his achieve-
nt most often passes unperceived. The picture is seen like all other
tures; the message between the lines is not seen into.

That is why we must analyze to some extent the artist's handling of
es in a picture. To the eye practiced in everyday judgments, an edge
contour represents an outline or boundary where a particular surface
her ceases and is neighbored by space or another object, or takes a
lden abrupt change of direction, as in the case of a cube where one
e adjoins another. In any event, in everyday practical seeing, each edge
it is scrutinized is as sharp or as soft as the substance that happens to
ipe it. The edge of a ruler lying on the table will be crisp, the edge
contour of a wad of absorbent cotton will be softly indeterminate, the
ge of a saw, jagged. The eye makes these observations by directing its
ze upon each contour that interests it. But there are occasions when
ipes are not of primary interest, just as there are occasions when in-
idual plants may momentarily cease to occupy the botanist as he
ccumbs to the aesthetic charm of a field of flowers. So, too, the piano
ner forgets the timbre of individual keys when he hears them played
a master. The quality of their individuality functions in a blend to
oduce something far above the fineness of their solitary virtues. In
her words, there are occasions when an artist comes along and sees all
apes and spaces blended also into something far above their several
stinctive properties, merging their identities like notes in a grand chord.
ow, to understand what happens to edges, contours, outlines when
ey are observed creatively as opposed to practically, let us return yet
ain to the meadow which we have been recurrently observing.

Let us now include in our field of vision several trees nearby and some
uses off toward the horizon. First look at just one tree, which in itself
ll be found to be a far more variable experience than is generally sup-
sed. We shall confine our observation to the trunk of the tree. The
st discovery we shall make is that it is impossible to focus simul-
neously on both sides of the trunk even if, theoretically, our attention
fixed on the center. The natural inclination of the eye is to see the

form more specifically from either the one side or the other. If we se
the right side of the trunk sharply, definitely, then the other edge seem
less precise. If we see the left side clearly, then the right side does no
seem so clear-cut as it did the moment before when we were focused o
it. One or the other side is seen exactly; never both at the same tim
Furthermore, if we are focusing at the lower portion of the trunk, the
even the side we are favoring loses its sharpness of outline gradually as
ascends away from our most attentive vision. In all directions away fro
wherever we may happen to focus our point of sight, contours, color
tones will tend to diminish the intensities of their actual characteristi
in ratio to their regression from the visual center. Keeping our sight fixe
upon this particular tree trunk, let us now take in the additional incider
of a neighboring tree. The second tree will be in no way so intense
experienced as the first. Its contours will be less palpable, its color an
tone vaguer, its mass less concrete in feel. Shift the gaze to the secon
tree, and the whole form of the context alters at once. The second tre
takes on all the more intimate qualities of centrality, and the first tre
subsides into the rhythm of incidence. A few exercises of this sort wou
initiate the layman into some of the first principles of plastic vision, an
would disabuse him once and for all of some of the basic fallacies
critical judgment. It would also help to clear up much of the pretentio
air of the esoteric that has been permitted to cloud the stuffy sanctun
of high art. At once, with a little of this sort of wisdom, the significa
can be rescued from the plethora of ornamental and banal produc
which necessarily flood the arena of modern isms.

We must not oversimplify the matter by concluding that a certa
amount of re-education of the visual process guarantees aesthetic insigh
But we must acknowledge such education as one of the essentials to
We must cease to see panoramically; each shift of the vision mu
register a whole reorientation of elements into a newly perceived forr
Hypersubtle, yes; but what ultimate truth and beauty is not? It is bett
to accept the necessity of subtlety and attune ourselves to it than
pretend an independence of it. There is a kind of impatient ambitic
today, as doubtless there has been in every age, to skirt the laborio
integrity of wisdom, to scorn the grace of spiritual serenity, and to cras

rough these difficulties with the deceptive authority of self-assertive-
ss. Because of the increasingly competitive nature of the modern art
orld, great numbers of practitioners have succumbed to the dominant
otivation—the "sell yourself" or "put yourself across" idea. And the
ost direct way to this sort of success seems to be via the sensational,
e monumentally forceful, muscular, impressive. Hence we find a temp-
tion to resort to the bold stroke, the impulsively sure but empty
sture, filled with spurious emotionalisms but devoid of deep spiritual
eling, of Love. There is always a great market in human gullibility for
ud assertion delivered with bravura fortissima. Many of the purest
ms out of the wealth of human creativity would be lost in the sur-
undings of such works were it not for the quiet authority of authen-
ity, which has greater surviving powers.

All the gusto, all the passionate enjoyment of life's high offerings, all
e emotional responsiveness to every facet of existence, however, will
ver by themselves produce the works that we most love and need.
dded to these elements of the creative faculty must be the innate or
quired technique for projecting them into some successful form of
alization. This art of painting has always been a superb vehicle. At
rtain crucial periods it has been employed by state and church to
omulgate some of the loftiest conceptions of social design and human
piration. Despite the wider familiarity and reach of verbal language,
has, at its highest moments, touched further pinnacles of spiritual
cension than words can tell. But its inherent possibilities are such
at it is still evolving, and from its great propagandistic virtues it has
een alternately shrinking and expanding into something as intensely
ersonal and soul-probing as thought itself.

It is now going through a phase of deep introspection, suffering all
e disadvantages and reaping all the advantages of this hazardous and
sential mood to further growth. And one of its great longings is to
ast off these limiting qualifications that have so often kept it the
ecially confined language of small inner circles who happen to possess
n aptitude for it. Since in its elementary simplicity it appeals to and
eaks to and enchants the multitudes, it must neglect no opportunity
o maintain a clarity of appeal at the more elevated levels of its maturity.

Many persons think that this is not possible; but many persons a
think that an art that is not intelligibly addressed to the univer
audience of mankind is defective. Certain it is that the healthiest p
cedure is to attain as wide a rapport as possible without inhibiting t
potential of the artist. The grimmest tragedy imaginable would be t
diluting and filtering of spiritual nourishment to suit the frailest dig
tion. The fullest verve and momentum of human genius must be s
tained at every instant; it cannot be tampered with or impeded by a
misguided attempt to modify and simplify for mass consumption. It
mass capacity that must be raised, and that is precisely why people shot
be familiarized with the need and methods and feasibility of cultivati
their dormant sensibilities. The problem is not nearly so much, as son
pessimists claim, a dearth of sense and sensibility, but rather of c
structed vitality.

For it is clear that the same frustrating complications of the hum
psyche which have been cited as impediments to creative power a
equally depressant to the general responsive capacity of individua
With all the will in the world to avail themselves of that which th
are intelligent enough to sense to be there, many brilliantly practic
minded people are utterly feeble-minded before great works of art. T
so-called "successful" type of person is frequently the most peculia
arrested of all aesthetically. The more a mind is busied with manipul
ing and managing the material fortunes of life, the more preoccupied
becomes with organizational minutiae, the more it is deprived of t
humility and devotional orientation so requisite to the ultimate si
plicities. It is as though such temperaments are so driven by their will
power, or so busied with their urgent sense of the need to establish t
authority of their intelligent ability to direct little or great affairs, th
their other, more spiritual needs recede into secondary consequence. (
course, this happens in many cases gradually and imperceptibly. For t
very qualities that equip such people for leadership often equip the
as well to understand and admire the purposes and achievements of fi
arts. In fact, they frequently believe themselves to be alert, appreciati
of and contributive to artistic endeavor; but if they are honest and con
prehending, they can judge the extent of their true sensitivity by t

gree of really anguishing division they must feel between material and
ritual necessity. There are indeed some rare, heart-warming examples
 men who divide their considerable talents between skillful, con-
uctive management of worldly enterprise and the kind of meditative
 creative activity that answers the appeal of their souls. They are the
es who can substantiate the statement that such an integration is as
il-trying as it is soul-satisfying! And yet that is the very accomplish-
nt toward which we must aim. The divided self, which is so clearly
ineated in modern times, and so poignantly revealed by Carl Jung
his *Modern Man in Search of a Soul*, must be reintegrated by animat-
; its faltering potentiality with love. Man must cease to feel himself
it between what has so long been considered two almost incompatible
eds, his material and his spiritual satisfactions. They should and can
 mutually related. The world anxiety neurosis would in great part
 dispelled.

So constantly perturbed are most of us by these conscious and sub-
nscious anxieties, which increase their empire over us in direct propor-
n to the growing civilized complexities of our times and tempera-
nts, that we feel a tremendous release and reactive buoyancy whenever
 high serenity of a more perfectly integrated spirit communicates
us some of its security and grace. We go to our wise men for it but
netimes even they are troubled. Yet, strangely enough, some of the
st troubled souls of all, the hypersensitive, struggling vitalities of
epressible artists, deposit impressions formed by the matrix of their
arching intuitions, impressions that we call works of art. In those
rks we gratefully sense and receive the inestimable catharsis which
the blessed gift of beauty.

That catharsis, that relief from tension and frustration, may be visited
on us at any instant that we happen to come within the influence
such works. For some, it is enough to walk into a cathedral and hear
few phrases of Johann Sebastian Bach. It is as though God had set
to perpetual availability the manifold and diverse works of men who
re near to him and transmitted by human arts some versions of his
ce. Many such men may never have thought in religious terms, nor
er might have claimed or suspected themselves to be within any aura

more special than that of merely being. For, after all, the greater t
artist the more miraculous is every slightest aspect of existence to ⟩
mind. He will be as enamored of God's most trifling effects as of l
supreme Majesty. Consider, for instance, the nature and works of su⟨
a man as Chardin.

The still lifes of this poetic painter never cease to thrill other paint⟨
by the eternally satisfying combination of qualities that they posse⟨
They are painted with a solidity of texture, a richness of pigment,
rightness of métier that are a delight to the craftsman. And in tl
masterly facture we have, besides, the most unerring conveyance
pure form, all apparently effortless, simple, matter-of-fact, as perha⟨
it was to Chardin. Whatever he elected to utilize for subject matt⟨
the most haphazard objects that chanced to fall under his scruti⟨
invariably revealed themselves to be consummative constituents of
perfect architectural abstraction. No previous arrangement, no bar⟨
imposition of a facilitating design, and no conscious striving to con⟨
the benefits of the artist's ingenuity, discretion or "good taste," mar t
self-reliant infallibility of his intuition. By the tens and hundreds
thousands, other painters have stood before similar subject matter a⟨
painted no more than in their blindness they have seen or in th⟨
ingenuousness invented. The insight of a Chardin is so utterly an aff⟨
of nuance that, to this day, only the so-called initiates are able to dete⟨
the immensity of difference between the beauty of his genius and t⟨
insignificance of the others. Indeed, it frequently happens that ma⟨
a suave and highly polished tour de force from the brushes of skillf⟨
but uninspired craftsmen is mistaken for a work of superior merit a⟨
distinction.

Chardin saw the immaculate grace of ultimate form by his sensitivi⟨
to the flawless continuity in which the revelatory light and sha⟨
wrapped it. Whether it might have been an overturned goblet wi⟨
wine spilling from it, or some musical instruments and manuscri⟨
lying in disorder on some dusty table, or an angelic mother with ⟨
angelic child would have made no difference to the perceptiveness
a Chardin, who caught the same message from anything that spo⟨
to his eyes. It was not the objects or the nature of the objects th⟨

red his love, though indeed they may have in other phases and
ects of his human make-up; it was their transcendental consonance.
every instant of beholding, whatever he happened to see must have
illed him, in eternally new combinations of disclosure, with the
ne timeless, beautiful truth. He shows it to us over and over again.
d one of the proofs of the timeless instantaneity of what we call
transcendental is in the fact that, however often we are treated to
elations of this same beauty, we are enraptured at each revealment
h an undiminished felicity as of a first and endless impact.

It should be gathered from this explanation of how highly integrated
painting must be that it cannot rightly be enjoyed for any isolated
tures that may seem pleasing. One often hears expressions of approval
ected at specific details of a picture, a graceful line, an eloquent
ntour, a lovely color, a sweet appearance of visage, an expressive
ssage. Unless the grace of these details is as intrinsically interwoven
to the essential indivisibility of the whole as a segment of a perfect
cle is into the entirety, it is meaningless to dwell upon them. A
ntour cannot by itself be beautiful, but must be apprehended in
njunction with those other contours which complement it by com-
eting whatever shape they are delineating. The most fluid and appeal-
gly graceful line of a shoulder may be deprived of its value by a dis-
oportion or disharmony with other parts of the figure. An exquisitely
oportioned hand may be out of drawing with the gesture that it
ould be making to fulfill the plastic attitude of which it should be
integral part. A head of surpassing loveliness may be out of rhythm
ith its torso, or even with the spatial organization of its pictural con-
xt, and thus lose all its functional beauty. A landscape may be filled
ith a thousand and one gracious and skillfully limned elements and yet
main a thoroughly unbeautiful picture. A color blue which on a color
rd might seem entirely charming may be either beautiful or ugly as
functions or fails to function in its pictorial employment.

The sculptor must be particularly aware of this tremendous issue.
he galleries of museums are flooded with sculptured figures exhibiting
olished recordings of human shapes and attitudes, but the great
chievements of modeling are not so frequently to be found as those

of painting. This is probably due to the greater literal tangibility form in three-dimensional actuality. It is so much easier to create image of a figure sculpturally by merely imitating the shape of figure under observation. If the great plastic continuity is not sen by the sculptor, his work can never exceed the bounds of skill imitation. But it is difficult to inject intimations of infinity into finite a medium as stone. To do so requires the very culminant s sitivity to nuance. Every minute facet of modeling must inhere to transcendent grace.

In the next chapter we shall study further some of the ways in wh. a great painter, via the pigments at his disposal, draws us nearer to tranquil immateriality of ultimacy. And we shall be obliged to c tinguish this exalted achievement from other creative processes sor. what more material in quality, which we might call temporal as oppos to supernal. For naturally I do not mean to say that the reach of ev artist attains to the spiritual summit. There are intermediate felicit along the way.

Chapter XIII

HERE AND NOW

〰〰

HE pictures which the greatest number of persons most readily
enjoy are likely to consist of descriptive vivacity. Forcefully
expressed ideas graphically proclaimed give great satisfaction
ause they give picturesque emphasis to aspects of life. Dramatic
tures of oceanic waves, tranquil pictures of seaside enchantment,
·nuously and earnestly painted commentaries of human behavior,
.ement expositions of the extremes of human comedy and tragedy,
·uliarly personal renderings of everyday scenes as well as unusual
·ctacles—all these representations are interesting because they charac-
·ize vividly, and add color to the average view of things. But however
·rmingly, however graphically a picture may describe the appearance
·objects or actions, however lavishly it may depict the charming, the
·cinating or the impressive, it falls short of its highest role until it
·nscends the specific subject matter and describes the universal cur-
·it of meaning that runs like electricity, omnipresent, through all
·tter, through all action.

·Once again it is profitable to have recourse to sculpture for a clearer
·derstanding of just what this implies. If we consider several examples
·sculpture by a genius of modeling such as Renoir, we shall see, even
·re exactly than by his paintings, what this universal current is. We
·ay look at a figure of his in bronze of a young girl standing in a simple,
·iet pose holding an apple in her left hand, gazing at it meditatively.
·'ithout trying to say another thing about it, the earliest thought that
·shes through my own mind whenever I recollect this particular
·onze is that it evokes instantly the quintessence of Renoir's charac-
·ristic achievement of plasticity, as it occurs in his filmiest pastel or
·ncil sketch or etching or painting, from still life to huge composition.
·ut then we may go on to see another bronze, this time let us imagine,

of a figure in full flush of hilarious motion, perhaps a young wom
in the act of flinging a rubber ball into the sky. Then another pi
may present to us the image of a nude figure reclining voluptuou:
and yet another a little child seated on the ground playing with
foot. In all these diverse figures and actions there will remain a ki
of common denominator that identifies them unfailingly as Renoiresq
Now, it is not merely a matter of superficial style, of "handwritin
that creates this atmosphere of Renoir's unique poesy. It is m
specifically his own singular rhythm, which is implicit in all that he s
and, consequently, in all that he performs. We recognize the rhyth
of his perception and creativity, when we are sensitive to it, as definit
as we would the rhythm of his approaching footsteps if he were c
familiar friend, or the sound of his voice. The attitudes or drama
implications of the subjects that he uses, while they provide grou
for stimulating interest and perhaps even provoking a relevant mo
do not confer the ultimate grace which we value in them as singula
Renoir's. For there are countless modelers in the round who can g
us such attitudes and lively actions as these even far more sensationa
proficient in technical effect, just as there are virtuosi who can perfo
miracles of skill that do not lead to beauty. After all, if we were
freeze into momentary fixity a human model of exquisite shape in
pose of utmost gracefulness, we should still have no work of art wh
soever in any significant sense of the term. And yet that is what t
average sculptor tends to do, with the exception that he consciou
tries to improve upon or idealize the traits and proportions of the figu
under observation. The plain fact is that the proportions of the mod
may be relatively fine or relatively far from fine and still be equally a
to the purposes of the sculptor with true insight.

Grace of shape is not essential to grace of form. But study the cc
volutions of such bronzes as Renoir's, see how absolutely every ar
of curvature blends into an uninterrupted harmony with every oth
area, so that the totality of expression seems to simplify itself into o
simple movement or gesture. Whether the mood of the subject
calm or violent, the plastic mood is eternally neutralized at the sta
of its sublimity. That is why I believe it may even be said that t

old dispute between classical and Gothic art must be ultimately
lved in the fact that at their supreme heights of fulfillment both
in to the same levels of spiritual equanimity, the one via its moods
wisdom, the other via its moods of passion and aspiration. In other
ds, once again we find ourselves confronted with the Schopen-
erian *World as Will and Idea.* The Greek temple is a symbol of
stic wisdom; the Gothic cathedral a symbol of the human will in its
ven-longing mood. "Sky-longing" is the term which the Chinese
sts, centuries ago, applied to the appearance of the mountains that
sfied their heaven-reaching instincts.

The great new discovery which we are on the threshold of making
our aesthetics, our science and our metaphysics is that form is not
ee-dimensional, nor even four-dimensional. It is not dimensional at
This is the concept that is so difficult for our minds to grasp because
have become habituated to think in terms of substances, boundaries,
tances. We are still obsessed with our earliest instinct for tangibility,
I when we are asked to think of final reality as being utterly intan-
le, immaterial, we tend to scoff at the whole idea as intellectual
gling, metaphysical theorizing. We do not like to accept the weird
dict that we ourselves are incorporeal any more than that our ter-
trial and ethereal element is. Our nervous system, our "common
se," seems so compellingly to testify to the contrary. We are so
Inerable to all the apparent laws of materiality, so habituated to
cepting physical standards as the inevitable measure of our being
d of our destiny, that the whole concept of spiritualism is relegated
the great majority of mortals to a reserved attitude of distrust and
epticism. The force and temporal appeal of our material illusions
ve such a hold on us that we are reluctant to recognize the testimony
our higher intuition concerning them. Like a child who naturally
ngs to his infantile faith in his own unassailable imperishability
spite all the doubts that creep in with the "disillusioning" evidences
at crowd the experience of his maturing years, we also cling to the
terpretation of nature that seems most comfortably substantial to
. Substantiality and reliability are synonyms in the idiom of our con-
ntional thought.

Among the many reasons for this pertinacity with which we ad
to our corporeal identity is the special enticement of our various l
gers. We are corporeally imbued with deeply seductive appetites w
are the mainspring of our élan, the vanquishers of our originally veg
tive inertia. We are preponderantly absorbed in the business of enjo
the satisfactions of these sensual and sexual cravings, and if even
horizons of our lives hold promise of such gratifications, we are ple
enough with the emotions of anticipation. Most lives are a cons
struggle for these gratifications, however disguised they may be
virtuous façades. When they are not affirmative struggles for gratifica
they are often tragically negative struggles of frustration. In ei
event, human nature is characterized by the profoundest reluctanc
submerge or tamper with these palpitating urgencies. Satisfied or
satisfied, torturing though they may be by the very contradictory
tensity of their voracity and insatiability, these hungers remain prec
to human beings. They are considered by ascetics to be perversion
the soul which the human patient clings to because he does not w
to try the alternative felicity of being rid of them. Hence we fin
great antagonism on the part of many persons, particularly of
extrovert type, to the serenities of spiritual sublimation. And we
great schisms in the world of consecrated artists today; on the one ha
intolerance of any form of expression not directly tangible and soci
relevant; on the other hand, intolerance of soaring generalities
abstractions. But there will be a growing understanding of the feas
middle course, communion with the ultimate entirely via, and in te
of, temporal actualities. And we are already beginning to learn t
even our sensuality is a perfectly integral and healthy element of
spiritual metabolism, when it remains within the proportions of
elemental role and does not spread its exuberance cancerously bey
the bounds of its beneficence. We have nothing to fear from
material environment or from our own corporeality as long as we b
in mind their transiency. We must come to rely less upon the finite a
temporal, more upon the infinite and eternal content of ourselves.

That is why it is so important to distinguish between mere st
telling, even exquisite storytelling, in pictures, and truly signific

mplishment of form. And the difference is sometimes so delicately
atter of nuance that in many instances there is never total agree-
t among connoisseurs as to the aesthetic value of a specific work.
vever, in the instances of supreme accomplishment there is little
n for question. For example, when we compare Leonardo da Vinci's
: Supper with other pictures that have been painted on the same
ect by able painters we are at once overwhelmed by the ineffable
tuality of Leonardo's genius. Contrast the static organization of
landaio's fresco to the current of plastic emotion that rushes like
usical wind through da Vinci's version. Admire though we may
decorative splendor and superior technique of Ghirlandaio's impres-
mural, the Leonardo is caught up in the stirring serpentine line of
vement that Leonardo spoke of as the inherent expression of each
viduality and of all things. But far beyond what he achieved in his
v disintegrating Last Supper, La Gioconda sits in majestically supernal
lence of what can be done by the wisdom, love and graphic genius
in advanced insight. Here for all who are sensitive to the perfectly
crete demonstration of sublime abstraction, is form in its breathing purity. Cathedrals, prayers, all the poetry of humanity at its
t, form the implicit aura of such gentle finality. The perfectly quiet,
n assurance of infinite authority animates the brush of this dis-
angled spirit. Had it been a Christ head, a wave in a wheatfield,
eavenly cloud, the timeless stature of this form would breathe the
ie message. It is a great man's summation of his incontrovertible
turity, the positing of an unquestionable serenity, humanity's intui-
n of its own divinity. Fully entering into the immanence of its con-
uing fulfillment, a susceptible spectator is enveloped in an emotion
t lifts him away from all the impedimenta of life's temporal and
sory perturbations. The awkward puckers and distortions of our
itual misinterpretation of time and space become resolved into a
se of an all-inclusive Now. There is the feeling of a miraculous
akening from a life-dream of turmoil, an aesthetic deliverance out of
htmare tentativeness into final integration. The here-and-now quality
La Gioconda and other works of art of similar virtue, if once, then
all time, dissolves the tortuous fabric of our immature, mistaken

concepts of material dimension. He who understands Leonardo's fo
is an untroubled soul.

I accent the quality of what I have called here and now. By
spontaneous grace with which every passage of light into darkne
darkness into light, and every line and plane seem all at once to f
so immaculately into the timeless revealment of Mona Lisa, the mi
of the beholder is absorbed and released into an empathic identificati
with Leonardo's vision. He is being taught the further possibilities
how his eyes can function in their environment, just as he might
taught how to swim. After all, every normal human body has
capacity for swimming, but is under the necessity of being acclima
to the special nature of water as an element in which to function.
too, human sight can be educated toward insight. A great sense
nearness, physical and spiritual, is aroused by the structure of t
picture in such a way that one feels nothing intervening between
and himself. In other words, one feels as vis-à-vis with it as though o
were Leonardo himself. All the tactile qualities are so heightened th
one's natural sensations are raised to a higher intensity than they wou
enjoy normally. The ordinary experience of seeing a woman, howev
suggestive of nobility, would not reach the pitch that Leonardo's tact
enhancement effects. This heightening of natural sensation, combin
with the exalted emotion that is inspired by the superlative dignity
inherent in the artist's spatial composing, fills the beholder w
quickened and exhilarated apprehension. What purer religious atm
phere can be created for elevated minds than that suggested by t
beauty of Leonardo's loving insight? In a letter to a friend, Mar
Proust spoke of the fusion of moral emotions with natural sensatio
as the only great poetry.

Hence we arrive at the realization that the great painting extrica
its spectator from his habitual entanglement with the petty confusic
and constraints of day-by-day uneasiness, and precipitates him into
own mood of resolved serenity. The ease and affirmative zest impart
by this persuasive consonance are similar to the salubrious effects
profound religious faith such as have been attested to by the mo
rigorous, scientific medical authorities. The restless, uncertain, troubl

nd breathes a deep and grateful breath of reassurance; it is relieved
its tensions and strengthened by the influential revealment of
;olute form. Absolute form constitutes a negation of all that seems
be chaotic. He who develops his character and sensitivity to the
te that permits him to see it dwells forevermore in its radiant
neficence. For its nature is that of the Deity in whom we have
rsonalized its attributes. To have looked upon it is to have been
se to Him. For surely He has chosen form as the nearest manifesta-
n of Himself to mortal sense. To mortal sense, I say, because it would
a presumption to ignore other avenues of intuitional approach.

The profound artist is aware of the sublime areas that he is probing,
d that is why his task is always so anguishingly exacting. Nothing
s than the most formidable exertions of his heart and soul can suffice
realize even the most fragile intimations of the perfection that he
ises. This will explain the almost universal plaint of creative per-
nalities, that the initial conceptions, the "inspirations," are mysteri-
sly effortless compared to the excruciatingly urgent labor of con-
mmating them. How many of us are filled with the occasional excite-
nts of half-sensed ultimacies, which at last are illumined for us by
e further powers of those geniuses who are able to confront us with
;ible translations and concretions of our own fugitive intuitions. We
l our inarticulate selves to be somewhat fulfilled by their enunciation.
deed, if those shortsighted individuals who consider fine arts to be
imarily an embellishment were to have a full imagination of what
e would be without the arts, they would have a colossal shock. It
not at all a question of how much John Doe personally may profit
m direct contact with the arts; the momentous issue is what John
oe would be in a world bereft of them. It is now a truism that a
ltural élite is an outmoded snobbism. We are learning by the most
igic lessons that a successful culture must be a universal culture. It
high time that we reawaken ourselves to one of our most neglected
atitudes—that the inspiration of our highest moments be the law
our daily lives.

One of the tragic lessons indicating the need for a more universal
lture came with the outbreak of the first World War. Thoughtful

and spiritually alert minds were dismayed at this twentieth cent
debacle, so incontrovertibly a proof that the dignity and value of
human individual was still submerged by his failure to surmount
desolating tidal waves of mass fears, cupidities and deceptions. H
resolutions were born during that calamitous period. They were ba
on recognition of failure in spiritual intercommunication, and of
fratricidal consequences. In 1918, Ordway Tead wrote a vigorous p
which gives promise of eliciting a more understanding response at
end of our current conflict than it did at the time of temporary cessat
of hostilities in the year of its writing. It was somewhat ahead of
time in the sense that mankind had not yet purged itself thoroughly
its martyrdom, and still had ahead of it the terminal convulsions
political and social folly. In *The People's Part in Peace*, he wro
"The new world, the world of the next generation, is unmistaka
destined to swing about a new center—the human individual. A
our discovery—or more accurately our rediscovery—of the supre
value of the individual becomes the criterion in the light of wh
we judge institutions and ideas. We have set up an ethical touchsto
which puts the thwarting absolutes out of business, which makes v
for a new evaluation of human affairs. Let there be no misundersta
ing, this is no recrudescence of 'individualism.' This is no effort to
up again an old utilitarianism or hedonism. It is rather the effort
make plain this truth: that the life of the community—interdepend
as it manifestly is with the life of each individual in it—gets its ju
fication and must derive its standards of value from the fact of
ministration to the body, mind, and spirit of every single individ
who is born into it. There is no value, there is no socially justifia
procedure which runs counter to the fostering of personality, to
growth of free, happy, disciplined individuals." And apropos the d
solitudes to which so many individuals are confined: "The provinciali
of presumably intelligent people is still appalling; but it is accep
complacently because we have never set out to teach our children t
interest, joy, and spiritual expansion made possible by a knowledge
the arts, literatures, philosophies, and religions of the world."

As the endeavor of painters approached modern times, the insti

pure form became more and more conscious and deliberate. It is
t the function of this study to embark upon a critical evaluation of
the different schools and individuals which comprise the develop-
nt of art through the centuries. Excellent texts are available tracing
: movements and countermovements of aesthetic progression, and
: manifold influences that tend to shape the character of creative
ort. And it is important for a thoughtful person who is seeking to
rify his understanding of all art to read such books, in order to have
owledge of what the various contemporary artists are trying to do,
d why. Because, at the present time, the art of painting has arrived
a phase of divided beliefs and directions, which are the natural con-
quences of a long evolutionary process not only aesthetic but scientific,
ychological, metaphysical and political. The serious student should
himself to perceive what has happened along the way marked by
ch milestones as Masaccio, Poussin, Goya, Daumier, Corot, Courbet,
zanne, Monet, Picasso until we arrive at the current school of non-
jectivism. These names I mention not precisely because of their
ture as creative artists, but rather as certain key forces (of which, of
urse, there are many others) that represent new or renewed approaches
the eternal quest of the plastic creator. While it still remains true
at some of the most exquisitely endowed artists are not necessarily
eat innovators at all, nevertheless we do have at certain propitious
oments men who are acutely sensitive to fresh possibilities arising out
the special characteristics of their age.

Even in England the nineteenth century brought forth several painters
a more revolutionary trend than had ever before come out of that
nd, where painting had never been a prime outlet for English lyrical
nius. Turner and Constable particularly had a great influence upon
e evolution of modern art. Delacroix, Géricault, Corot, and other
ogressive Frenchmen were extremely sensitive to their fresh vision,
d the later Impressionists owed much to Constable's vigorous inno-
tion in the breaking up of color into juxtaposed touches of hue.
aumier made a formidable stride ahead in his masterful elimination
detail, to the enhancement of his supremely forceful sense of move-
ent. Not since Michelangelo, and then Rembrandt, had a painter

made such audacious simplifications in order successfully to increa
the dynamism of his concepts. Cézanne went further in his zeal
eliminate everything of superficial character that stood in the way
penetrating to pure form. Here we have the beginning of a recourse
frank abstraction, but only a beginning, because Cézanne was st
enamored of nature as it presented itself to his eyes, and he found hi
self able to perceive great abstract rhythms via the concrete experien
of his vision. It is only as we get into the twentieth century that Picas
and countless others lose confidence in the perceptible outer world
a medium of spiritual experience, and resort as completely as possib
to imaginative invention of abstraction. This is indeed a highly cereb
state of affairs; intellectuality is taking a strong hold upon large numb
of artists whose greatest determination is to break away from all co
nection with past performance in order to dissolve completely wh
they call the camera approach to graphic expression. So great is th
distrust of all visual actuality that their major premise consists of
insistence that no contemporary art can be significant unless it
entirely nonobjective. Representations of recognizable aspects of natu
become taboo. "Through art we express our conception of what natu
is not," writes Picasso.

At the end of the first World War a movement of antirational
increased its momentum out of emotions of indignation and desperatic
at the chaotic state of human conscience and relationship. Known fina
as the Dada movement, its aim was a complete subversion of tradition
values, based on a limitless cynicism and a sensational effort to capitali
upon the perversion of all conventional or familiar modes of expressio
Animated by a deep bitterness, and, of course, as in all movements
radical departure from the strictures of practiced, disciplined techniqu
exploited in many instances by opportunists, Dadaists flung their e
plosive epithets and challenging monstrosities at a bewildered ar
frequently indignant world. The prodigality of their fantasy was n
entirely without interesting results, and as Surrealism arose out of d
carded Dadaism, the various experiments with subconscious manifest
tions, such as psychic automatism, dream representation, etc., produc
works not devoid of psychological and aesthetic significance. If o

re to make a serious study of some of these nonobjective and fan-
tic productions, from schools such as those of Dadaism, Expressionism,
erzism, Vorticism, Futurism, Suprematism, Rayonism, Symbolism,
taphysical Painting, Neoplasticism, Synthetism, Minimalism, ad in-
itum, one would come to some profitable conclusions.

First of all, it is clear that these artists have rejected what we com-
nly call reality as a model from which to derive, or at least in which
observe, essential truths and beauty. They are convinced that the sub-
nscious mind of man is the only legitimate source of creative inspira-
n. "My painting," says Miro, "is always conceived in a state of hal-
ination created by a shock either subjective or objective, for which I
utterly irresponsible. . . . As to my means of expression, I strive to
ain more than ever the maximum of clarity, power, and plastic drive,
t to create a physical reaction, then to reach the soul." We must
te, before all else, the striking similarity of such a statement to those
literary and philosophical personalities as outlined in Chapter Seven.
is is a highly intellectual form of intuition, despite many violent
otional trappings. If its specific intellectualism is not apparent, it
comes so when you compare it to the thought processes as expressed
almost all painters antedating this particular era. Practically none of
em was so primarily preoccupied with his inner vision. Blake was one
the few who anticipated anything like Salvador Dali's "hand-painted
eam photographs."

Georges Hugnet, a Surrealist writer who describes Surrealism in a
lletin of the Museum of Modern Art, quotes Max Ernst as follows:
he investigations into the mechanism of inspiration which have been
dently pursued by the Surrealists, lead them to the discovery of certain
chniques, poetic in essence, and devised to remove the work of art
m the sway of the so-called conscious faculties. These techniques,
ich cast a spell over reason, over taste and the conscious will, have
ade possible a vigorous application of Surrealist principles to drawing,
painting and even, to an extent, to photography. These processes,
me of which were employed before the advent of Surrealism, are now
odified and systematized by Surrealism, making it possible for certain
en to represent on paper or on canvas the dumbfounding photograph

of their thoughts and of their desires. . . . Surrealism, in turning to
turvy the appearances and relationships of 'realities,' has been able
hasten, with a smile on its lips, the general crisis of consciousness wh
must perforce take place in our time." André Breton has this to s
"The narrow concept of imitation [sic] as the goal of art is at the sou
of the serious misunderstanding which we see perpetuated even in
own time. Basing their work on the belief that man is capable only
reproducing more or less happily the superficial image of that wh
moves him, painters have shown themselves much too conventional
the choice of their subjects. Their mistake was to suppose that
subject could be taken only from the external world at all. It is t
that human sensibility can give to the most ordinary object an un
pected distinction; but the magic power of the imagination is put
very feeble use indeed if it serves merely to preserve or reinforce t
which already exists. That is an inexcusable abdication. It is impossil
in the present state of modern thought, when the exterior world appe
more and more suspect, to agree any longer to such a sacrifice. T
work of art, if it is to assist in that absolute revision of values, up
which we all agree, must base itself upon a purely subjective inspirati
or it will cease to exist." Hugnet concludes: "To plumb the myst
of man too many roads have been neglected. Man is what he has be
made. It is important to reveal to him that which hides him from hi
self. With Surrealism all poetic and pictorial manifestations are situat
on the level of life and life on the level of dreams. In the night
which we live, in the carefully preserved obscurity which prevents m
from rebelling, a beam from a lighthouse sweeps in a circular path o
the human and extra-human horizon: it is the light of Surrealism."

Transubstantiation of values, shades of Nietzsche! Here indeed i
metaphysical aesthetic too; the world of twentieth century physics, w
all its reversals of ancient cause and effect theory, and its contradictic
of our orthodox notions of time and space, is of course a world
startlingly experimental aesthetics. A logic that had insisted for thousan
of years upon a rationality based on observation of all natural manifes
tion as specific effects of specific causations suddenly seems to discov
by its own scientific investigation that ultimate being is immaterial ar

st bewildering of all, entirely free of what we had hitherto deemed
iversal laws of nature. The atom has been reduced to elements of
rgy that behave according to no perceptible patterns or laws other
n their own spontaneous, wavelike, explosive free will. And we are
thermore under the new impression that what seems to be movement
nature is not movement at all. What we had formerly called common
se turns out to be nonsense in many instances. All of this fascinating
v physics, combined with the beginnings of a new science whereby
human mind attempts to examine its own workings and to penetrate
veils in which for millenniums it has shrouded its own deepest
esses, naturally combine to produce new phases of all the art mediums.
wever, while the spontaneous outpourings of these experimental
rks are psychologically revelatory and hence valuable, specifically
ause of their pure spontaneity in the instances where it is genuine,
l we must exercise judgment, by the very intuition which these works
n to fulfill, as to how much they accomplish in terms of beauty and
w much in terms of protest against banality, shattering of outmoded
bboleths.

As this latest aesthetic settles into the rhythm of its function in art
olution, we shall understand more clearly just what its virtues will
ve been, and there will be less ground for the violence of feeling
aracteristic of its protagonists and antagonists. It behooves us to
member that in the century just past an aesthetic of realism rather than
rrealism seemed to create as wild a ferment as today's most extravagant
straction. When Courbet shocked the romanticists and classicists
d general run of conservatives simply by freshening up his approach
it, there was as much of a furor as the twentieth century has brought
th in its turn. Courbet describes his realism in these terms: "I stupefy
e entire world. I have triumphed over not only the ancients but the
derns. . . . I have thrown consternation into the world of art."

Nowadays our susceptibility to consternation is dwindling. It is not
much that we have reached a point of saturation as that we have
t a great deal of what used to be deep spiritual certitude about things.
e are in a rather advanced stage of a materialistic era, which P. A.
rokin has called an age of incertitude, and our confusion is such that

all our values are tenuous and constantly challengeable. Naturally tl
weighs heavily on the creative impulse of man. It results in an atm
phere of insecurity, fear and transience. We have lost the great adva
tages of the kinds of fervency that characterized human spirit during
less materialistic phases. The political catastrophe to which our cc
fusion has led us is as severe a sign of our desperate condition as we c
stand at this time. We shall not be able to re-create ourselves by ov
hauling our ethical concepts and arrangements. We cannot hope
make a beautiful world by changing a few rules of behavior, any mc
than we can paint beautiful pictures according to specific direction
Contrary to the bland optimism of those who have faith in the essent
soundness of contemporary values, there will have to be a tremendo
resurgence of the will to better ourselves, to purge ourselves of o
petty and pusillanimous vices which lead over and over again so i
evitably to tragic disaster. This is the only hope of any happy desti
for mankind. And we can see by the gyrations of contemporary a
that they are for the most part caught up in the little whirling vortic
of our troubled current, when they are not languishing at the outlyi
edges of stagnant pools. When the arts and sciences evolve into
radiant new dawn of spiritual revelation we shall know ourselves to 1
on the path of higher civilization, leading toward such happiness as
now impossible. When Swedenborg the realistic engineer turned in
Swedenborg the mystic, he became symbolic of the problem that co
fronts us. A healthy future lies in the hands, the hearts and the minds
those who once again, like St. Francis of Assisi, shall find within tl
breadth of contemporary knowledge a wisdom founded on inner mea
ings and a love not of things but of being. Modern man is indeed
search of his soul, as Carl Jung has put it, and the growing psych
neuroses which threaten our stability and sound existence have bee
defined as the "suffering of human beings who have not discovere
what life means for them."

Who can deny that our world is floundering in deep neurosis toda
with neurosis defined as "an inner cleavage . . . the state of being
war with oneself"? We are most terribly torn between our unprecedente
wealth of command over matter and our poverty of wisdom to prof

by such wealth. We know ourselves to be threatened with spiritual bankruptcy. Rich with strength, but destitute of grace, our life movement becomes a fierce struggle when it should be an inspired dance. Many have come to think that our scientific rationality no longer allows the enlightened psyche to have any faith in religious dogma. Jung has found that among the thousands of confused souls who have sought his medical help in their psychic dilemmas, only a small percentage are religious persons. Even a somewhat blind faith seems to protect the psyche from breaking under the strains of modern tension. A real revival of intuitional love, not in the old forms that inspire neither confidence nor hope in enlightened modern minds, but in a framework of vivid contemporary reality, would bless our world with new and illuminating faith—faith in ourselves, in each other, in a continuing felicity. It would enable us to curb our sensate gratifications in favor of a more pervasive happiness, and to temper the passions of our lusts by the grace of our love. A human being who has not discovered what life means for him, or a human being who feels that he has discovered that life does not mean enough to him, is of course a spiritual invalid. That is why so many dissatisfied mortals consciously and unconsciously turn to the arts and artists, not for consolation, but for a quickening of their spirits, a revival of their faith in values, a breath of their afflatus. For the real artist is what Nietzsche used to call a Yea-saying individual, a man in the full flush of divine affirmation. The artist sees beyond things, loves beyond things, and finds his enduring happiness in expressing and communicating his insight. The artist who labors not for vanity, not for reward, but out of the impelling fervor of his love for the beautiful glory of every instant of living, is a tonic and a savior. He has cast aside all else to follow his Love. Those who labor only for their food and raiment, those who contend all their lives for comforts, vanities and little pleasures, and are consequently depressed by the frustrations that are the inevitable accompaniment of such competitive objectives, find a sustaining satisfaction in the example of him who has the good fortune to love what he does because he courageously does what he loves, rather than dissipate the miraculous gift of living by succumbing to standard criteria of success. In the enlightened activity

of the artist, the layman frequently sees fulfilled the man he wants t
be, and yet does not truly want to be because he does not want to tak
the risks and make the sacrifices required. We love our Thoreau, ou
Emerson, our Whitman for their fortifying messages of self-reliance
of brave resolution and adherence to lofty objectives; we make littl
spurts of tentative self-assertion while injected with the spirit of thei
ardor. But the sustained integrity demanded by the arts is more readi
admired than emulated, and the majority stimulates itself with rese
vations. How many Christian mortals would accept the role of th
Savior were the divine privilege vouchsafed them? No; man is made t
give and to receive. It is therefore wise and in the province of eac
of us to fit ourselves to give the best of which we are capable, but n
less vitally to receive the best that, by the grace of church, science
philosophy or art, is given us.

Albert Einstein puts it this way: "I agree with Schopenhauer tha
one of the most powerful motives that attract people to science an
art is the longing to escape from everyday life, with its painful coarse
ness and unconsoling barrenness, and to break the fetters of their ow
ever-changing desires. Man seeks to form a simplified, synoptical view
of the world conformable to his own nature, to overcome the worl
by replacing it with his picture. The painter, the poet, the philosophe
the scientist, each does this in his own way. He transfers the cente
of his emotional life to this picture, to find a surer haven of peace tha
the sphere of his turbulent personal experience offers." I should want t
quarrel a bit with the phrase "escape from everyday life," and wonde
whether we might not substitute "amplify and exalt."

Bertrand Russell, and countless others down the corridors of history
feels that "it is preoccupation with possessions [security?] more tha
anything else that prevents men from living freely and nobly." On
thing is certain, I believe. We must pound away at the importance c
living soundly each present moment. Too much of human folly is th
result of fears, anxieties, lustings projected into the future. Most persons
efforts are siphoned off for the purpose of shaping the course of futur
events. It is even instilled into us as the higher wisdom constantly t
take thought for the morrow. We must establish a sounder and mor

ourageous principle governing our division of effort between the full esthetic good of the present and the expediency that governs so much f human conduct. Havelock Ellis comes to the unreserved conclusion nat "the highest attitude attainable by man towards life is that of esthetic contemplation." We must purify ourselves of our utilitarianism, nd recognize the sanctity of man with all the essential obligations hat his sanctity imposes. Today the arts seem more than ever to bear reat promise and the high guarantee of man's faith and loving endeavor nd achievement. That is why when a great or, let us say simply, a ood picture reveals instantaneously a human being's passionate recogni- ion of the beatitude inherent in the here and now of being, via any nd every most casual aspect, it is Braille for the spiritually blind.

Chapter XIV

THE FALLACY OF ESOTERIC ART

PERHAPS great works of art are less important in themselves as entities of beauty than for the value they have as "eye openers," as conditioners of the psyche that takes lessons from them. It is easy to understand the pleasure that a possessor of a picture or a collector of pictures may gather from such possession and constant experience of enjoyment. But the true artist himself furnishes a sounder indication of the value of an accomplished work; the continuing quality of his being, of his growth, keeps him in a sustained ferment so that each concept and realized picture is in reality not a separately achieved and satisfying entity, but rather an indivisible attribute of a flowering process. There are and have been, for instance, many men of wisdom who have spoken many truths, expressed many beautiful and noble sentiments. And while their contributions excite our admiration and are stimulating in detail, it is the totality of each man's character formed in the accumulation of his creative process, that inspires us When the name of Bach is mentioned a whole atmosphere of spiritual creativity is evoked. True, it is separate works which comprise the totality of our impression, but once they have been heard, even the most fragmentary phrase of his music is enough to launch us into the empyrean of his exuberant and devotional genius. The works themselves once experienced, both by creator and by creative appreciator, are, in the long continuum of the evolutionary current, somewhat like the consummated gestures of a great dancer, never again quite so vital when reviewed as in the grace of their original becoming. It would be fool hardy to deny the pleasures enjoyed by the re-experiencing of great works; but pleasure is small change in the fortunes of the human soul. Happiness is an eternally spontaneous state of being, singing an eternally new music because every instant of truly experienced being

194

eternally new. Nor, when we say "new," must we make the common error of confusing voluntarily contrived novelty with the natural and inevitable freshness of that which has not yet been. If Bach were alive today, his spirit would be nurtured by his past creation, but he would be writing another music now. And it would be another music not because he would make any conscious effort to alter the form and content of the early Bach, but only because his music would be the outpouring of his spontaneous, contemporary insight, which could not possibly be identical with the intuitions of centuries past.

It is a perplexing question, this matter of the "value quotient," to invent a term momentarily, of works of art that have been created and assimilated. Moreno's concept of what he calls the "cultural conserve" is shocking to the art lover who feels convinced that he is responding with maximum appreciation to works with which he is deeply and fondly familiar. But if we study our reactions profoundly we discover some startling facts. I believe it is safe to declare that in a truly adequate appreciation of any work of art the response process may best be described by a rising curve of intellectual and emotional assimilative capacity, reaching a peak level at the high point of total grasp, and then falling away somewhat to what we might call a level of habituation. Only the most creative minds are able to sustain a perpetual spontaneity of reaction over unlimited repetitions of the same works. Each renewal of acquaintance with a great work serves as a refresher and a reminder of that summit of emotional response to which one mounted at the moment of full revealment. Naturally, the more perfect the work, the more it is capable of maintaining a constantly renewed sense of here-and-now immediacy, which releases the spectator from that fallacy of human intelligence which is its most pernicious obstacle to expansion, that is, its habit of separating itself from, and breaking up into factitious particles, the continuum of ultimate grace. It is that marvelous quality of immediacy, of intensely urgent immediacy, which projects the Bible so powerfully and enduringly over the centuries, and maintains its potency in the hearts and minds of men. From its majestic pages speaks the authentic voice of timeless conscience. Even the naïveté that so inevitably characterizes some of the mental processes of that distant age

fails to destroy the impact of its essential meanings upon the contem
porary mind. Once again we see that it is the spirit rather than th
substance which lives perpetually. The great magic of Homer seizes th
sensitive imagination of today over a span of several millenniums by
similar integrity of spirit. The maximum creativity of any epoch i
likely to perpetuate itself over the entire evolutionary process of unfold
ing, because at the height of its highest inspiration the human spiri
transcends the barriers of illusory temporality.

In his *A.B.C. of Aesthetics*, Leo Stein comes to a similar conclusion i
respect to the responsive process: "A permanently satisfactory aestheti
object, for a fully competent observer, cannot exist, because it is alway
an attempt to give in arrested form the quality of movement. In ele
mentary symmetry the movement is at a minimum, and the success i
expression is at a maximum. But with increasing richness of the move
ment, there is increase of fallibility. The movement can only be sug
gested, it cannot be rendered, and it tends to go dead when it is looke
at too long. Therefore, a work of art is like a sunset, in that the perfec
moment for leaving it is when its splendor is at the fullest. Even as th
colors of the sunset fade to ash, so the vitality of rhythms dies out in th
perceived fixity of compositional elements, which can no longer b
brought to vibrant coherency but fall into a group of inventorial objects
Ichabod, Ichabod, the glory is departed! So has many a masterpiec
gone its way to the ash heap. Some have returned in answer to a resur
rected sensibility, but many have remained on the ash heap forever."

A most pressing problem of today, which has been a pressing problem
at all times, is pushing its way into the awareness of more serious peopl
than perhaps at any other time in human history. We want to know
whether the finest products of human genius have to remain beyond th
understanding, appreciation and love of the great majority of people, o
whether something can be done to heighten the sensibilities of hu
manity-at-large so that a fusion between its creative and receptive power
may be effected at a high level on the broadest possible basis. We wan
to know whether we may ever attain to that happy state wherein it wil
be natural for the majority to function on an aesthetic plane that wil
remove "art" as a separate concept from our idiom. Shall we ever arriv

t that thrilling and conceivable stage of development when most per-
ons will be equipped and inwardly driven to communicate to one
nother their highest and subtlest inherencies rather than the lowest
ommon denominator of their materialistic habituation? Will the artist
ver speak to everyone instead of to a few who are almost artists them-
elves? Or do we resign ourselves to the negative notion that we are being
nuch too precious about this entire business, that "beauty" is there for
hose who happen to see it and get excited about it, and that life can
e lived satisfactorily by a great majority who feel far from "starved" on
ess spiritual diet? Within any sensitive individual this baffling question
ages from time to time.

In the creative temperament it takes a different form. What man, bent
n the imperious mission of fulfilling himself at his highest potential
evel, has not at one time or another wondered whether he was not
naking a "great deal of fuss about nothing"? The artist who finds at
very instant so much that is excitingly and absorbingly beautiful has
noments when he wonders why it is not enough to sit back and enjoy
is experience. What is this obsessive urge to perform, to register one's
cstasy, to communicate one's fervor? Is there not a great element of
anity that drives a sensitive person to exhibit and spread the influence
f his genius? Would it not perhaps be a higher function of choice spirits
o dwell quietly in the felicity of their special awareness, merely spread-
ng the warm glow of their incandescence within the orbit of their
riends? The answer is eternally No. It is only the vegetative, the
ethargic side of our natures that tempts us from time to time to yield
o these sluggish tendencies. The more positive side of our nature is more
ften characterized by an instinct toward the most dynamic possible
unctioning of our energies. We feel the individual to be identified with
he group, and thus to incur a perpetual obligation to fulfill himself at
is highest potential level, as his minute yet essential role in the universal
nd creative unfolding. We know that the whole virtue of a society is
letermined by the predominating influence of its most excellent mem-
ers. And while all our creative leaders may not exercise their talents
rom the impetus of a social conscience, nevertheless, they are imbued
with what is frequently called an instinct to express themselves. This

"instinct" serves its purpose just as certainly as the song and plumage of the male bird, which announces itself to females in the offing. These so-called motive impulses are susceptible to a great deal of psychological analysis.

An important question is just how much the total personality of a creative human being is benefited by the activation of his potentialities. It is easy to say that such a person "feels better" when he has satisfied an urge to express whatever his exuberant sensitivities conjure up. But is there not also a stage of wisdom, of serenity of spirit, that may no longer require any articulation and yet constitutes a sufficient creativity within the self? Is the Oriental concept of Nirvana so foreign to the Occidental temperament as to be no challenge at all to our complacency in respect to our aesthetic assumptions? Shall we not say that there are meditative areas in which the human spirit may profitably and virtuously dwell and flower without taking any other than a devotional attitude?

Here, indeed, is where religion in the purest quality of its intuitional insight may claim a superiority to all but the most immaculate aesthetic achievement. There are saints who in their simplicity transcend all need for our world of sensuous beauty, of aesthetic sensibility, of intellectual aspiration. There are saints who make of themselves what artists make of rhetoric, clay and pictures. The artist must be something of a saint before he can produce the noblest specimens of human insight.

From studies of the evolution of animal and cellular life we learn that co-operation is the ultimate necessity for survival of higher forms. Many animals are shown from experiment to grow faster in moderately crowded conditions than in relative or complete isolation. Hence we conclude that systematically co-operative aggregations are most highly productive. The energies of the best types serve to rouse those of less élan to a quickened effort. So awakened are we to the desperate need for the best spirits in our world society to spread the light of their vision as swiftly and as persuasively over the wide masses of their less awakened, less enlightened brothers as possible, that we are beginning to lose patience with forms of art and science which do not draw their inspiration at least partially from a recognition of this need. Of course, we know that the motivations of the best minds in any age correspond to and spring out of

special conditions pertaining to that age; and it is understandable
efore to find today's most sensitive human beings consumed with a
1ary passion to do something about the appalling infirmity of spirit
mind that characterizes a world submerged in disaster originating
of that infirmity. It is due to the sad depletion of moral fiber in a
ety sinking deeper and deeper into the grip of a materialistic civiliza-
, that we find ourselves confronted with a prospect of catastrophe if
do not bend every effort to avert it. We can no longer consider our
as anything less than essential aids in the emergent struggle for
th-while survival. Just as in the actual emergency of war the most
rse talents all turn their energies toward successful prosecution of
battle, so in the anguishing conditions of a seemingly tottering
lization must every highest effort go into the final hope, the quicken-
of the general human will power toward grace and away from
tiality. No minor efforts of little fanciers in the fine arts are going to
m of much consequence in times like these. An artist with a manly
science today feels impelled to stretch the sinew of his hungering
tition to the breaking point, or else to sacrifice the aesthetic momen-
ly in favor of the moral. We seem, indeed, to have reached a point in
materialistic era where the ultimate values seem overrefined and too
fied to the great majority of people. The great truths and the beauty
the great truths must be brought within the horizons and the reach
multitudes, not of aesthetes and scholars.

Yet this must be done without attenuating the quality of the best
ducts of our available genius. We certainly cannot afford to dilute
essence of our loftiest intuition in order to bring it down to the
prehension of wider audiences. The alternative is the only healthy
look. We must elevate the greatest possible numbers by sound and
erous educational process to a familiarity with these higher languages.
ere was, after all, a recent time when only an "elect" minority were
possession of the gifts of reading and writing. Now it is time for the
e arts to be brought closer to the lives of all people. These arts too
be acquired by the many. We must not allow ourselves to fall under
misapprehension that the fine arts must always remain restricted to
h as are born with special sensibilities and equipment. A proper

training would make it feasible to prepare all children from the instar of birth for a far richer capacity in these intuitional fields than is no dreamed of. There is no question as to the reason for the prevailir inadequacy of the average person to a rich appreciation of the arts. It far less a problem of lack of sensitivity, far more a problem of unde developed sensitivity. So great has the stress been upon the so-calle practical arts and sciences that the aesthetic, the spiritual side of o natures, has been allowed to develop or not to develop in the most ha hazard way. I do not mean to imply that we can set up systems of schoc ing that will automatically guarantee generations of creative artists. B we can create atmospheres of stimulation, by setting children at the most formative periods in close and ready familiarity with these high languages, so that they are not left for discovery and special study in tl curriculum of colleges, when it is already late for the establishment real appreciation. We can produce generations of responsive person and out of greater responsiveness will certainly come greater creativit

We must not let the fine arts remain over the edge of the averag man's horizon until he decides to investigate, to acquaint himself wit them, to "cultivate" himself. They must become one of his nativ mediums, just as literature is gradually becoming so. It is much clear to us now than it has ever been before that the major part of mar capacity is determined during the earliest years of his life, during infan and early childhood. It is then that his perceptive faculties, his imagin tive faculties, his tendencies toward disciplined and sustained effort opposed to the desultory and superficial are basically formed. That when the greatest shaping of our destinies occurs. All the guidance ar disciplinary measures and education of ensuing years, valuable thoug they be, are of secondary influence as compared to the subtle molding those first years. And such is the potential sensitivity of infancy th every nuance of the atmosphere to which it is subjected will contribu toward determining the nature of the child's malleable character, ter perament, disposition. These are the breeding years of the healt potentialities and of the neuroses. Because of our knowledge of the facts, much is already being done to improve the techniques of chi care and training. Much remains to be done.

Of course, the constant exercise of our mental and spiritual energies is essential condition to a rise of the level of our sensibilities. And a it part of the atmosphere of contemporary civilization deters us from necessary condition of real culture. We are surrounded by temptations to easy amusement which plunge us into the shameful sort of cosis which is the inevitable fate of those who succumb to the contemporary floods of automatic entertainment. A generation brought up the factitious excitement of motion-picture and radio techniques will readily turn toward the subtle world of fine arts for either its pleasures or its profit. The transition is too demanding. The art of the cinema requires no effort of its audience. It is simply an intensification of life's most elementary emotions, and even when it rises to an occasional level adult entertainment it rarely serves to awaken human intuition or stimulate human reason. These modern mediums of entertainment do supply a constructive need in the community, but we have not yet learned to balance the spiritual and educational diet of growing human beings in a way that will protect them against too much of this sort of thing. Easy entertainment threatens to monopolize the leisure time of the majority of people. This tends to encourage a passivity of temperament, a dullness of wit, a spiritual anemia. It leads toward a culture of mediocrity. It recalls the atmosphere of disintegrating Rome. Only the fanaticism of Christianity saved a culture for the posterity of that era. We shall need a purification of spirit in our own times if we are not to overwhelmed by the material aspects of our modern genius.

Educators are thinking about this problem. They are bending every effort toward the development of well-integrated personalities. Obviously will be a slow process, since so much depends upon the cultivation of good parenthood. The tastes and general character of parents constitute the atmosphere in which the child takes his own form, and the best schooling in the world can be invalidated by negative home influence. The multiplicity of factors determining the character of human beings presents us with a complicated picture, but at least we know what some the essentials to the aesthetic development are. An early environment cultivated taste is of primary importance.

However, my major aim is confined to an assessment of creativity in

the plastic arts. And it requires a different book to outline method
which the aesthetic faculty can be more widely and richly cultiva
But in this second project it would be essential to understand the wl
question of talent, of "special aptitude." It is too widely believed
"art" is primarily a matter of being born with special endowment,
there are multitudes of people born without the ability to "dra
straight line," etc. The fact is otherwise. Experience and observa
bear out this contention as we study children under special envi
mental influences. Sensitivities can be stimulated to further acuter
and the susceptibilities to various art idioms can be definitely canal:
by subjection to the constant influence of personalities accomplishe(
those fields. Parents need not be creative geniuses to raise cultiv:
children. But they must be cultivated persons. And they can be.

"Painting, Poetry and Music are the three Powers in man of conver:
with Paradise which the Flood did not sweep away," according
William Blake. Yet how many of us are left out of the conversai
because we haven't learned the language in which it is carried on. '
problem would be a hopeless one if multitudes of us were born witl»
the capacity to learn these languages, without the potential sensitivit
their nuance. But the plain and happier truth is that we are born v
far richer capacity than we ever utilize, because so much of the pare1
dullness blunts the bright possibilities of the growing child. Someth
happens to most human beings as they "mature" which is tragic. T
lose the qualities of childhood that are most precious, and from gen
tion to generation the vicious circle swirls on at the expense of the l
qualities of naïveté and spontaneity. "Every genius," according to Sc
penhauer, "is a great child; he gazes out at the world as at someth
strange, a spectacle, and therefore with purely objective intere:
Whereas the average person quickly loses all sense of the world's stran
ness, its quiet, perpetual mystery, because he is trained by pract
parents and practical educators to adapt himself to familiar patterns
life, to master the proper techniques for comfortable survival, and her
to have a subjective interest in all aspects of life which determin•
successful course in the competitive struggle with nature and with
fellow men. He comes to the conclusion, which is considered the pi

l conclusion, that "gazing out at the world as at something strange"
:served for children who have not yet reached an age of obligation to
e with and master the "strangeness," and for luxurious moments of
's leisure time, "lest we neglect the 'cultural side.'"

Vordsworth's Ode on Intimations of Immortality swells with a recog-
on of the darkness that descends upon the souls of so many growing
dren. "Heaven lies about us in our infancy! Shades of the prison-
ise begin to close upon the growing Boy . . . At length the Man per-
·es it die away, and fade into the light of common day." The magic
itions of childhood melt away before the imperious process of "grow-
up," when all the grace of spontaneity yields to systematic imitation
he old by the young. The art of manhood and womanhood presents
lf as a formula to which most ambitious youth is keenly attentive.
: kind of self-reliance which permits a youngster to develop more
lusively along the paths of his own innermost will and insight, acting the influence of creative elders and rejecting patterns of con-
tional rigidity, is rare. Indeed, most parents are fearful of the conse-
:nces of such independence of spirit, and generally consider it safer
guide, conduct and mold the growing child into stereotyped con-
nity and security. One of the most persistent questions flung by
ilts at youngsters is "What are you going to be when you are grown
·" The compulsion to direct the new generation into rapid familiarity
h the tried and approved ways of coping with the material trials of
ng and procreating deflects and discourages even the most adventur-
 parent from risking the encouragement of nonconformity to safe
terns of behavior. Furthermore, there is so often the additional mis-
tune of the unfulfilled parent attempting to make more perfect in his
ld the particular type of character that he had aimed toward as his
n unattained goal. Nothing can be more destructive to the creative
intaneity of a growing child than this sort of constant pressure exerted
the well-intentioned parent. One of the most depressing spectacles
it life so frequently offers is that of the unhappy adult who struggles
ring all the decades of his maturity against the subtle, implacable
traints that inhibit his natural expansion, restraints which he does not
ognize as having been imposed upon him by the ardent vanity of a

parent who has sought to re-create himself in the life of his offspr
The stimulating influence of the finest teachers, friends and lofty leac
may fail to break the bonds of such parental power over an individ
For it has been exerted at that vital formative period when, from
conscious to the subconscious, a whole web of inhibitory authority wi
itself around the pliant psyche. Even recognition by the individual v
has been so subjected does not always suffice to clear away the fett
though it is one of the first requisites to undoing the mischief. It is
within the province of our purpose here to go into the psychological a
other forces which combine in numberless ways to deplete the avex
human being of his best energies and freedom of momentum. Suffic
to say at this point that our best thinkers are increasingly aware of
vital problem, to say nothing of the Greek dramatists of more than t
thousand years ago. We are still at the beginning of our effort to
something about it.

Among the tremendous forces at work upon human beings of this
is that of the dominance of reason as the ultimate faculty whereby ju
ments are made and truths established. We are living in what we h
come to call an "age of reason," and even if it were not so predominax
a materialistic age, it would still suffer greatly from the limitations
posed by the intellectual approach to most things. Immanuel Kant w
about as far as human intellect at present can go in an effort to appro
the ultimate truths by means of logical, rational processes of thoug
The structure of his intellectual gesture is superb and beautiful, but
still find ourselves intuitively convinced that many of our deepest qu
tions remain unanswerable by the faculty of reason alone.

Hence the peculiarly acute sense in modern times of a deep need
recourse to the arts. Many a sensitive person is filled with a restlessn
and a growing despair without understanding the deep-seated cause
his unhappiness. There is such a growing split between our skill
manipulating the forces of nature and our failure to make parallel stri
in the shaping of our spiritual destinies. Only twenty years ago
average person's concept of success was that of functioning suitably
a stable economy, to the extent of providing himself and his family w
satisfactorily conspicuous comfort and a secure surplus. Only the dra

ortunes so directly consequent to this shallow philosophy of ma-
lism have served to shake that complacency.

his A.B.C., Leo Stein remarks that "if aesthetics could be recog-
d as the important thing that it would be in a world that refused
ubordinate almost everything to a possessive interest whose mag-
ent consequence is conspicuous expenditure, if pure aesthetics could
a place—there would be little or no difference between knowing and
ying." He comes to the conclusion that the basic value of the aes-
ic experience is its capacity to serve for the unification of the self,
nake knowledge of the self available, and consequently to further its
elopment. Whenever that self gets too far away from its essential
e, which is the urge to find answers to the questions of what and
the self is, and what is its destiny, a profound anxiety sets in. The
lt is that no materialistic age can endure permanently, for whether
ave smooth sailing or rough sailing, invariably the questing self
s ascendancy over the complacent self, if only in the negative shape
he neuroses that form a protective covering around the soul endan-
d by spiritual anemia.

ertainly one does not expect to pluck a great truth here and a great
h there as one picks daisies in a summer meadow. One does not
ect to be on close conversational terms with God at any casual
ment that one may decide that this would be convenient or desirable.
more can one be in communion with any of the best things that life
to offer unless one is in the constant process of qualifying himself
the privilege. At present, however, this process of qualifying is far
m being man's foremost preoccupation. It still remains the special
vince of an all-too-small minority of poets, artists, philosophers. The
at majority of the world's children still feel themselves to be under
necessity of being "realistic" before they dare indulge in the extra
l dangerous luxury of toying with the transcendent. And the multi-
les of realists swiftly lose, from disuse, almost all the sensitive equip-
nt with which they were endowed and which would have enabled
m at least to receive more than the minimum stimulation and
fit from the labors of their more spiritual brothers. Yet it is fantastic
witness the ignorance of many of the world's most energetic and

often useful citizens when it comes to assessing their own compe
sensitivity to the various arts. They are blind to the vast areas of cer
art forms which their perception does not even touch, while yet
think themselves to be in close rapport with them.

Examine, for instance, a little more insistently than is deemed p
by the average amateur, the extent of understanding possessed by
fairly enthusiastic music lover. When one points out to such a person
inability of his mind to envelop a continuity of music sufficientl
apprehend the grace of form as conceived and developed by the c
poser, the usual answer is that one need not be an architect to apprec
a cathedral or a poet to love a poem. The trouble is that people are o
more concerned with the matter of their pride than with the final tr
Nobody could convince me that I am getting more than the merest f
tion of what great music contains when I am listening to it. Both
logic and my intuition assure me that I receive no more than a small
of what Mozart's genius offers me. My logic tells me this by compa
the insight I derive from music with that which I derive from paint
sculpture and literature. Words fail me to describe adequately the q
ties of sound that enchant me, the breathless moments when I fall
the measure of some marvelous part of a great composition, when
an intuitive flashing recognition of the quality of a passage I infer so
thing of the significance of the whole. Yet, with all these delight
the ear and partial delights of the mind, my soul weeps with the
ment of my inadequacy to the full revealment which I sense to lie beh
and within the sounds and silences that are music. Pleasures, yes,
course, there are pleasures to be had in hearing music without full c
prehension. There are pleasures to be had in seeing pictures, watch
dancing, reading, living, with only partial understanding. But th
pleasures do not constitute the main and majestic purpose of revelat
art. While I love the sound of God's voice, my passion is to sense
meaning. I have heard musicians go through fine scores, seen the e
with which they scan and grasp the whole as well as any of its parts.
form of a sonata is as clear to them as a children's melody is to me. I
plain that they are comprehending an entire symphony as spontaneou
as I comprehend a picture. But to me the symphony is a long success

component parts, none of which I am able to relate to any but its
immediate predecessors or followers. I have seen large concert audiences
main almost totally unaware that a pianist has shattered a composition
forgetting large portions of the score. I have seen sensitive and serious
music lovers" not realize that an earlier portion of a composition has
en repeated for them during a hearing of gramophone recordings,
stead of the proper ordering of the records being adhered to. It would
: absurd to say that these people are not enjoying music. The point is
at the supreme function of great art is not to supply enjoyment at all,
y more than the mystic could be said to enjoy a revelation, though he
ight conceivably enjoy the colors or sounds that happen to be mediums
its representation. Here lies some of the explanation of why hordes
semimusical persons adore Wagnerian music, whereas pure Bach,
en unadorned by spurious orchestral transcription or added coloring,
mains relatively "unexciting." The former, regardless of its essential
ntent and form, is expressed in an easily perceptible, sensuous display
highly colored texture. The latter is primarily confined to a realm of
re abstraction, wherein the nuance of inspired form is everything and
sational color practically nonexistent. This is not to say that color is
itself always necessarily formless and insignificant. Debussy alone
uld disprove that.

But until people cease to conceive of the fine arts as an adjunct to
eir way of life, as an ornamentation growing out of leisure time and
rplus energy, the human personality will not be well-integrated. The
ing about the artist himself that seems so enviable to the layman is
: fact that the artist has made the major business of his life the pur-
it of his major interest and satisfaction. This is in direct contrast to
: life program of the layman, whose major occupation has been chosen
imarily as a means of livelihood, and only secondarily as an answer to
ter urges and needs. True, the average person tries to choose a business
profession most suitable to his apparent abilities and temperamental
edilections; but how many people derive the thrilling sense of self-
fillment out of their economic function, comparable to that of the
ist who practices his art? I have seen successful businessmen more
eful over some modest achievement they have attained in an amateur

pursuit of some art form than over the whole triumph of their economi
careers. Were they able to feel assured that a primary pursuit of art woul
net them a scale of pecuniary success and prestige on a par with that o
their practical activities, they might be tempted to give it a greater plac
in their life program. However, since practical work has to be done, an
well done, if laymen and artists are to live, it is obvious that the ide:
aim would be for the two activities to merge. If everyone were somethin
of a creative artist and something of a practical worker, we should hav
a greater social dynamic than we have today. And the language of th
arts would not be confined to aesthetes and specialist practitioners c
the arts. It may be objected that the truly productive artist has no tim
for practical work, and that the hypersensitivity which enables him t
be creative tends to render him less useful in practical matters. This poi
of view seems to me to have grown out of the artificiality of our preser
attitude toward the whole question. I am ready to admit that at presen
it is perfectly true that there is only a small and select audience fc
great truths and great beauty. But I am not ready to admit that th
sorry state of affairs is unalterable. The sooner we emerge from tl
absurd habit of surrounding art and artist with a hushed atmosphere, :
though creative genius were a peculiar deviant from the normal behavic
pattern, meriting special indulgence as though the creative soul sufferc
from a divine malady, the sooner we shall be on our way to a healthi
understanding. Only the neurotic state of our social psyche today driv
the sensitive, creative spirit into protective states of apparently mo
extreme neurosis than the normal. In a different, healthier society, is
not probable that creativity would find a wider, sounder base of oper
tion? With the miracle of life for subject matter, and the miracle of tl
human mind for activating agent, every human being is potentially
poet. Those of us who are not poets are simply retarded.

Chapter XV

YESTERMORROW AND THE MIRACLE
OF THE COMMONPLACE

〰〰〰

WHY do many of us find particular and unusually sustained pleasure in sitting at a seashore, looking hour after hour at the sea and the sky? "I could sit here for a week," has been [sai]d numberless times by many different kinds of people contemplating [the] sea. What is it that reveals itself more clearly and compellingly there, [tha]t keeps renewing its forces of enchantment so that we stay with it [lon]ger and more intensely than we stay with most other aspects of our [en]vironment? We cannot, of course, ignore the tonic stimulation of the [spe]cial air, sunlight, and general quietness which characterize a seashore [in] its moods of serenity. To those who live the greater part of their lives [in] cities and crowded communities, these qualities alone would seem [to] explain much of the special fascination. But those of us who have [real]ly been with the sea and received some of the favors that it extends to [tho]se who love it, know that there is something more, something subtle [an]d yet amazingly widespread in its influence. So much of the beauty [of] things and concepts comprising this sensitive life of ours is dependent on the very qualities of exquisite subtlety that make them inaccessible [to] all but a few who are attuned to them. But here, in the mergent [sp]aces of sky and sea, we have one of the supreme subtleties reaching a [gr]eat many of us, stirring us with a feeling for certain infinitudes which [so]me of us only meet so closely under just such special circumstances. [O]thers sense in the merest wisp of a cloud, or a smile, a ripple or a [sh]adow, implications of the same ultimate immensities. But those are [on]ly a few of us. At the seaside many of us respond. It is one of the rare [su]btleties that seems to project itself magnanimously. How does it do so? We shall find some of the answer to this question not in what there [is] to be seen, but rather in what is not there. At most times, in our more

habitual life situations, we find ourselves surrounded by quantitie
little and large things, truly vast complications of interlocking substa
and spaces that clutter up the scenery of each moment. Pause to
account of and to analyze from time to time the agglomeration of it
and sensory perceptions that constitutes our experience at a given inst
Only a mentality of surpassing stature, orderliness, and well-nigh e:
sensory intuition can readily sense an ultimate, spontaneous simpli
behind and beyond all the immensity of confusing detail. True, as I l
said, the mind of great intuition does see the infinite a thousand ti
a day within the intricacies of life patterns. But the average mind
proaches the concept only by staring into the midnight heavens or i
other apparently boundless areas of mystery. As a general rule, we do
realize even remotely how cluttered our lives are with jostling minu
that keep prodding us from every direction, diverting our attention f
the main and grand currents, provoking and inhibiting our nervous r
tions alternately and even simultaneously. We accustom ourselves t
much extraneous stimulation that invades our conscious and subc
scious sensibility that we gradually become insulated against much o
or else we are hampered by it. But when we transpose ourselves to
seashore we find among other fine things an impeccable perfectior
atmosphere, particularly on a cloudless day. Uninterrupted by de
the sea and the sky encompass within their limitless simplicity all of
awareness. No sudden or harsh changes of fragmentary shapes, tonalit
or colors mar the smooth transitions from near to far. Time and sp
are caught at last in the intimacy of being joined in prayer. Quietnes
punctuated by the oceanic ebb and flow, and even the visible eviden
of the tide recede into the immaculate tranquillity of the barely
ceptible horizon.

Here we have a great, untroubled form of space, luminous, enraptur
by the force of its compulsive perfection, and unhampered by bounds
competitive distractions. It is one of the nearest visions of form with
dimension. Here we are close to the magnitudes of being as we se
them only cloudily from day to day through the more usual maze of li
intricacies. I have seen these magnitudes in great works of sculpture a
in paintings of many concrete and abstract representations, and yet I

think I have often seen a painted sea that is not a dead image of
f. Why, when it is so good to look at in nature, is it so elusive to the
h of the artist? As a rule it is rendered plastically only by little
ons of its immense behavior, waves against the shore, boats and gulls,
es in the surf, and scudding sails; in other words, auxiliary elements
nst which to dramatize the spaces of which we have been speaking.
tself it lacks the tactility and the susceptibility to implied rhythms
hich any but the most magic brushwork could aspire. Most versions
his sort of pure form fall flat. They disappoint us, because they are
· vulgar reminders of loved atmospheres, rather than atmospheres
nselves. But the average person who is entranced by this rare close-up
· of cosmic implications is seeing for once a little of what the more
ly developed sensitivity of the creative artist perceives at almost every
ant of existence. There are those who find it excruciatingly trying to
victims of such heightened awareness. The experience can be so con-
tly poignant and the imperious urge to communicate, exchange,
·e the impressions of all that one loves with all whom one loves so
suming, that, without the release of actually communicative crea-
ty, a state approaching that of hysteria supervenes. There are acres of
ibition walls filled with samples of overexuberant outbursts, enthu-
ms unmodulated and unschooled by the composure of an integrated
it.

ust as such simplified vistas at a seashore lift us into an awareness of
e spatial form, so too are we developing a better comprehension of
e, that other dimension of being. Our growing sense of the con-
ity connecting the past to the present to the future and our envision-
of the architecture of events as an integrated form like that of a
sical concept make us more and more alive to the unseparateness of
cessive moments. We can no longer conceive of a single instant of
e as in any way isolated or complete within its own identity. Nor
we conceive of reality itself as anything less than vast totalities of
e, of which we ourselves and our own measure of duration are the
rest atoms. Our new apprehensions of reality make a million years
m quite as understandably a spontaneous instant in eternity as they
m in our personal measure a dizzying magnitude. Today was yester-

day's tomorrow; and it is tomorrow's yesterday. Today is yestermorr
At every instant it is vibrating in its dual role of child and parent; i
a result of its past and a cause of its future. Actually there is no fi
yesterday or tomorrow in the instantaneity of eternity. These terms
merely a result of human intelligence and its inability to encompas
whole gesture of eternity without breaking it up into its apparent se
of component instants. Today is always yestermorrow to our grow
sense of evolutionary continuity.

Hence our contemporary notion of here and now, while it seems to
getting nearer to the true state of affairs, also seems to the average m
to be growing more complicated. For it is still difficult to grasp as
idea. Understanding of such truths necessitates a kind of gradual accli
tization to new symbols of measurement. For a long time our fine
have been preparing the human mentality for just such physical
metaphysical innovations. Music has been doing tremendous things w
time integration, and the plastic arts with space. Literature is now d
ing intensively with the same phenomena. Now let us examine a li
more penetratingly just how a successful painting affects our relation
time and space.

Let us project ourselves into any imaginable situation that might
into the pattern of our daily lives. Let us, in other words, "isolate" a s
cific moment of existence to the extent of focusing on the appearance
whatever we may be looking at at that specific moment, and on
accompanying state of mind. A state of mind is, of course, an immens
incalculable magnitude, but since states of mind do exist at instants
time, they must so be spoken of. Let us say that I am on a country ro
walking along an avenue of elms. I stop and observe and meditate
feel. At this instant, among other simultaneous experiences, I am
tainly having a visual experience. It is an experience that never again
all the aeons of coming time will occur exactly as it is here and n
occurring. Even if I were to return to this same spot another time
were able to find nothing in the thousands of elements that combine
make up the scene the least altered, still my experience could not p
sibly be the same, for I myself alter at each instant of my evolution, a
must see differently a moment hence that which here and now seems

roughly established. If there is no apparent change in the appearance
hings, we ourselves are everlastingly in flux. But as I stand in con-
plation of this scene, I have a deep sense of utter satisfaction with it;
ll into a mood of complete absorption with the timeless and infinite
fection that I feel in the unblemished harmony of the instantaneous
v. Though time is passing, and so am I, even in the very midst of
process of beholding, yet there is stirred up within me an emotion
t has no interruptive consciousness of anything that could disturb
infallibility of my spontaneous impression. In other words, true spon-
eity is independent of what we call time; it is simply kinetic response
being, uncorrupted by the frustrative afterthoughts and reservations
ch, in the involved processes of civilized thinking, tend to obstruct
intrinsic sensitivity to the perpetually new unfolding of all things.
s possible for me to walk along this same road, if I preserve the in-
rity of my insight, day after day for many years, and see what it has
offer in the eternally fresh and exciting versions which are ensured
its and my own continual evolution. But let us say that I have an
ent desire to communicate the specific feeling that I am having at
here-and-now instant of which we have been speaking. And I have
desire not only to communicate it, but to perpetuate it by "freezing"
image of it into a preservable form of itself.

And so I endeavor to paint a picture of what I feel in my visual ex-
ience of the road. If I am at all successful, the resultant picture will
tray a plastic image of an appearance of road profoundly modulated,
cted, influenced by the character and style of my own mentality.
st of all, as I observe the scene, I have a sense of my own identity
rging with the time and place that constitute the theater and sub-
nce of my present consciousness. At this moment the road and all its
ipheral aura, constituting a form within my apprehension, are so
rinsic to my very sensation of existence that it would be hard for me
objectify them. Were I asleep and dreaming them, they would be
only vibratory emergences from the oblivion that characterizes total
ep. That which I see in fullest concentration of my wide-awake sensi-
ities becomes as totally enveloping of my consciousness as the most
npulsive dream. Nothing else is permitted by my incorruptible at-

tentiveness to intrude upon this communion with the absolute.
longer is it just a patch of road and its environment; it has yielded tc
penetrant and everlasting quest for further intimations. It is
longer one among millions of views that compose the kaleidoscopic
orama of day-to-day exposure, any more than the person for w.
one conceives a passion is seen as just another human being. At the
nacle of aesthetic ardor one's ego becomes as absorbed as in the
summations of love. Even the summits of religious emotion are descr
in these terms. And out of the mood of fulfillment comes an inces
craving to conserve, perpetuate and irradiate all that it has been to
Hence the poet sings and celebrates his love, and the painter paint:
finite versions of the infinite.

The point is that we have a deep longing to hang onto the high pc
of our spiritual flights, and a great reluctance to let ourselves
through these avenues of miracles without effecting some firm record
that will endure. Our memories alone can never revive in fullest,
like intensity the emotions of our past visions. Only a great work o
can capture and retain and transmit through long reaches of time
unadulterated purity and power of them, and communicate then
other hearts and minds. If I have found the road beautiful, I am
much enriched; if I can reveal the particular beauty as I find it, th
shall have successfully shared my wealth with those who want it.
sooner we can arrive at that stage wherein such wealth and its fluid tr
mission will be the rule rather than the exception, the sooner we s
have achieved some of that spiritual dignity for which our intuition
man to be destined. The world and our life within it are as beautif
they are perceived and revealed by those who most beautifully see th
The average man's recognition of life's deeper meanings comes to
primarily from the articulate probings and enthusiasms of the poets
substantiate human intuition by the eloquence of their images.

That which will give significance and value to my painted pictur
the road on which I stand has nothing whatever to do with the su
ficial resemblance of the painted to the actual scene. Indeed, there
instances of good painting in which the image evoked on canvas b
no recognizable relationship to the thing portrayed. The supreme f

1 of the finished picture is not at all to render a photographic repro-
tion of a specific place at a specific time. It is to portray my own
sonal vision of the scene in the full vibration of my response to it.
ere are some painters whose vision responds to nature's stimulation
h such abstract experiences of plastic form that the resultant pictures
not at all scenic, but merely tonal and color symbols of an aesthetic
ction. The water-colorist Marin frequently enters this category of
ist; when he does, his works do not present us with representations of
ws as seen by the average eye, but rather with suggestive expressions
what he feels in his own unique way about the absolutes he finds
erever he happens to be looking.

The value to the observer of such pictures lies in the personalized
thm transmitted from the mentality of the artist, via the canvas, to
t of the beholder. To a Marin, the road on which I stand may be
scribed onto his canvas by such lines and touches of color as I could
er dream of seeing or inventing. The important thing to remember
hat his translation of the view into an abstraction of it does not at all
stitute the sole manner of achieving a picture possessed of abstract
nification. A Rembrandt canvas of the same subject might give us a
fectly concrete version of a road with magnificent feeling for the
tle and the abstract connotations of the view. There is absolutely no
ticular style, approach, concept, manner of realization that can
thoritatively be said to achieve the highest aesthetic result in the paint-
of pictures. The entire matter depends upon the spirituality, the in-
rity, the sensitivity of the artist. And if he is truly the poet, it will
t matter a jot whether he sees "objectively" or "nonobjectively," for
is impossible to see purely objectively anyway. Even the most banal
lividuals see in their own unique fashion, and it would be interesting
d instructive if such persons really had the capacity to convey to us
th complete fidelity that which they see and feel. There is a definite
lue in the intercommunication of accurate pictures of what each per-
n experiences. At present, our means and powers of communication
still so much inferior to what goes on inside our heads and hearts
at we frequently appear to be much more obtuse and uninteresting
an we really are.

Once I succeed in creating a picture which will involve others so c
pletely in the process of my own being and feeling that they are mon
tarily identified with the sensations of my own psyche, then I shall t
created not only a transference of mood but also a projection of
time dimension. The representation of my spontaneous response to
road, once it is firmly fixed in pigments, is capable of maintaining a
within me, and within anyone who is receptive to plastic imagery, a
sation of timeless actuality. The here-and-now immediacy of that wl
I find beautiful in the road that I paint survives plastically in a uni
fashion. Though the painter grow old and die, the fingerprints of
spirituality are everlastingly stamped in the strokes of his brushw
Nothing that I can contrive by all the effort and ingenuity of my e:
memory is ever able to restore to a feeling of present actuality my
periences of the past as can my pictures. That is not their prin
purpose, but whatever emotion I may have had at the time of pain
becomes a permanently activated emotion once it is preserved in
ment, and it is not to so great a degree lost as it might have been
simply disappearing into the areas of my subconscious memories.

The world cannot be the same world to our eyes after we have s
it for even an instant through the eyes of a Rembrandt as it was bef
We do not often pause to realize to what a vast extent our whole sp
uality is shaped by the insights we have had from our multitudes
creative teachers. The most unconcerned man in the street is differen
some extent from what he would have been had Plato never lived. I
paintings never been painted, the eyes of a sensitive person would l
out differently upon his world. The sensitive person catches overtone
many beautiful moments which remind him of this or that poetic ge
whose works he has loved. Even the most gigantically personal of art
cannot avoid the delight of seeing from time to time through the sp
of other equally gifted creators. Some of the grandeur that life has
offer is this very emotion of sharing the insights of those to whom
are attuned. What greater privilege can we enjoy than that of lov
together that which by virtue of our natures we are forever destined
see separately?

Those who would understand modern art must be aware of the stra

hich contemporary sensitivities are subjected. It need not here be
onstrated that the development of our culture has inevitably resulted
he production of more and more complicated mentalities and tem-
ments. The more complicated we become, the more we suffer from
confusions and the pressures created by our own expansions. We
e pitiable attempts at correctives impossible of attainment. One of
most common of these is the effort to return to primitive simplicities,
irable enough in its intent, but hopelessly shallow in its comprehen-
of what is possible and what is impossible. It is a fine thing that
have the perception and the wisdom to appreciate the qualities of
mitive" aesthetics, and it is understandable that we long for such
ification as would seem to be in store for us if we could return many
cts of our current lives to the simpler and more apparently spon-
ous behavior of our earlier, more childlike selves. But for twentieth
tury man to idealize the aesthetic values of primitive societies as the
est aims toward which he can aspire is as regressive as though, in
enchantment with the charm of childhood, we were to bend all our
lt effort to restore ourselves to it by successful imitation.

t is naïve to imagine that at our age we can, or need to, create forms
he particular spirit of the ancient Babylonians, Egyptians, Etruscans,
of the Africans. It is equally naïve to suppose that in order to avoid
the banalities of romantic or "traditional" art as it has been exercised
the uninspired, we must abandon every manner, principle and ideal
t ever operated in past motivation, in order to achieve a Nietzschean
substantiation of values. To overthrow every last vestige of dimen-
as to which we had become accustomed, because new dimensions are
ealing themselves to our intuition, is not even revolutionary, it is
rely erratic. Exploration is one thing; even nihilism is something; but
beautiful is not susceptible to the advances of the revolutionary-for-
-sake-of-revolution.

Ience the intellectual conceptions or, more frequently, the intellec-
l gropings and stutterings which give birth to many modern art mani-
tations are not the proper wellsprings from which we may hope to
eive great benefactions. Adolphe Basler, in his work on *Modern
lpture in France*, has a lucid historical perspective in this matter.

"To pretentious academism, to morbid mannerism, to stylized extra‐
gancies, the love of the true which characterizes rare creative works l
always risen in opposition in France. . . . Enlightened historians
ancient sculpture observe in all peoples at decadent periods a pench
for archaism. The archaistic coquetteries of the present era are superfic
and originate, if not from a tormented intellectualism, then certai
from a confused aestheticism."

The artist who goes forth to seek beauty is not yet an artist, for t
artist is a lover, and he is no lover who goes forth to seek love. If I
along the road of which we have been speaking, and come to a halt
some spot which I hope is a likely spot to present a view in whic
intend to find suggestions and clues to the creation of a beautiful pictu
then I am on the wrong track. Yet this is exactly what the great major
of would-be poets and artists do. They are in love with the idea of bei
poets, being painters, just as many youngsters are in love with the id
of becoming doctors, largely because they are lured by the atmosph
of special awe, authority, and almost oracular omniscience that seems
emanate from the skilled physician upon whose words the anxious p
ents have hung in a breathless sort of esteem mingled with gratitude su
as they seem to exhibit in no other circumstances. The true painter l
no need of consciously inventing and arranging on a canvas; in fact, t
moment a painter does feel this need, it is an indication that he is r
stirred by an authentic emotion, an aesthetic insight. The painter w
musters the resources of his laboring imagination to contrive what
wishes to be contemporary and revolutionary expressions may be co
pared to the multitudes of men who try to alter and enhance in th
imagination the physical and mental attributes of a woman who do
not truly quicken them in the precise fashion of which they dream.
art one simply cannot be a successful lover by trying to make the b
of an ungenuine passion. It is a realm wherein it is unwise to preter
If one is possessed by that visual form of ardor which makes life a co
stant miracle at every instant of being really alive to it, then there is
need or desire for efforts to improve upon one's impressions. Only t
impressions of the unpossessed stay dead to the miracle which th
neither see nor feel; they may paint with every wild or scientific devi

fashioning works of genius, but nothing which their inventiveness
ates can match the priceless boon of natural intuition. In the pure
icture of inspired art there is little fabrication. Communicative skill,
; but the inner meanings are dictated by intellectual and emotional
ponse to beauty already apprehended, not by beauty that a man
ends by art alone to fabricate. Cézanne himself was awkward in his
ft; the art was altogether one of insight. There were and are thousands
more skillful wielders of the brush than he. The "words of God" have
t always been heard and transmitted by the most fluent, and surely
ver by the exhibitionist. They are the progeny of only the purest love.
That universal architecture of space which seems to inhabit the works
so many of the masters, giving an underlying serenity to even the most
multuous surfaces, is a sign of the recognition which large spirits have
the ultimate tranquillity that awaits our understanding. This is the
essage of Bergson, that most enlightened of modern minds in the
icial judgment of durations and extensions in time and space. With a
mplete discernment of what can and what cannot be accomplished by
e logic of the intelligence and the aesthetic of intuition, he apprehends
esolution of all agitation and anxiety in our eventual comprehension of
e Nirvana toward which wisdom and love never fail to lead us. This is
e calm perfection which people sense as they sit at the seashore, facing
e tranquil mergence of sea and sky, with their backs to the turmoil,
rs and confusions of the kind of reality that seems to victimize them
most moments of their lives. For them the immaculateness of this
eanic and heavenly atmosphere is a symbol of the life to which they
pire and which they know in the deepest recesses of their undefiled
nsciences is far more attainable than they generally want to believe.
or the cost of this serenity, though well within their capacity to pay, is
t at all to the taste of their smaller selves. Their greater selves fully
derstand the temporal pleasures, petty ambitions, vanities, lusts to
hich they sacrifice all possibility of real, self-convincing virtue and real
anquillity of spirit. Their greater selves are in ceaseless conflict with the
cessant demands and inertias of their weaker sides. Few human beings
e so integrated as to be assessable in final terms. We are all at war with
rselves, primarily because few of us have the character and sagacity to

relinquish the relative pleasures and conceits for absolute felicity
self-obliteration. We cling to the ego as though it were our only
on life; to transcend itself is the ego's worst nightmare. How many o
with imaginations capable of embracing the consequences, would
fully accept the privilege of being the Messiah? How many of us ac
the privilege of merely following his precepts? What courage it ta
what abstinence—abstinence from the poisons that taste so good!
want serenity but not at the expense of more exciting things. In o
words, we rarely truly want it, except as a surcease from the trials
tribulations with which the inferior sides of our natures sometimes o
whelm us.

Furthermore, the stability that we associate with an integrated, se
spirit is not a static quality such as can be achieved by a withdrawa
our energies; it is dynamic and concentrated on the more transcenc
excitement of the eternally new smile of unblemished actuality. "
self which we all drive to protect and give scope to, has a certain
bivalence between a search for stability and a yearning for novel
according to Ordway Tead. The consecrated mission of the sincere a
is to find that stability in the serenity of insight, and that novelty in
everlastingly spontaneous process of creativity. Nothing is more abs
ingly new in its impact than the beautiful.

That composure which the average man finds so hypnotic and uplif
in his vision of the sea is found by the artist everywhere. In roads
blades of grass, in brooks and streams and waterfalls, in a million asp
of persons, places and things, he finds an indwelling essence commor
them all. For they mirror back to him that nature of themselves wl
responds to his own virtue. The disordered and distracted menta
finds chaos in the same world which to the finely balanced mind rev
itself in purest equilibrium. And just as a person who retains
equanimity in circumstances of upheaval helps to preserve the s
possession of others less stable than he, so does the poised dignity of
artist spread its steadying influence. The animation of the artist's
thusiasm is exhilarating to others; his absorption in the positive busi
of his art points to an ideal state of concentration. In many ways
artist is the soundly developed child who has managed to retain so

nection with those "clouds of glory," and considerable preoccupation
h them. He has not been deprived of his essential innocence as so
:n happens in the process of maturing. He looks out upon the world
 as something to cope with, to conquer, to fear, to hate, to envy, to
ust to as though it were something outside of and alien to his own
; rather, he sees himself and it identified inseparably in the same
sterious newness of every instant. The road he stands upon is not
: a road for travel; at any instant he may infer within its beauty such
/es and patterns of emotion as in other mortals could be aroused only
 the occasionally marvelous. For unnumbered centuries men in their
veté have tried to envisage God, as though his presence does not
anate from every properly regarded pebble, weed, typewriter key or
n-made teacup. The light reveals as the shadow formulates, trillions of
es an hour, the image of his grace. Watch the light and darkness
ld temples of equilibrium within the accidental folds of a fallen scrap
paper, a mountain range, a petal, a pillow creased with the memory of
ecent tenant. "All merges," in the words of Walt Whitman, "toward
: presentation of the unspoke meanings of the earth."

No experience of the past, no matter how stupendous it may have
en in its actuality, can compare in intensity and tangibility, once it is
t, with one's experience of the present moment. You may say that the
ite faculties of a sound imagination will re-create immense moments
the past into present emotions that will be greater than reactions to a
atively uneventful present instant. But only great works of art can
complish this; they project a great instant into timeless forms of in-
ntaneity. Five minutes ago I was lying on a couch, looking at a note-
ok, and seeing beyond the edges of the book a portion of the couch
d then the rug on the floor, and a little of an easy chair some feet away.
uddenly became aware of how utterly unreal all else seemed as com-
ced to the impact of everything that was comprising that most real of
 moments. A half hour before, I had been discussing with great in-
isity some matter of interest with students in a classroom, and at
it time the meditation on the couch, which was a half hour away in
: future, was only being conceived in the evolutionary womb. The
ssroom scene was everything to me in its own moment. Now, the

word "now" for its fugitive instant, already passed away, as I sit h
before my typewriter, forms the momentary center of my intens
awareness, and the memory of reclining on the couch so recently
already cool compared to the heat of this developing sentence whicl
now draw to a close, wondering just what thought and mood awaits t
formulation of the next sentence, the next paragraph, this evening,
morrow, the midsummer still many months off, and the time beyo
my limited mortality. Already the notion above expressed melts ir
the wonder-world of that which has been, and my mind now searches t
the next words which shall materialize out of the vaporous immaterial
of my thoughts an actualized expression that will say something to t
reader. And it turns out to be this. If I had painted a picture of t
experience while lying on the couch, a picture possessed of the f
plastic significance of that which I perceived in the blending of mys
with all that I then was seeing, the beholder of such a picture wou
find resurrected visually, as verbally could be performed only by a po
that state which memory alone cannot possibly delineate. We may rea
back and caress our memories of the treasured past, but we are in r
touch with only the actual present. As I now reassemble some of t
numerous details of conscious and half-conscious observations that co
stituted that particular moment on the couch, I recall how my visi
started with the sight of my own hand visible just under my left e
as my head rested its weight upon it, and how I told myself that a
true picture of what I was then feeling would have to include the feeli
of that hand's imminence as it made itself felt out of the corner of t
eye. I resolved then and there to paint such a picture, showing the ha
of the painter in just such position as would convey the fact that t
artist was lying on his side, head resting on hand, book before him, b
gaze fixed in reverie on the edge of the couch just beyond the boc
Here was, then, the geometric pattern of my world, and one of certa
colors too, of course; and were I to have tried, as indeed I did, to dra
some divisional line between myself and that which was outside myse
I would keep falling into dreamy apathy to such an effort, feeling i
tuitively the lack of validity to the very idea. Things that I see are
real to my identity as things that I dream I see. It means little to me

onalize about the objectivity of objects and the subjectivity of self. ay remind myself that the couch was there before I came to lie upon nd will be as substantially there when I am risen from it; but still my inct insists that during the moment that it enters into the plastic tinuity of my vision, it and I, and all the other items that combine to n that instant's meaning, are ideationally in procreative mergence, so speak.

At these moments of almost trancelike absorption it is impossible to arate the self from the nonself. Indeed, when one tries to imagine the stence of any kind of self-aware ego in a void, it becomes inconceiv- e. We do not often realize to what an extent our consciousness of f is based upon our relationship to an environment. And since we are rning and thinking nowadays, both physically and metaphysically, in ms of ourselves and things outside ourselves as being ultimately of a ilar composition, we tend to accept the apparent interpenetration of f and nonself as valid. In *Creative Evolution*, Bergson summarizes this t of concept in the following terms: "Everything is obscure in the a of creation if one thinks of it in terms of 'things' which may be ated and of a 'thing' which does the creating, as we do habitually ink and as our understanding insists upon doing . . . This illusion natural to our intelligence, an essentially practical function designed represent to us things and states of being rather than changes and ts. But things and states are merely instantaneous glimpses taken by r intelligence of the process of becoming. There are no things, there e only actions." What we see and accept casually as things, we now ow to consist of constellations of electrical activity. In this respect ings and ourselves are unceasing activities; and it is not strange that begin in this era of physical revelation to be peculiarly sensitive to e implications of this ultimate immateriality of ourselves and of all se. Through our scientific acumen it looks as though we are at last nerging from that uncomfortable era of materialistic reasoning into a discovery, on a loftier, more satisfying and convincing level, of our trinsic spirituality. This restores that element of mystery to ourselves r which we have such an inherent preference. Civilization's develop- ent has been characterized by eras of extreme terre-à-terre realism alternating with less rational, more intuitional periods. However, during the most scientific phases of our progression, we find the m of our ablest physicists drawn toward the ever-tempting realms of my speculation. Perhaps to our most logical, clairvoyant mentalities, the called mystical is reasonable. We call those concepts mystical which unapparent to our senses and not clearly discernible to our intellige But now that we reliably know how much exists beyond the touc our senses, and now that our confidence is fortified by the fact tha many of the old intuitions have been corroborated by the plodding te nique of intelligence, we begin to accept the invitations of our spiri insight with renewed assurance. After all—and this is so much the ticular message of the good artist-painter—nothing is less mystery than anything else when fully seen. The commonest object is miraculous as the marvels of our highest flights of imagination; we born into such mystery as still challenges all the genius of mankinc fathom. Its beauty is illimitable and incessant. The artist, the lover of treasures each particle of nature, each sacred instant of eternity, as lover of a woman treasures the very shadow and faintest perfume of presence, the merest fleeting expression of her body or her soul. painter restores its property of wonderment to so much that familiarity has reduced to illusory commonplaceness. In so doing not only dissipates the deceptiveness of what we call the "ordinary"; also invokes and revives the mystic potential of our own primor uniqueness. He liberates us from the deadening self-diminishment t atrophies our spirits the moment we accept boundaries to our self pansion. The mystery of our selves is no less wonderful than that of universe. The measure of the latter preserves for us that indispensa humility without which we can achieve no final Virtue.

Chapter XVI

THE IMMEDIACY AND BEAUTY OF THE PRESENT INSTANT

~~~~~~

T IS necessary constantly to remind ourselves that at the beginning of our lives everything which entered our experience seemed marvelous until we became so used to many things which repeated :mselves and seemed to follow familiar patterns of cause and effect t the marvelousness faded away. There seem to be two great phases human receptiveness, one at the beautifully naïve stage, which may called that of the First Simplicity, and finally in the rare instances matured capacity, that of the Last Simplicity. Few persons have the urage to traverse the long and trying fields of development that lead m first to last. The modern philosophy of art in particular often clings the relatively easy initial phase, exalts the childlike primitiveness of trained creativeness, frequently mistaking reversion to infantilism r mature genius. That is what puzzles the general public when it tries discern the differences between what it knows to be first simplicities t of its own nurseries and what it frequently suspects to be similar though mounted on museum walls. The great and the essential difrence between first and last simplicity in art seems to revolve around isdom. There is important charm to the spontaneous gestures of the ncomplicated creator, the child who loves the brand-new world, and presses his love in explosive bursts of artistic exploration. But the ind that can grow into fuller familiarity with life, mastering much of s logic without ever losing the initial recognition of the full wonderent behind it, the mind that both Understands and Loves, is productive n a higher plane. Between the beauty of naïveté and that of supreme tuition lies the dangerous area of the largest quantity of fine-art enavor, primarily motivated by egoistic desires to make impressively eautiful things rather than by the fervent yearning to share the emo-

tion of incessant mystery. Hence one may conclude that at the beginni
and at the end of human genius there sounds a music of mysteri
apprehension that becomes imperceptible to the great majority w
outgrow childhood without reaching the final grace. Those of us w
do not hear it may be drawn toward it by a human instinct which yea
for the miraculous beyond the commonplace. The artist shows us t
the miraculous lies within the commonplace. He revives the mystery
the familiar at an elevation of beauty.

Around those whom we call the "great" there is always something
an aura of mystery. We like to think of their powers as a little beyo
the merely rational. Human beings have a great longing for magic. F
the average person the supernatural is much more marvelous than t
natural. Only the wise understand that nothing in this wide world
ours is more explicable, less wonderful than anything else. But as t
mentality rises to conversance with the subtleties of what we call Tru
it perceives how little of separateness there is to existence. It becom
clear that what seems to be a vast disorder of neighboring entities is
reality permeated with a coalescent interfluency wherein even the m
apparently contrasting forces merge into the consonance of their ul
mate harmony. All of the illusion of separateness melts away, until t
whole universe is apprehended as an uncomplicated, spontaneous g
ture. No contributive part of it is any less mysterious than the who
The very term "harmony" was originally a mathematical conception
the ancient Greeks, who felt the entire cosmic order to be a beautif
quantitative and geometrical abstraction. Mathematics is rational to
point, but no more limited to reason than is the music which is
singing voice. In this regard, apropos of music as a reflection of t
world, Thomas Mann has written that "music is number, the worsh
of number, hallowed computation, resonant algebra. But does not t
very essence of number contain an element of magic, a touch of witc
craft? Music is a theology of number. . . ." To Mann "music is a gre
mystery. By virtue of its sensual-spiritual nature and the amazing unic
it achieves between strict rule and dream, good form and magic, reas
and emotion, day and night, it is without a doubt, the most profoun

st fascinating and, in the eyes of the philosopher, most disquieting
enomenon."

We are drawn to the mystic by a great hunger that underlies all our
ensibly well-fed twentieth century realism. Secretly, in our heart of
arts, we never altogether repudiate the visionary murmurings that
e and fall in the fermentations of the universal subconscious. We
come tremendously excited when certain rare occasions seem to testify
our possession of a clairvoyance beyond that of reason. Sometimes we
e our premonitions fulfilled in a way that makes us hope that some-
ing more magical than good sense or "coincidence" has been at work.
'e make as honest and scientific investigations as our intelligence can
ntrive to ascertain whether we do not possess the potentialities for
trasensory perception and for telepathy. With all that has been accom-
ished by the resolute and adroit workings of the human mind, still the
ind itself remains a baffling mystery to us. The obvious difficulty of men-
lity studying itself under the auspices of its own faculties and processes
eds no elaboration. But fortunately, such is the healthy vitality of its
wn nature that it never surrenders, never acknowledges a state of im-
asse in its efforts to comprehend itself and its destiny. And one of the
ings that it seems most recently to have clarified for itself is the fact
at "intellectuality" alone is destructive to the apperception of finalities.
ome of our highest types of mind recommend rather startling abandon-
nent of confidence in the powers of reason. In their recognition of the
hortcomings of mere thinking, perhaps they lose sight of the fact that
mere" intuition, unfortified by the structural implementation of in-
elligence, can be just as sterile in its emotionalism. The highest crea-
ivity seems to be compounded of a fine mixture for which no recipe can
e too readily proffered.

However, the important fact is that in the background of our con-
ciousness remains always a regard for the possibility of mystic revelation
s a way of having the unknown explained to us. With some it may
e a sort of last hope, tinged with skepticism. But with those possessed
f the most sensitive types of minds, the unknown and the "known"
like present such an equal enigma as to leave the so-called "common-
lace" things of life still just about as finally unexplained as the totality

itself. Most human beings oscillate between what they call their sci
tific and their religious attitudes, making great but rarely proficient
forts to amalgamate the two. Most modern people's conceptions
common sense tend to glue their feet firmly to the solid earth, relegat
the angels of divinity to the category of charmingly ancient mytholog
and religiosities. The age of technology burst upon us with an intens
of hopefulness that has already faded somewhat, leaving us in states
anxiety. Those who dwelled once upon a time in comforting proxim
to the guardian angels of their faith were not so troubled. Our meth
ical genius has momentarily incapacitated our other gifts of appreh
sion; we have perhaps become temporarily biased toward the rational
of our recent skillful inventiveness. It has yielded such materially fruit
rewards as to have momentarily dazzled us; but already the vitality
our better judgment is beginning to assert itself. For instance, Alfr
North Whitehead, in his Lowell Lectures of 1925, was acutely consci
of the situation when he pointed out that "the greatest invention of t
nineteenth century was the invention of the method of invention.
new method entered into life. In order to understand our epoch, we c
neglect all the details of change, such as railways, telegraphs, radios, sp
ning machines, synthetic dyes. [Think of the fantastic expansion that h
occurred in the two succeeding decades!] We must concentrate on t
method in itself; that is the real novelty, which has broken up t
foundations of the old civilisation. The prophecy of Francis Bacon h
now been fulfilled; and man, who at times dreamt of himself as a litt
lower than the angels, has submitted to become the servant and t
minister of nature. It still remains to be seen whether the same act
can play both parts."

Our confidence in thought, in the beautiful art of human reaso
must not be disturbed by the fact that it tends at times to become orna
rococo; this happens periodically to all the arts by which man celebrat
the miracle of being. At the present time the art of reason is doi
itself a great mischief by invading fields in which it does not rightfu
function and belong. Man has found himself progressing so sensationa
along the legitimate paths of reason, and suffering such considerab
discomfiture and bewilderment from his inability to adjust all of h

to the new conditions arising out of his scientific triumphs, that he
empts to apply the same rational faculties to situations requiring
er kinds of touch. Sir Thomas Beecham was reported by the New
rk *Herald Tribune*, on February 15, 1944, to have made some interest-
remarks in a lecture at New York's Town Hall, on the subject of
"decline of music." It will be to the point to examine a few excerpts
this quoted talk. "Sir Thomas Beecham asserted . . . that the
cline of music in the twentieth century' might be averted if com-
sers would be 'socially stupid' and 'intellectually puerile' . . . He
clared it an incontestable fact that in the last forty years the 'creative
rrent of the world in music is running dry.' . . . Sir Thomas said
had come to his conclusions about traits necessary to produce good
mposers after a study of the lives of great musicians. The things that
od out about such men as Bach, Handel and Beethoven, he said,
re their intense personal religious convictions and their lack of intel-
ctuality as the word is understood today. 'After all, music came into
istence primarily to express something that words could not. There is
finality about words, but not about sound. A composer therefore is
ncerned with an element to which the ordinary rules of sense,
alysis and mental criticism in respect of definite terms do not apply
all.' He defined a creative artist as 'primarily a clairvoyant creature,
most a medium in a trance condition receiving revelations that are
nied to everybody else. Let's please pray our creative artists to be
cially stupid, intellectually puerile, to shut themselves upstairs in an
ory tower and be as they used to be, outrageous, preposterous, impos-
ble and almost outlaws from society, but to recover the pride in their
aft and the faith in its all-supreme importance.' "
Here you have violent and contestable reaction to an overrationalizing
a. No significant artist is ever in an "ivory tower," for no significant
t fails to touch and to nourish the human conscience. However,
eecham's main point is being made in every field. Let us inspect one
ore quotation, from a contemporary critic of poetry this time. E. E.
ummings had offended social-minded persons in the 1930's by "dwel-
ng in an ivory tower." But today we find Theodore Spencer writing:
Cummings' reputation as a poet went partly underground. He seemed

to be merely an oddity, apart from the main stream of contempora
writing. He mentioned social issues only to attack them, and his i
dividualism seemed to flourish in its own queer way in a climate qui
removed from the contemporary scene. But as we look back at tl
thirties and see that the emphasis on social issues, from which Cur
mings was so far removed, produced little good poetry, Cumming
work stands out with increasing clarity. The artist, by remaining alwa
the artist and nothing else, has triumphed . . . By concentrating wil
complete honesty on his own response to individual objects and em
tions, he has not merely perfected a personal idiom, but in his be
poems he has achieved a special depth and insight which few of h
contemporaries can equal . . ."[1] If a poet achieves and gives dept
and insight to his brother man he is not in any isolated tower. We a.
simply witnessing the age-old battle between the ways of intelligenc
and those of intuition.

Once again we cannot do better than to attend to Whitehead
recognition of this important fact. "We quickly find that the Wester
peoples exhibit on a colossal scale a peculiarity which is popularl
supposed to be more especially characteristic of the Chinese. Surpris
is often expressed that a Chinaman can be of two religions, a Confucia
for some occasions and a Buddhist for other occasions. Whether th.
is true of China I do not know; nor do I know whether, if true, thes
two attitudes are really inconsistent. But there can be no doubt tha
an analagous fact is true of the West, and that the two attitudes involve
are inconsistent. A scientific realism, based on mechanism, is conjoine
with an unwavering belief in the world of men and of the highe
animals as being composed of self-determining organisms. This radica
inconsistency at the basis of modern thought accounts for much tha
is half-hearted and wavering in our civilisation." He finds the perplexit
insinuating itself into poetry of the nineteenth century, as even thi
fine art grows vulnerable to the tortuous convolutions of thinkin
divided against itself. For instance, Tennyson's opening lines of I
Memoriam:

[1] New Republic, April 3, 1944.

Strong Son of God, immortal Love,
Whom we, that have not seen Thy face,
By faith, and faith alone, embrace,
Believing where we cannot prove.

And so we return at the end of this meditation on art to the atmosphere of its first chapter. In a sense, we are ready now to embark on a
new adventure into the fascinating question of how the arts tend to
invest the commonplace with its inherent mystery as well as to draw
the ultimately mystic nearer to the groping touch of human apprehension. It is this achievement which must form both the climax to
our present study and the suggestive basis for further contemplation.
Great painting, great art, helps us to overcome that deadly human
fallacy, that insidious enemy of truth, the familiarity complex. When
we look upon a great picture, if it exalt but a blade of grass, our eyes
are reopened to the full glory of what is there to be seen when it is no
longer depreciated by the almost universal bad habit of growing blind
to the subtlety of familiar things. Even Christ had to renew the impress
of his beauty from day to day with reiterated signs of his miraculousness
in order to reassure his apostles lest they lose faith while dwelling in
such dear familiarity with him. Because man accustoms himself to his
environment until it no longer awes him with the wonder of its infinity,
he has had to build churches wherein to re-create by architectural
fantasy an impression of that atmospheric divinity which his imagination attributes to the infinitude of holiness. While the purpose should
not be discouraged, nevertheless, it is obvious that any man whose
spiritual intuition is intact surrounds himself with his own cathedrals
wherever he may be standing, and it is good to be near such men as
these, for they are towers of strength to their friends. And they are the
hope of the world.

So it is with good painting, as it is with the creation of any other
beautiful recognition. To recognize is to know again something previously known. How often we have the strange feeling as we contem-
plate a work of art that here is revealed a certain inherent perfection
which is generally imperceptible to us in the ordinary experience of
daily living but which, when demonstrated by the artist, is not exactly

a new marvel to us at all but simply a marvelous evocation of somethin
we have long since subconsciously and incompletely surmised. Muc
of our emotion flows from this stirring recognition. We love to fin
perfected for us in articulate works of art those vague cognitive sens
tions that underlie our thinking and feeling, which we cannot su
stantiate as definitive thought, and yet which form the structur
pattern of our innermost intuition. The very immensity of our respon
proves the latent capacities that are in us. In an artist's picture we fin
that he has recognized via the images and spaces of his world a for
which transcends the touch of his and our near intelligence but whic
sends an even more authentic ring of truth reverberating through th
temples of our more ultimate perception. Is it the grace of his ow
equilibrium that he bestows upon an impassive reality which we ca
nature? Or is it his possession of a little extra modicum of sensitivi
that enables him to see and to show to us what we cannot see throug
our own eyes but can somewhat see through his?

In any event, the intangible form implicit in all great art provid
an element of mystery not unlike that surrounding the personality
saintly persons. We do not make catalogues of all the definable facto
which we observe and put together when we form an impression of a
individual. Even at the first moment of meeting a new person we ca
not avoid an instantaneous presumption of far more than actually o
verbalizing intelligence could explain concerning his character. In th
bearing, in the many telltale features from head to foot, the tone
voice, the glance of eye, we read in a flash some of what has been forme
by years of evolution, molded and drawn by powers and inertia
puckered and lifted by vice and virtue, ad infinitum. And in our visic
of what we call the "saint" we usually find more mystery than in th
ordinary man. Beauty and mystery in the minds of those profound
susceptible to either are drawn closer and closer to synonymy. C
course, the saint would insist that the mystery and the beauty are
be found no less in one soul than in another—and the artist wou
insist that they are simply everywhere. This, then, means that he sa
they are here and now.

Hence if we examine a hundred paintings of the same scene by

undred different painters we are likely to find that whatever few of
them may have come from the brushes of true artists will be distinguished by a certain elevation above the matter-of-fact—they will be
imbued with a quality that emerges as a distillation of the artist's and
the outer world's intrinsic natures. To ourselves, with our limited perspectives, such works properly have a vast meaning. If we soar in our
imagination above the boundaries of our human measurement of time
and space, and visualize our molecular little earth spinning its rather
unimpressive course through the indifferent heavens, we shall scarcely
notice the faint man-made aesthetic murmurs and gestures that dot the
surface of its astral experience. The mystery and the beauty then are
in the firmament with all its uncrowded trillions of celestial orbs, and
in the further universal vastitude that dwarfs the heavens of our earth.
Only one thing in human experience matches the momentous import
of this totality, and that is—oneself. Even in the fullest health of
humility we need not escape awareness of the immense wonder and
power of the human ego. Men of great spirit are not crushed and overwhelmed by the size of themselves relative to the universe. To humble
oneself before the infinite is not at all to humiliate oneself. The poet
is one who expands into and is exalted by the grandeur of his world
concept. The wider his scope the greater his own stature. He does not
measure his size and his value against those of his fellow men or against
those of the universe; if he measures at all, it is only against the standards
of his own conscience. The rest is a matter of loving the miracle and
the beauty of it all, which is furthest removed from self-love. Nothing
dissipates the malady of egotism so thoroughly as true love. Part of the
comfort of contemplating fine art is the self-forgetfulness engendered.
Momentarily at least all one's petty vanities and anxieties are obliterated
as one becomes empathically involved in the artist's persuasive version
of the soul-embracing sufficiency of our natural affinity to all things
at all times.

There are those, of course, who scorn the very word "mystery," so
greatly have they come to rely upon the ostensible evidences of intelligence as the only credible factors in human comprehension. However,
it is quite certain that nobody sensitive to the nuance of what we call the

beautiful can be without a sympathetic understanding of what we me̵
by its mystery. In the most elementary terms, it is "mysterious" by t̵
mere fact that nobody has ever succeeded in intelligently analyzing ̵
the phenomenon of beauty has never been completely explained. ̵
formula has ever been devised to which one might reliably adhere wi̵
a guarantee of aesthetic success. However, to any creative temperamer
the atmosphere of mystery that envelops a beautiful thing, and henc
when fully seen, all things, is, like the pervading air, both within ̵
and beyond us. If there is the slightest mystery to time and space, l̵
and love, fear and death, then there is no less mystery in every mome̵
of all time, every fragment of substance, every shadow of reality. On̵
again we must remind ourselves how sadly our freshness of visi̵
deteriorates as we "grow up" unless we are careful and fortunate a̵
well-guided. We lose our excitement about the wonderful, we succun̵
to the cultural patterns which exert such deadening influence up̵
our virginal ebullience unless we contrive a conformity to soc̵
exigencies without imbibing the poisonous narcotic of indifference. K̵
Hung-ming explains the eternal youth of the Chinese people by t̵
fact that the average Chinese has managed to maintain within hims̵
the head of a man and the heart of a child.

Our explanation in earlier chapters of how the artist's own rhythm̵
tempo carries over into his picture and thence into the mind of ̵
audience has a great deal to do with the hypnotic force of success̵
painting. Since under ordinary circumstances individual minds a̵
separated from each other by the impossibility of fusion, they a̵
generally incapable of inhabiting each other's worlds except under t̵
diluted conditions of verbalized translation. And as we so regretfu̵
know, it is only by the highest art that one of us can say enough a̵
say it well enough to another to translate his deeper meanings a̵
emotions efficaciously. To translate a visual experience from one mir̵
to another with such fidelity as to have the second individual "se̵
exactly the same way as the first is, in the verbal idiom, impossib̵
Even plastically, it is prodigiously difficult. The nearer we come to ̵
accomplishment the nearer we approach possibilities of spiritual fusio̵
which is one of the high aims of the social conscience. When the go̵

inter touches his vision onto a canvas, his picture is never so exter-
lized in the process as to become a thing separated from himself.
ne images he projects are flung forward in the same controlled way
is employed by one who spins a top by casting it from himself and
lling it toward himself but never letting go the string which in its
winding sets the top aspinning. The rhythm with which the painter
sts his form of space upon the canvas is characterized by a grace of
ntinuity, as explained in the chapter on Form. That grace of con-
uity, frozen into its pictorial translation, does not stop at the surface
the pigment but carries back to the sensitive observer, who, the more
nsitive he is, gets a feeling analogous to the queer sensation one has
nding in another person's shoes or occupying any intimate place
bitually belonging to another person, particularly one of strong
rsonality. Strange, is it not, how even using a friend's comb, or
untain pen, or topcoat casts a slight, subtle spell of fused identity?
nere is ground for prolonged study in this important phenomenon
  how one's personality clings in the minds of others to the objects
th which one has been associated. How much more, then, does the
irit of the artist inhabit the works which are his soul's most ardent
d most intimate labor!

If one spends merely a brief evening in the company of an acquaint-
nce who happens to be a person of powerful individuality, one comes
vay momentarily influenced, sometimes so noticeably as to have
quired overtones of his mannerisms and style, or vice versa, depending
on whose is the predominating force. One feels oneself acting and
sponding at various times in the ways of those whose influence has
ayed upon one. An introspective person knows that he is not at all
mes definable in exactly the same pure terms, but that he is a com-
ex, and even feels himself to be on different occasions a different sort
 person. But somehow, an individual seems to rise to his highest
vel of integrity when he is in rapport with works of art. He then tends
ward fusion with the artist's intuition.

Man at his best seems much the same sort of creature all over the
orld. A study of comparative religions will bear this out. At the apex
 his spirituality he is in high accord with himself! When he comes,

therefore, under the influence of an aesthetic experience, he undergo
what amounts to a catharsis. This in itself, when it is intense, is n
unmystical in its emotional impact. It is possible, in contemplating
picture of supreme merit, to undergo an extraordinary exaltation, whic
at an abnormal level, may easily result in reactive manifestations simil
to those characteristic of religious fanaticism. Any human being who
sensibilities are developed to a stage where he is no longer insulat
against the electrifying stimulus of aesthetic insight will unquestionab
encounter moments of startling revealment when he is in contact wi
an art that touches him. There are, of course, those whose sole art li
deeply within themselves, requiring them to be audience to nothi
other than life as it presents itself; by their own virtue these rare spir
radiate a goodness that is a sufficient equivalence to all beauty. Tl
was recognized by Confucius two thousand five hundred years ag
and today we have thinkers who feel that practice of the fine arts
only the symbol and symptom of man's self-insufficiency which w
eventually be supplanted by the fully integrated personality. As Co
fucius saw it . . . "There are men who seek for the abstruse ar
strange and live a singular life in order that they may leave a name
posterity. This is what I never would do. There are again good me
who try to live in conformity with the moral law, but who, when th
have gone half way, throw it up. I never could give it up. Lastly, the
are truly moral men who unconsciously live a life in entire harmor
with the universal moral order and who live unknown to the wor
and unnoticed of men without any concern. It is only men of ho
divine natures who are capable of this."

As Otto Rank sees it . . . "The new type of humanity will on
become possible when we have passed beyond this psycho-therapeut
transitional stage, and must grow out of those artists themselves wl
have achieved a renunciant attitude towards artistic production. A ma
with creative power who can give up artistic expression in favor of tl
formation of personality—since he can no longer use art as an expre
sion of an already developed personality—will remould the self-creati
type and will be able to put his creative impulse *directly* in the servi
of his own personality. In him the wheel will have turned full circ

om primitive art, which sought to raise the physical ego out of nature,
the voluntaristic art of life, which can accept the psychical ego as a
rt of the universe. But the condition of this is the conquest of the
ar of life, for that fear has led to the substitution of artistic produc-
on for life, and the eternalization of the all-too-mortal ego in a work of
t. For the artistic individual has lived in art-creation instead of actual
e, letting his work live or die on its own account, and has never
holly surrendered himself to life. In place of his own self the artist
its his objectified ego into his work, but though he does not save his
bjective mortal ego from death, he yet withdraws himself from real
fe. And the creative type who can renounce this protection by art
d can devote his whole creative force to life and the formation of
fe will be the first representative of the new human type, and in return
r this renunciation will enjoy, in personality-creation and expression,
greater happiness."[1]

In evaluating the faculty of sight as a medium toward insight we
ust not forget that there are also other paths leading to the same
prehension. The main thesis of this book is simply that, since our
ajor sentiency is ocular, we should bestir ourselves to a livelier, fuller,
ore mature capacity for the visual arts. And the weakness is far more
n the receptive than on the creative side. The pictures are there,
regnant with meaning, while multitudes pass them by. To illustrate
e force of an audience's indifference, it is a familiar fact that some-
mes when a person who greatly loves some work of art shows it to
nother person or to a group unequipped to catch its significance, the
riginal person suddenly finds his own appreciation dwindling, until
e realizes with a start that he has begun to experience the work
mpathically through these other minds rather than purely through
is own. How impossible it is to See when you are busy showing the
ing to others! You are trying to see what they are seeing in order to
ake sure that they are loving it. You lose contact with the grandeur
f the thing, which seems to shrink to the proportions it has in the
yes of the less sensitive ones of the group to whom it is being shown.

There is no doubt about the undertow that is exerted upon creativity

[1] *Art and Artist*, by Otto Rank. A. A. Knopf.

by general mass inertia and incomprehension. "To have great poe
there must be great audiences too," said Walt Whitman. Every mor
has his role to play in the human ascension toward grace. The awkwar
ness of a single soul breaks the continuity of total communion. As t
ultimate design of Christians is to find universal union in God, so t
virtue of high art is to exalt all of mankind to the grace, which is t
beauty and the truth, of its highest intuition.

To give further point to the vital function served by the artis
concentration upon the immediacy and beauty of the present insta
and the uniqueness of this attitude, let us draw a parallel to Jun,
conception of what constitutes a modern man. "The modern man—
let us say again, the man of the immediate present—is rarely met wi
There are few who live up to the name, for they must be conscious
a superlative degree.—Since to be wholly of the present means to
fully conscious of one's existence as a man, it requires the most intensi
and extensive consciousness, with a minimum of unconsciousness.
must be clearly understood that the mere fact of living in the prese
does not make a man modern, for in that case everyone at present ali
would be so. He alone is modern who is fully conscious of t
present. . . .

"The man whom we can with justice call 'modern' is solitary. He
so of necessity and at all times, for every step towards a fuller cc
sciousness of the present removes him further from his original 'p
ticipation mystique' with the mass of men—from submersion in a co
mon unconsciousness. Every step forward means an act of tearing hims
loose from that all-embracing pristine unconsciousness which clai
the bulk of mankind almost entirely."[2]

The latter paragraph constitutes one of the grimmest tragedies,
few words, that arise out of human inequalities. And it is certainly o
of the loftiest aims and obligations of high art to restore that "p
ticipation mystique" between the creator and his fellow men. What l
worthy function than this could adequately and consistently inspire
true artist? Indeed, it is of this very participation mystique that we ha
been speaking in connection with the emotion that arises when he w

[2] *Modern Man in Search of a Soul*, by Carl Jung, Harcourt, Brace & Co.

ιtemplates a work of art enters into total communion with him who
de it. The mystery is not at all in the picture, if we wish to be scientific
ɩ precise about it; but a sensation of mystery envelops the momentous
ːurrence of true contact between two souls. And this true contact
ιot made at low levels. The artist and his audience must be charged
ɩ activated at least to some extent by the same current, if there is to
junction. E. N. da C. Andrade, in his fine clarification of modern
ysics, makes a statement in his preface to The Mechanism of Nature
ιich applies as well to receptivity in art as to understanding in science.
ferring to the important task of making clear to the inquiring lay-
ɩn "this or that achievement of our modern physics," he says: "It
quently happens that the task is rendered extremely difficult by the
ːt that the questioner is without the first beginnings of a knowledge of
e matter and the method of the science, and is, as it were, like those
emical compounds which are apt and, so to speak, anxious to absorb
e vapour of water, but cannot do so easily if they are already very dry;
ey require a preliminary infection with moisture if they are to drink
with facility a further store." But once the requisite susceptibility
attained, then the layman's eyes begin to open in exultancy to the
eath-taking disclosures of the physicist's genius. Every human art
ɩ science affords some access to that final insight to which we all
pire. Those of us who disclaim the aspiration are often either some-
ιat defiant or somewhat defunct.

Let there be no misunderstanding of the artist's personal motivation.
he painter of good pictures does not set himself before his easel with
ι audience in mind. Even the great actor, literally confronted with a
ːge audience, immerses himself in the dynamics of his role; and the
ore totally he plays to the circumstances of the drama, rather than
the gallery, the more successfully he involves his audience. The real
tist is simply responding spontaneously to that which touches him
ost poignantly. The nature and quality of his response depends upon
ɔw beautiful a person he is. A Cellini is not a Fra Angelico. Must we
ɩnfess that at our present stage of personal relativities there seem even
 be degrees of beauty? There are many Cellinis, but they are not
ɩite mysteriously beautiful. Their selves are not so wonderful as their

talents. By my own humble taste I should count the world richer
the song of a Schubert than in the ejaculations of a Wagner, howev
musically géniale. Through all the genius of the works one feels d
ferences that are referable not to the skills but to the souls of th
authors. There is often more genuine power in a quiet statement th
in thundering passion. And the passions of great men, if they do ari
are tempered by what seem to be the gentle laws of authentic love a
wisdom. It still is safer to say that the great speak quietly. Men
wisdom do not react with agitation to the diseases of the human spir
by maintaining the poise that comes of their understanding and t
love that comes of their virtue, they sustain and exalt those who kn
them. When you hear much noise and see much show of power y
are not most likely to be in the presence of an artist. One cannot tou
the ultimate too heavily.

But one yearns to touch it, and particularly now, when man fin
himself at one of the lowest moments in all the undulant history
the human soul. We mortals of today, in the paroxysm of our soc
and psychic conflict, present a tragic spectacle of human hopes, cul
vated through the ages, shattered more violently than ever before. T
philosophy, faith and aspiration of all the centuries of Christian ide
stagger under the concussion of global war. This is a formidable sho
to modern man, and as a consequence we find him fallen into a mo
of profound uncertainty. The modern conscience cannot escape t
pall of self-reproach, the sense of failure that accompanies such cat
trophe. Modern man's faith in himself and in his intrinsic virt
properly trembles in the balance. Hitherto he had believed that t
moral strength of the few was always working upon the destiny of a
and that mankind was mounting gradually and resolutely, despite
temporary setbacks, toward a high integrity. Now there is no individu
of any perception who does not feel himself involved in the gener
shameful deficiency that proclaims itself in the debacle of our age. T
many of us have lost faith in the old dream of an eventually tranq
world that was to be erected as the final monumental reward to t
exercise of human reason and moral purposefulness. We begin to dee
ourselves congenitally incapable of elevating ourselves to the height

best inspiration. We succumb to the easy skepticism which accepts
outlook as incontrovertibly gloomy and, knowing the root of all
trouble to be within ourselves, we yearn for a magical serenity and
purity to take the place of our tumult and confusion. At such a time
this some of us turn our eyes back nostalgically toward the apparently
ater composure of man's spirit at an earlier era, when he enjoyed
comfortable asurance of God's love and protection and the faith
it by alternating repentance and virtuous effort he could surmount
corrosive forces of his weaker mortal nature, and ascend to an
rnity of blessedness.

Our religious faith today no longer imbues us with that unquestioning
w of confidence in divine revelation. Scientific materialism demands
er, more substantial and more rational, bases for a credo. Modern
n is becoming spiritually famished as he wavers between the dominion
intelligence, which sets up ideals of material security and social wel-
e, and his subliminal hunger for a felicity that is more soul-satisfying.
s progressive materialism has plunged him into chaos and catastrophe;
dwindling spirituality leaves him more exposed to the corruptibility
ainst which his faith was once so strong a protection. Modern man
s lost much of a sublime self-confidence he once enjoyed; but his
w humility is already recharging his spirit with the irrepressible
wers of will and clairvoyance that are the natural forces of his destiny.
Art plays a mighty and a prophetic role in the coming restoration of
an's faith in himself and thus in the brotherhood of man, and in the
trinsic virtue of the human soul. In this mysterious Form of which
have been speaking, in the inviolable beauty of it which man so self-
sly loves, survives our deathless intuition of man's ultimate capacity
r integration. Here is tangible evidence of the potential order and
renity which overlies and underlies the world's illusions of tem-
rality and divisibility. The artist's vision, disclosing to us the radiant
uth that from every aspect of life's most common gestures may be
ferred the harmony of ultimate grace, fills us with an emotion such
comes only when we stand on the threshold of revelation. At every
aterial sight glowing with spiritual insight we rejoice in our recognition
the perfection that beckons to us. Illusions of separateness and dis-

cordancy are dispelled by the plastic revealment of totality. Cons
lations of objects and intervals which constitute our perceptible wo
merge into interpenetrant fusion. Substance and space blend i
marriages of lightness and darkness. The ego of man is reabsorbed i
the impersonal stability of the absolute. Every successful communicat
of the artist's intuition of these truths brings us the heartening mess
that our chaos is transitory and resolvable. All the testimony of
wisdom points to the immanence of equilibrium. Every touch of
love embraces us in its magnanimity. At the summit of his genius
artist locates and defines the beautiful as here and now.

INDEX